The Operating System

An Anarchist Theory of the Modern State

The Operating System

An Anarchist Theory of the Modern State

Eric Laursen

Foreword by Maia Ramnath

The Operating System: An Anarchist Theory of the Modern State
© 2021 Eric Laursen
Foreword © 2021 Maia Ramnath
This edition © 2021 AK Press (Chico / Edinburgh)
ISBN 978-1-84935-387-8
E-ISBN 978-1-84935-388-5
Library of Congress Control Number: 2020946158

AK Press   AK Press
370 Ryan Avenue #100   33 Tower Street
Chico, CA 95973   Edinburgh, EH6, 7BN
USA   Scotland
www.akpress.org   www.akuk.com
akpress@akpress.org   akuk@akpress.org

The addresses above would be delighted to provide you with the latest
AK Press catalog, featuring several thousand books, pamphlets, audio
and video products, and stylish apparel published and distributed
by AK Press. Alternatively, visit our websites for the complete
catalog, latest news and updates, events and secure ordering.

Cover design by John Yates | www.stealworks.com
Printed in the United States of America on acid-free, recycled paper

To the memory of David Graeber

February 12, 1961–September 2, 2020
Scholar, anarchist, rebel, friend

CONTENTS

The New Idol

Somewhere there are still peoples and herds, but not with us, my brethren:
here there are states. . . .

A state, is called the coldest of all cold monsters. Coldly lieth it also; and
this lie creepeth from its mouth: "I, the state, am the people."

It is a lie! Creators were they who created peoples, and hung a faith and a
love over them: thus they served life.

Destroyers, are they who lay snares for many, and call it the state: they
hang a sword and a hundred cravings over them.

Where there is still a people, there the state is not understood, but hated as
the evil eye, and as sin against laws and customs.

—Friedrich Nietzsche, *Thus Spake Zarathustra*

Foreword

by Maia Ramnath

When I first received a message from Eric Laursen inviting me to comment on his new book and possibly write a foreword, I was standing in line. It was a bathroom line, snaking out of an art space that had opened its doors to protesters and spilling into the COVID-emptied evening streetscape of Lower Manhattan. There, at the height of the Black Lives Matter uprisings in June 2020, a vibrant autonomous encampment had sprung up outside City Hall, waiting in suspense for the City Council's budget vote—which might or might not include defunding the police. Everyone was masked.

It was a long line, and I had lots of time while checking my messages and waiting for a toilet to think about Eric's project in the context of the urgent critiques being enacted all around me.

What Eric offers us in these pages is an illuminating theoretical model of the modern State as operating system. (The aptness of the analogue is no coincidence, reminding us of the concrete linkage between the development of the Internet and state-funded military research for networking communications of command and control.) The operating system is an all-encompassing master software for the functioning of, well, everything: a networked and distributed set of commands that control the deployment of all our institutions, organizations, financial entities, corporations, parties, coercive instruments, and common-sense assumptions.

Outside, a different, bristling complex of individuals, organizations, and emergent networks of actors demanded a radically

1

transformed people's budget for New York City that would defund the police and instead prioritize housing, education, mental health and drug treatment services, and other social programs. All of which, if flourishing, would nudge toward obsolescence the perceived need for policing, penal, and carceral systems—deactivating, in other words, much of the apparatus and logic of the operating system itself.

Voices in the camp offered a spectrum of tactical views: from the pragmatism of presenting a list of concrete, tangible, quantifiable demands, amounting to a slate of line-item reforms in the city budget, on the one hand, to more immediate radicalization, calling for unconditional abolition and reflecting many organizers' dissatisfaction or disgust with piecemeal reforms, on the other. Perspectives about the encampment itself included those who argued that the spontaneous prefiguration of a community based in mutual aid, cultural revitalization, and self-organizing to provide one another with respite, protection, food, and medicine was its own visionary argument, its own world-making achievement, its own reason for being. Others, however, saw the encampment purely as a base camp for staging confrontational actions.

There were debates on the meaning and ownership of Black leadership—particularly the uplifting of women's, youth, and queer leadership—and on the role of white or non-Black POC allyship. There was also a proliferation of artwork, a people's bodega, a people's library, an electrical charging station, and a bounty of food. There were discussions, presentations, workshops, and cultural events. There were bridge-takings, street blockades, and loud nocturnal visits to council members' homes.

Then we reached the eve of the climactic budget vote. What would the long night bring? Would the budget be passed, disregarding protesters' demands? Who would stay or go if it passed? Who would stay or go if it didn't? What would the consequences be in either case? Would we be locked in pitched battle with the police? Would there be mass arrests? Would they try to kick us out? Regardless of the outcome, some organizers had stated their intention to leave voluntarily after the vote while others were committed to staying indefinitely.

The budget passed, controversially, with half measures. It wasn't nothing, exactly, but it was abysmally short of what had been hoped.

Disappointed activists vowed to continue a much longer fight. A deliberative decision on the camp's future was taken in the predawn hours, prioritizing the wishes of Black participants. The original organizing body withdrew, along with the infrastructure for which a détente had been negotiated for a set period of time, the police promising relative noninterference until the council vote. But many chose to stay on, without material support or protective cover. For them, the goal had never been limited to securing a budget deal, and it had certainly not been reached.

Abolition Park was evicted three weeks later. If only for one brief month, nevertheless, in confrontation with the mechanisms of the State, activists had posited another kind of society and set it on a course of fluid self-discovery and self-creation, debating the unfolding and meaning of its own existence. Here, other codes beyond the operating system were being written and test-run.

II.

Eric urges us to bring antistatism back to anarchism, restoring it to the center of our analyses of power, oppression, domination, and authority. The need to recall anarchist attention to the State, or even to mention or emphasize the State, may seem funny or ironic, given that antistatism is assumed to be at the core of anarchism. Nevertheless, it's gotten somewhat lost in the shuffle, Eric observes, given the necessarily expanded critical awareness of systemic hierarchies linked to race, gender, ability, and other interlocking structures of oppression.

Remembering this doesn't mean forgetting about the rest of it. Antistatism in itself need not be opposed to all forms of hierarchy, authority, domination, or coercion. An antistatism that tolerates or indeed actively promotes white supremacy, patriarchy, capitalism, colonial dispossession, extraction, and exclusionary chauvinism is in no way emancipatory. Which is to say that antistatism pure and simple is not the equivalent of anarchism. Anarchism, by contrast, is comprehensive and holistic in its critique of power. Its beautiful chaosmongers can walk, chew gum, and juggle, all while dodging snowballs.

Anarchism is comprehensive and holistic in its critique of power. Its beautiful chaosmongers can walk, chew gum, and juggle, all while dodging snowballs.

But we can't forget about the State, with its unparalleled coercive power, reach, and conceptual dominance. So how do we distinguish a comprehensive systemic analysis from a far-right "deep state" conspiracy theory? Or, for that matter, from a bureaucracy staffed with career public servants?

For those suspicious of governmentality, what explains the difference between the image of a ubiquitous operating system and the notion of a globalist-Zionist-Islamist-Satanist-Communist cabal? Another way of asking the question: How do we distinguish left and right antistatisms and be sure which vision prevails as the mainline State breaks down?

As Eric notes, we need both social and political revolutions. Whereas "political" means power structures and governmental organization—who's running the place?—"social" includes relationships, values, mores, and the texture of the cultural fabric. Perhaps the social addresses content where the political addresses form. What makes the difference between right and left antistatisms is their social content, incorporating an analysis of interlocking structures of oppression, most prominently race and gender. Furthermore, an anarchist antistatism requires an awareness of historical context: of the ways in which all subjects are situated in relation to the past and present unfolding legacies of capitalism, colonialism, and empire.

When you overthrow the state, or establish your autonomous zone or liberated territory, what values are prevalent there and what relationships will you systematize: patriarchal white supremacy or egalitarian polyculture?

III.

The second line was even longer than the first. It spiraled around all four sides of a city block on the Lower East Side of Manhattan, buffeted by a cold October wind. Everyone was masked. This was a line for early voting in the 2020 presidential election. I had peed first, and brought a book (on anarchism) to pass the time—and there was plenty of time: for reflecting on the tactical choice, as an anarchist, to vote, on how to wrap up the foreword to Eric's book, and on what these things had to do with each other.

Various hecklers made the rounds. A white man, maybe in his late fifties or early sixties, walked down the row, addressing each person waiting: "Communists! Look, a communist! Another communist!" I couldn't tell if he was speaking as an antiauthoritarian leftist or a right-wing conservative, or whether his jeers were intended as serious or whimsical. Then a Black man, maybe late twenties or early thirties, castigated us from across the street, growing more vehement as he strode the block. "What, are you all stupid? Gonna choose another slave master? The fuck are you doing? You think this is helping anything?" A little later he came back the other way, so animated that one pass hadn't been enough.

Finally another white man, maybe late sixties or early seventies, approached the line. (Do only cis males feel the need to harangue people standing in line?) He wore a MAGA hat and no face mask. His words were barely coherent, but the rage and hate in his tone were unmistakable. "No freedom . . . for me. No shopping . . . for you. No restaurants . . . for you. My grandkids? No Christmas . . . for them." He seemed to be denouncing pandemic-related shutdowns. It was very confusing. "No health care . . . for you. No . . ." Someone in the line called out, "Put on your mask." This enraged him further. "Why don't you just put a bullet in my head!" he spluttered. "Come on! Put a bullet in my head and then you can put a mask on me!"

The line inched forward stoically, doggedly, in dread and determination. Each person had their own reasons for being there. To me, it didn't feel like reformism, or selling out, or settling for increments, or acquiescence to a problematic system, or "harm reduction" in the sense of adjusting to the ongoing existence of the source of harm. It felt like forming a provisional united front among radicals, progressives, leftists, and liberals in the face of rising fascism, as was experienced in the 1930s and 1940s. It felt like teaming up, all hands on deck in a desperate emergency, in the way that you wouldn't ask about ideology when trying to put out a fire or turn a car from hurtling over a cliff or stop a gunshot victim from bleeding out. It felt like a last-ditch defensive measure, linking arms against impending destruction. It felt starkly necessary and utterly insufficient. In this sense it was a negational act, not a generative one. This vote in itself would not lead to emancipation, abolition, transformative justice, equality, sustainability, cultures of creative potential, horizontality, mutuality, participatory nonauthoritarian social organization, degrowth, redistribution, ecological sustainability, interrelational community, or—in Eric's words—"a directly democratic system that can then address our problems honestly and equitably" and allow people who fall outside of the State's Core Identity Group to determine their own futures free of violence. It would not decolonize a settler regime. It would not remove capitalism or extractive industry. But it might just counter the incipient annihilation of any conditions of possibility for seeking all those things.

"Despite its power and pervasiveness," Eric writes, "the State exists because we choose to let it." The state running this election could not offer us security, identity, or a path to material well-being: the benefits that Eric notes people have traditionally looked to it to provide. It would not save us from the twenty-first-century challenges that we earthlings face: crises in ecology, the economy, and the mass migration unleashed by these crises, by wars, and by other modes of violence. Eric is unequivocal that the State is culpable in these problems, with no possible capacity to provide solutions. Even if there was ever a time when it was possible to imagine progressive reforms enabling more radical change within the context of the State, he warns, that is no longer true. The crises are features, not bugs.

In the last few years, the systems and hegemonic norms of liberal democratic American governance seem to be breaking down, its institutions hollowed out. Or were its true colors simply being revealed (and, therefore, its legitimacy questioned)?

And isn't that what we wanted?

Not this way.

But here's an opportunity.

If the most recent administration served as a demolition crew wielding a wrecking ball on establishment architectures, if it exploited the fatal economic and social flaws revealed by the pandemic as the operating system glitched up to the point of systems failure, here perhaps is an opportunity *not* to restore the existing architecture but rather to build something else in the newly available space, cleared of the rubble of the status quo. A fresh chance to create in that space the radical alternatives that we have long imagined, or have begun to prefigure autonomously, here and there, whether ephemeral or more sustained, publicly or off the grid, anchoring rural communities or outside New York's City Hall. What if instead of building back the battered institutions, we decide now to scrap them, redesign, reimagine, open wide the Overton window, and venture outside the operating system into other scripts, other improvisations?

This book demands that we do just that, and points us in some possible directions.

Maia Ramnath lives in New York City and is the author of *Decolonizing Anarchism* and *Haj to Utopia*.

Acknowledgments

In a previous book, I argued that pacifists play a vital political and social role, even in an easily justified conflict like World War II, by asking the essential question about war: If not now, when? If we all agree that it's an inhuman, murderous scourge that destroys human societies and poisons the earth and is only becoming more so, when will the boundaries of acceptable public discourse expand sufficiently for us to demand its complete abolition—and not be patronized as naïve, unrealistic, and dangerous?

In this book, I ask a similar question in another context: If not now, when will we finally be allowed to look at the modern State squarely, judge it on its merits and faults, and propose alternatives— without being patronized as naïve, unrealistic, and dangerous? *The Operating System* is the opening installment of a larger project to explore and understand the modern State from an anarchist perspective: an overview, to be followed by a series of closer-up, more detailed studies. I hope it will also be the start of a conversation, as more people offer their critiques and their own ideas of the origins, mechanics, and motivations of the modern State, from an outsider's point of view.

I first discussed the idea for this book with David Graeber and Chuck Morse, who were generous with advice and encouragement along the way. I regret that David is not with us to see the result. Other friends and comrades who advised and lent an ear as the argument took shape include, especially, David Goodway, Andrej Grubačić, Chuck Munson, Robert Nedelkoff, Keith Nightenhelser, Stevphen Shukaitis, Marina Sitrin, Seth David Tobocman, David Wyner, and, of course, Mary V. Dearborn. As always, the New York Autonolistas— Melissa Jameson and Christopher Cardinale—were instrumental in keeping me on track as I juggled competing claims on my time, including the need to make a living. I'm deeply grateful to Carwil Bjork-James, Michael Herzfeld, Maia Ramnath, Kevin Van Meter, Kristian Williams, and once again, Mary V. Dearborn, for reading and commenting on my manuscript and for their encouragement.

The modern State is a huge subject; I can't begin to mention all the scholars, theorists, journalists, organizers, and agitators whose work—in writing and in the streets—has informed my approach to the field, going back decades. Peter Kropotkin, Rudolf Rocker, Emma Goldman, Lucy Gonzalez Parsons, Cindy Milstein, Joan Robinson, Immanuel Wallerstein, Rebecca Solnit, Angela Y. Davis, Charles Tilly, James C. Scott, and Crimethinc. Ex-Workers Collective are just a few of these. Finally, I'm enormously grateful to a few friends who've passed away—Clara and Sidney Solomon and Robert Erler—who were my personal bridge to earlier generations of anarchists, anti-authoritarians, anticapitalists, and rebels who dedicated their lives to critiquing and overcoming the State.

Finally, I'm very grateful once again to AK Press for giving me the opportunity to write this book, bring it to a larger audience, and, I hope, provoke further discussion of the nature of the State. AK helps give a voice and a presence to authors whose anger and outrage are matched only by their love of humanity and of the earth. Please support AK Press.

INTRODUCTION

Toward an Anarchist Theory of the State

The state is, to some extent at least, an alien power; though it is of human construction, it is not within human control.
—Chandran Kukathas, "A Definition of the State"

Hoping to soak up every last bit of partisan advantage in the face of continuing mass protests against African American deaths at the hands of police, U.S. president Donald J. Trump picked a most familiar ideological scapegoat. On July 27, 2020, he tweeted, "The Fake News Media is trying to portray the Portland and Seattle 'protesters' as wonderful, sweet and innocent people just out for a little stroll. Actually, they are sick and deranged Anarchists & Agitators who our great men & women of Law Enforcement easily control, but who would destroy our American cities, and worse, if [Democratic presidential candidate] Sleepy Joe Biden, the puppet of the Left, ever won." A day later, testifying before the House Judiciary Committee on the federal government's militaristic response to protests in Portland, Oregon, Trump's attorney general, William Barr, stated, "In the wake of George Floyd's death, violent rioters and anarchists have hijacked legitimate protests to wreak senseless havoc and destruction on innocent victims."[*]

Meanwhile, deaths from the COVID-19 virus, the rapid spread of which was in large part the fault of a chaotic and disastrous response by the State, reached 150,000 in the United States and the number of infected topped 4.4 million.[1] In addition, a U.S.-backed Saudi Arabian assault on rebels in neighboring Yemen had left almost half of that nation's inhabitants on the brink of starvation and racked up more than 70,000 killed since the conflict began in 2016.[2] By 2020, between 185,194 and 208,167 civilians alone had died in various conflicts in Iraq that followed the 2003 United States invasion of that country, according to the Iraq Body Count project.[3]

Getting back to the reasons for the protests Trump and Barr were so anxious to quell, a *Washington Post* analysis found that since the start of 2015, 4,927 people across the United States had died in police shootings, of whom more than half—2,499—were non-white. Since Blacks made up only 13 percent of the U.S. population, they were victims in a disproportionate number of cases: thirty-one deaths per million compared with just thirteen per million for whites.[4]

In other words, while Trump and Barr argued that force was the only way to save the State from havoc and destruction at the hands of dangerous anarchists, the State was busily destroying nations, botching its response to the worst public-health crisis in a century, and failing to keep its citizens safe from its racist public servants. Which, then, was the greater danger to order, security, and social progress?

[*] Less than two months later, the U.S. Department of Justice directed Barr, along with Homeland Security secretary Chad Wolf and Russell Vought, head of the Office of Management and Budget, to identify and review federal funding of jurisdictions "that have permitted violence and the destruction of property to persist and have refused to undertake reasonable measures to counteract these criminal activities (anarchist jurisdictions)." Allan Smith, "Justice Department Deems New York City, Portland and Seattle 'Anarchist Jurisdictions,'" NBC News, September 21, 2020. New York City, Portland (Oregon), and Seattle subsequently sued the Trump administration for violating Congress's spending power and localities' authority to provide public safety as they saw fit. Veronica Stracqualursi and Kristina Sgueglia, "NYC, Seattle and Portland Sue Trump Administration over 'Anarchy' Designation and Threat to Withhold Funding," CNN, October 22, 2020.

Granted, the Trump administration was an uncommonly authoritarian one by American standards. And anarchists have furnished a convenient scapegoat for opportunistic politicians for the better part of two hundred years. But why was this particularly the case in 2020, with a pandemic raging and public opinion turning in favor of African Americans in the debate over police violence?

Perhaps what anarchists say as much as what they actually do was what made the Trump White House so eager to single

> By emphasizing direct action, anarchism reflects a growing disillusionment with the State and democratic government as engines of progressive change.

them out. By emphasizing direct action, engaging in horizontal and leaderless organizing, and rejecting conventional pressure-group politics, anarchism reflects a growing disillusionment with the State and democratic government as engines of progressive change, and particularly as means to modify capitalism. As corporate-friendly economic policies have become ever more tightly hardwired into the functioning of the State, from the most highly developed to the most impoverished countries, the possibility grows fainter that any form of conventional politics, practiced within the system, can modify those policies.

Meanwhile, the world seems to have rediscovered the fact that the anarchist movement is a wider and more imaginative field than its caricature as a collection of bomb-throwing assassins and antigovernment nihilists. In the 1970s and 1980s, Murray Bookchin and the Institute for Social Ecology established the link between anarchism, radical ecology, and small-scale, municipal-level self-government. Subsequently, anarcha-feminism became a hot topic, anarchists in developing countries challenged the stereotype of the movement as made up largely of white people from the West, and the Occupy movement demonstrated (yet again) that nonhierarchical organizing can pull together a large and disparate resistance with lightning speed.

Anarchism remains small as a political movement, but its influence and reach are widening. Anarchists have been active in struggles like the Standing Rock Sioux's opposition to the Dakota Access

Pipeline and Palestinian resistance to Israeli occupation and apartheid policies. The anarchist community in Athens made the Exarchia neighborhood a haven for refugees entering Greece and a stronghold of resistance to the country's increasingly xenophobic government. Anarchist writers and thinkers—among them Colin Ward, Ruth Kinna, David Graeber, Noam Chomsky, and Cindy Milstein—have exposed readers to the anarchist take on everything from anthropology and education to media, economics, democracy, and grassroots organizing.

Anarchist theory, and some elements of anarchism in practice, have become fashionable areas of inquiry for scholars. Anarchist theory has even found its way into the specific assignments of top-tier academics. To give just one example, French philosopher Catherine Malabou was named the Spinoza Chair of the Philosophy Department of the University of Amsterdam in February 2019. The announcement of her appointment noted, "This year's central topic is philosophy and anarchy. . . . Different, sometimes contradictory, signs are making manifest the necessity of a new interrogation on anarchy in the current global political situation, far beyond the idea of a violent strategy against the State. How are we to understand and interpret those signs?"[5]

Discouragingly, none of these developments—or, indeed, the global resistance in general—have had more than limited impact on the further entrenchment of corporate-friendly economic policies, which continues as if the past decade-plus of economic collapse and grossly uneven recovery had never happened. Globally, the greatest beneficiary of the outrage that followed the economic crisis of 2008 and 2009 has been the Far Right, whose quasi-fascist appeals to nationalism and vitriolic racism proved a convenient distraction from the real economic causes of the crisis and the punishing austerity that followed. Even a disastrous, and preventable, global epidemic appears to be consolidating state and corporate power rather than weakening it. The System, as it was once known, seems to have weathered the storm in relatively good shape.

* * *

Why has the anarchist movement not been more successful at bringing together a serious opposition to the State and its offspring and intimate partner, capitalism—especially given the disasters they have inflicted lately and the attractions of anarchism as an approach to politics? A partial answer may involve the direction that much of the movement has taken, both in practice and in theory, over the past few decades.

What set anarchism apart from other forms of socialism in mid-nineteenth-century Europe was its firm opposition to any form of authority, but especially the State, and its assertion that capitalism can't be abolished—as other socialists hoped it would be—without at the same time abolishing the State. The Russian anarchist Peter Kropotkin put this emphatically in "The State: Its Historic Role," in 1896:

> There are those who hope to achieve the social revolution through the State by preserving and even extending most of its powers to be used for the revolution. And there are those like ourselves who see the State, both in its present form, in its very essence, and in whatever guise it might appear, [as] an obstacle to the social revolution, the greatest hindrance to the birth of a society based on equality and liberty, as well as the historic means designed to prevent this blossoming. The latter work to abolish the State and not to reform it.

With the exception of fringe groups like anarcho-capitalists, almost every anarchist today would doubtless endorse this statement. What sets anarchists apart from democratic socialists or mainstream progressives is that they do not regard the struggle against the State as something to be put off for tomorrow in order to fight for more limited, immediate reforms or to support one more "really good" candidate for office. Shaking off the State, as we'll discuss in chapter IV, is the job *now*. (A word of encouragement to nonanarchists: you don't need to agree with this conclusion to draw some valuable lessons from an analysis that doesn't take the State as a given.)

But anarchist scholars, theorists, and publicists in recent decades have generally directed their attention elsewhere. A recently published anarchist anthology includes twenty-eight essays by anarchist scholars—only one of which directly addresses the subject of the State.[6] Inspired by movements and intellectual tendencies including feminism, Black studies, postcolonialism, poststructuralism, and queer studies, anarchists have concentrated instead on studying authority in general, including how it bears on the oppression of women, people of color, gender nonconformists, the Indigenous, and more; how capitalism aggravates these injustices; and how we might visualize a self-directed or directly democratic society to replace it.

These new approaches are vital and have greatly enriched and updated the tradition. Anarchism today wouldn't have any place in a strategy of social, political, and economic change if it had nothing to say to these issues. But anarchists seem to shy away from directly addressing the State: what it is, how it continues to evolve, how it expresses itself as a specific form of authority, how it incorporates capitalism, and, above all, how it induces us to obey. (Oddly enough, Chomsky, who is sometimes accused of not being sufficiently anarchist, is one of the exceptions, since his media and communications analyses directly address how the State and one of its vital components *work*.)

Anarchists aren't the only ones who skip past these questions: academics, activists, and other leftists often appear to be interested in every aspect of anarchism except its critique of the State. Recall what the University of Amsterdam declared when it announced its Spinoza chair: "Signs are making manifest the necessity of a new interrogation on anarchy in the current global political situation, *far beyond the idea of a violent strategy against the State.*"

But what's wrong with a "strategy against the State," violent or nonviolent? Can a movement that avoids creating such a strategy be called anarchism at all, or is it just a general preference for a less authoritarian, less hierarchical system? Is the State still "an obstacle to the social revolution"—to the fight against racism, sexism, economic inequality, and more—or is Kropotkin outdated in this respect? Isn't it important—maybe more so today than previously—to understand, criticize, and work actively to bring down this increasingly sophisticated, powerful, and ruthless force?

The answer has to be yes. The anarchist critique of the State can enhance our understanding of racism, sexism, and economic inequality, and potentially can help us see what's needed to overcome them. By the same token, however, anarcha-feminism, for example, isn't really "anarchist" unless it addresses how and why the State perpetuates and benefits from sexism. The same goes for anarchist analyses of white supremacy, Indigenous struggles, queer oppression, and economic exploitation. Without incorporating the State—and not just power in a generalized sense—in each discussion, anarchism can offer only a partial understanding of these issues. When anarchists critique capitalism, patriarchy, and other forms of oppression from a materialist perspective, but omit any direct analysis of the State or give it only a secondary role, they risk practicing not anarchist theory but a kind of Marxism Lite. While they may make some valuable contributions here and there, they're unlikely to solve the big problem anarchism faces today: how to make itself once again an effective mass revolutionary movement—and, in so doing, pull the rest of the Left out of the dead end it has occupied for the past half century.

Neither of these goals is achievable unless anarchism refocuses on the institution that's the foundation of our social, economic, and political order and directly addresses the question of how to overthrow it. Today, this is not just a socially desirable outcome to work toward, but an existential necessity.

Humanity faces three enormous challenges: first, the advancing and interrelated catastrophes of climate change and ecological destruction; second, increasing economic inequality and concentration of power; and third, the need to adjust to a vast increase in human migration that for the first time is turning the entire globe into a genuinely multicultural society.* The first could render the earth uninhabitable. The second devalues human labor and, with it, the value of human beings outside a narrow, favored group. The third could result in either a richer human world than we have ever had or

---

* Marxist philosopher Slavoj Žižek poses a list of "four possible antagonisms" that partially overlap with these three challenges. One of these, perhaps equally important, is "the socio-ethical implications of new techno-scientific developments, especially in biogenetics," whose practitioners play with the very nature of plant, animal, and human life. Their potentially calamitous work is generously supported and directed by the State and shielded from community oversight. Žižek, "How to Begin from the Beginning," *New Left Review*, May/June 2009.

a violent new regime of racial exploitation and exclusion. The State has failed to meet these challenges, at times deliberately refusing to do so. Working within the system has not worked, and we're all—anarchists and nonanarchists alike—running out of time to replace it with something that does.

* * *

The irony of anarchists' inattention to the State is that plenty of mainstream and Marxist scholars and theorists labor obsessively over the modern State, its history, and its component parts.

I'm looking at the March 19, 2020, issue of the *London Review of Books*, a highly regarded political-cultural publication with a left-of-center slant. Of seventeen substantial articles, eight—almost half—are about some aspect of the State. The subjects include the condition of the contemporary Japanese monarchy, the foundations of the modern State in England under the Tudors and in seventeenth- to nineteenth-century Prussia, the Chinese state and its relations with the world, the migration of peoples from Africa and Asia into Europe since 1945 and its geopolitical consequences, and the impact of upsurging Hindu nationalism on the Indian state.

Like so much recent mainstream writing about national and global politics and political economy, these pieces all implicitly address the same fundamental issue, one that goes back to writers of the early modern era, including Machiavelli and Shakespeare: Can the State establish itself firmly (in newer states), and can it survive (in older ones)? The specific set of dramas is always the same, too: Can the State rise to a particular challenge, such as industrialization, economic modernization, increasing racial diversity, or secularization? Can it legitimize itself, or preserve its legitimacy? Can it defend "progress" and civilization, or will it give way to some variety of xenophobic, authoritarian populism? Whatever the specific issue—war and peace, poverty and inequality, racial injustice, or capitalism and technology—the State is the framework for the discussion and the setting in which the problem must be solved, if it's to be solved at all. Is the State important to the extent that it can help eliminate malnutrition, or is malnutrition important to the extent that it is a test of the State? In this discourse, the State is consistently the protagonist: the hero we're meant to root for to score the winning goal, the general who pulls victory from the mouth of disaster, the Moses leading us to the Promised Land of order, prosperity, and contentedness. The vast majority of mainstream political practitioners and observers typically accept this institution, which is merely five hundred years old, as a given that can be reformed but not superseded. Outside the State is the void. There is no alternative to working within the system, because outside of it there is nothing and no one. If we attempt to organize or create a society without it, we are doomed to irrelevance or disaster—an assertion that pundits rehearse whenever any evidence crops up that the State is beginning to wobble in one place or another. The horror of the "failed state" is that it forms a kind of black hole, breeding centrifugal forces that can suck other states in.* Deep acceptance of the State, coupled with this equally deep anxiety, is why the ringleaders reflexively assume the task of recouping or reproducing the State each time a revolution succeeds in overthrowing an oppressive regime.

Among the nonanarchist Left, the problem is somewhat the same. For 150 years, democratic socialists have generally framed their struggle as being against capital, not the State, and have repeatedly run aground because they ignore or set aside the deep connection between the two. Socialists often fail to see the State as much more than a facilitator of policies set by the capitalist elite to secure their profit-creating ends, on the one hand, and maybe as a tool for opposing and controlling capitalism, on the other. As a result, the Left all too often finds itself building the very thing that cements capitalism's grip on the economic life of the human community. The language of protest reflects this: a random search of writings on the Standing Rock protests against the Dakota Access Pipeline,[7] racism,[8] climate

---

* The Fund for Peace uses four criteria to define a "fragile state" that may be on the road to failure: "1) loss of control of its territory, or of the monopoly on the legitimate use of physical force therein; 2) erosion of legitimate authority to make collective decisions; 3) inability to provide public services; and 4) inability to interact with other states as a full member of the international community." https://fragilestatesindex.org/frequently-asked-questions/what-does-state-fragility-mean/.

change,[9] the expansion of oil and gas extraction,[10] the COVID-19 crisis,[11] and the problem of rural dispossession in Brazil[12] turned up multiple references to capitalism's causal role in each case, but hardly any to the State, even though state policy plays a central part in each one. We talk about state oppression as well as capitalist oppression, but the latter is generally assumed to be more fundamental.

This is where anarchism becomes a necessary tool, and anarchists need to once again be part of the conversation. Anarchism is the only theoretical approach that fully recognizes the connection between capitalism and the State and completely denies the assertion that there is no alternative to either. Viewed through an anarchist perspective, the fundamental problem isn't capital or the wage system, it's the State. It's not the police or the military, it's the State. To be more precise, it's the State and the role it carves out for each of these institutions and practices within itself, since the State provides the edifice and the collective direction without which they could not exist. When we address problems like economic exploitation, racism, and oppression based on sex and gender roles, the anarchist perspective frees us to look outside the theoretical and practical framework of the State system for solutions. We're free to conclude that there are problems that, by their nature, the State is not equipped to solve, and we may realize that some are not solvable at all as long as the State exercises its influence.

Anarchists view the demise of the State as a wonderful opportunity for humans and the earth, not a tragedy. It may be our best hope. We criticize the modern State because we know it's only the latest form of human domination, with no greater claim to permanence than any of the earlier ones. We also know, thanks to Kropotkin and the many researchers who succeeded him, that humanity has lived successfully in cooperative communities built on mutual aid, and could do so again. We are free to consider the fundamental strengths and weaknesses of the State, how it works in theory and practice, what's likely to bring it down, and what we can do—what kind of politics we can practice—to hasten that day.

* * *

This book is an introduction: a first step to building a new anarchist theory of the modern State. The starting point is to propose a new and more comprehensive way to think about the thing itself. In chapter II, we'll look at several useful and commonly cited definitions of the State and flesh out a new one, but for now, let's note that the State is more than just government. It's a form of human organization that aspires to create an encompassing social, cultural, and functional environment for every one of its inhabitants, one built on the creation of wealth, enabling the State to continuously expand and deepen its powers. Individual states compete and cooperate, depending on the circumstances and their particular ambitions, but collectively they, too, work to preserve and extend the State as a form and apply it to new territories and environments.

The State is more than just government. It's a form of human organization that aspires to create an encompassing social, cultural, and functional environment for every one of its inhabitants, one built on wealth creation, enabling it to continuously expand and deepen its powers.

The State is not a thing, then, so much as a form and a set of institutions, a way of thinking that's inculcated into us that we perpetuate at the same time that many of us resist it. In chapter II, I'll argue that the thing the State most resembles is not any other human form of organization, but a human-created mechanism: a computer operating system like Windows or iOS, an environment that aspires to create an encompassing social, cultural, and functional environment for its users. Like an operating system, the State works to make the environment it creates so enveloping that we hardly think of functioning outside it because doing so would require too great an adjustment for us to feel motivated to try, whatever annoyances and even injustices this might cause us. Like an operating system, the State becomes reality—or at least, attempts to persuade us that it is. And as this implies, while the State is a creation of human beings, it also molds and directs them, limits and guardrails their aspirations and ambitions such that they conform to and support its objectives.

The modern State embraces every organization or grouping on which it confers legitimacy, official or not. It encompasses political parties and pressure groups of all sorts, households, small and large businesses, nonprofit organizations, trade unions, and neighborhood and community associations. Both private and public education are parts of the State; both benefit from its assistance, follow its prescribed curriculum and cultural fundamentals, and use their voices—and money—to influence it. Patriotic and religious organizations are components, since they encourage us to be loyal to and work through the State. Criminal organizations are part of the State, too, insofar as they depend on it for infrastructure and perform favors for it from time to time. Most importantly, capital is part of the State, supplying the economic engine it needs to grow and reproduce itself while depending on it for the conditions necessary for capitalist enterprise to function—and for protection and rescue when it (regularly) overreaches.

These and many other entities are tightly interlocked with the legal and organizational structure of the states they inhabit and so are implicated in its larger project; we'll explore them in more detail in chapter III. All, in other words, are invested in growing and reproducing the State, whatever their professed objectives. That's why I spell *State* here with a capital *S*, and reserve the lowercase *s* for individual states.

As this implies, while the State is a creation of human beings, it also molds and directs them, limits and places guardrails on their aspirations and ambitions such that they conform to and support its objectives. It induces us to accept a system that makes decisions for us rather than bending to our needs and desires, however democratic its governmental framework may be. It persuades us to regard racial and gender discrimination, atrocities committed in its name in warzones and inner cities, and the economic disempowerment of working people as tolerable, necessary, or reformable only in the fullness of time. It tells us that violence or the threat of violence is the price of peace and order. It manipulates us into accepting environmental destruction as the necessary trade-off for economic growth, and economic growth as the human race's highest material value. Above all, it persuades us that it's all there is.

What are the boundaries of the modern State, geographically and otherwise? The State does not contain Indigenous peoples who've never accepted the rule of a state and never adopted a functional role within it. Outside of it, too, are minorities and subject populations whose only choice for survival, often, is to organize in defiance of the State: people of color, sexual and gender minorities, political refugees and dissenters. Outside of it are cooperatives and groups practicing mutual aid, often in the urban heart of the State itself. Outside of it are artists who create for themselves and for a community, not a "public" or a paying audience molded by the State and capital. Outside of it are all of us when we center our thinking on progress defined by self-generated human needs and desires rather than the imperative of infinite wealth-building.

The State cuts across functional areas and even specific aspects of our individual lives: health care, for example. For-profit and nonprofit hospitals all lie within the State, since both are recognized and operate according to its rules, including accepting payments drawn from state subsidies, assigning patient IDs, and staffing with doctors and nurses licensed by states. Free clinics, street medics, and practitioners like midwives, as well as some doctors and nurses, sometimes operate within the State and sometimes outside, according to their desire to make their own path and fulfill their duty to the community as they understand it. When we accept their services, we, too, may be either operating within the boundaries of the State or stepping outside them.

As a first step on a longer road to understanding this complex system we call the modern State, this book focuses more on drawing parallels and commonalities than exploring all the many differences that emerge as individual states are born and develop: why some attributes deliver advantages to some states and not to others, why different social formations display different strengths and weaknesses, how larger states exercise dominance over smaller ones. We won't explore why the British state developed differently from Prussia-Germany or tsarist Russia, why representative institutions flourished in some states but not in others, or why tensions emerged between capitalists and the landed class in nineteenth-century Europe. Many of the examples and generalizations in these pages are gleaned from the experience of larger states with developed economies, and particularly the United States, although they apply to smaller, less industrialized states as well.

So it's important to keep in mind the limits of our analysis. No two states are interchangeable; each occupies a unique situation in the world and is molded by its geography, populations, and cultures, not just by its effort to succeed at the same game as other states. Culture and politics are made at the bottom, not just the top; communities and subcultures aren't always defined by the State, but define themselves; revolutions, social movements, and liberatory desire force states to make accommodations at different rates of change. Sometimes these movement directly oppose the State itself.

States don't operate on an even playing field. Some are far more powerful and some more successful than others, lasting longer and responding to crises with greater resilience. And, of course, states quarrel, go to war, and fight each other to the death, with devastating results for their people. Not every state proceeds at the same pace of development or weakens or collapses for the same reasons.

Today's states are quite different from the developing modern states of the sixteenth century, despite their similarities. Among other things, one state—which calls itself the United States—has achieved an unparalleled position of dominance and cultural hegemony over all others and now aspires to be recognized as a superstate or effective world government. From its political and economic capitals in Washington, D.C., and New York City, the United States attacks its perceived enemies at will, makes and breaks regimes and social systems, innovates and provides a role model for states and statespeople everywhere. The United States and its doings appear more often in what follows than any other government or institution. But this book is not about the United States.

We'll try to grasp instead not a particular state or states, but the State: the model that has been evolving over the past five centuries and that has expanded to take in almost the entire planet and more and more of our individual and collective consciousness. Where did it come from? What are its components? How does it impact us? What are its aspirations? And how can we reassert our free will against it?

I

The State and COVID-19

The ultimate expression of law is not order—it's prison. There are hundreds upon hundreds of prisons, and thousands upon thousands of laws, yet there is no social order, no social peace.
—George Jackson, *Blood in My Eye*

The modern State is a relatively new institution, dating back only a bit more than five hundred years. By comparison, from the founding of the Roman Republic to the collapse of the Roman Empire was more than nine hundred years, China's Zhou dynasty lasted almost eight hundred years, and the Tiwanaku state of the southern Andes is thought to have survived for as long as eight centuries as well. The (mostly) culturally unified Christian Europe of the Middle Ages waxed and waned over close to a thousand years. But history moves faster in our time than it did in earlier days, thanks in part to faster communication, more widespread literacy, and more rapid technological change and economic growth, all of which the modern State is responsible for, to a considerable extent. So at five hundred years, is this particular form of human association reaching its limits—and the end of its usefulness? Or is it the last and best social model we'll ever need, the culmination of all that came before?

By virtually any standard—geographic, economic, cultural, technological—the modern State has been more successful than any previous system at imposing itself on humanity and the earth. Over five centuries, it has harnessed capital, labor, science and technology, and firepower to remake almost the entire world through conquest, slavery, innovation, economic exploitation, the subjugation or evisceration of societies that followed other models, the systematic stripping of the planet's natural resources, and the inculcation of its worldview into every one of us.

These were not by-products or unintended consequences. They also didn't have to happen. But these practices were integral to the State's goals and ambitions; they are part of its DNA. In the past century, the atrocities have grown in magnitude as the State has grown more powerful: over six million killed in Nazi Germany's death factories, millions imprisoned and dead in the prisons and forced labor camps of the Soviet Union and Maoist China, and an unprecedented incarceration boom in the United States that's created a powerful new private industry of prisons and detention centers.

Today, the State is well on the way to creating, for the first time in human history, a worldwide monoculture tied to a uniform economic model and a single pattern of governance directed by a self-selecting global elite. More remarkable is the speed with which this project has advanced in just the last hundred years, bringing with it a slew of unprecedented problems including climate change, mass migrations, and a startling rise in economic inequality. We may know in the course of the next fifty years whether this vast system of domination and cultural hegemony will overcome these challenges or will capsize or be overthrown.

The drive to achieve that monocultural vision, the longed-for "end of history,"

> Today, the State is well on the way to creating, for the first time in human history, a worldwide monoculture tied to a uniform economic model and a single pattern of governance directed by a self-selecting global elite.

inspires the elite who direct the State and serve as its ideologists and cheerleaders. It has driven them to brush aside the mounting evidence of its failures, deny them, or compromise by offering ineffectual half measures in response. Fundamentally, however, the State itself is the problem. In the early modern era, its colonial and profiteering incursions depopulated the Americas through disease and pauperization, destroyed and deskilled sophisticated economies throughout the Americas and Asia, turning them into dependencies of the industrial West, and created enormous enslaved and disadvantaged populations: all to further its path to dominance.

Why, then, isn't this great Leviathan meeting massive resistance? We'll examine this complex question carefully, but one factor stands out. Over the five centuries of the State's rise to dominion, we've all acquired a perceived stake in its success.

This has been its greatest achievement: to convince us that the State itself is indispensable. It has persuaded us that any major societal problem, from racism to nuclear proliferation to climate change to affordable housing, can and must be resolved within the context it sets and that outside the present form of the State (whether democracy or dictatorship) there is only something worse (right-wing authoritarianism, chaos, dissolution). Any failure of the State—any systemic failure—tends to be written off as a failure of leadership, implying that the solution is more or better leadership and that any alternative that moves away from leadership as a principle is unrealistic. Especially in the last century, the State has thus established itself as the locus of political activity; if you're outside it, you (seemingly) consign yourself to political voicelessness and irrelevancy.

"It is the state which men [sic] constantly encounter in their relations with other men," wrote the Marxist sociologist Ralph Miliband; "it is towards the state that they are increasingly driven to direct their pressure; and it is from the state that they expect the fulfillment of their expectations."[1] In this sense, the State is the greatest beneficiary of status quo bias, by which humans tend to take the current state of affairs as the baseline, whether they actually like it or not, and approach any change with great caution for fear it could result in loss.[2] We may not believe in capitalism, the predominant religion, or monogamy, but we're still inclined to cling to the institutions and processes of the State—even when there are plenty of reasons not to—on account of the day-to-day reassurance it provides. We just can't take the chance.

The State works hard to reinforce the belief that it is what there is, that it underlies and informs everything, such that we conflate our deeper hopes for human society—for peace and prosperity, for freedom and self-determination, for the preservation and growth of cherished traditions—with the health and growth of the State. We're conditioned to think of government as impossible in the modern world without the State, that "primitive" peoples who exist outside such a structure lack government. In fact, every human community "governs" itself in some way when it decides to form a polity, or political entity, anthropologist Michael Herzfeld points out;* the State is just one way of doing so. What makes it different is its comprehensiveness, and the depth of its penetration into our consciousness.

Almost unwittingly, we find ourselves focusing not on creating a new world but on making sure the current one—the one defined by the State—is moving in the "right direction" (by whatever definition). So long as we do this, the State has succeeded, and, for the most part, it can't lose for winning because the answer to any failure or shortcoming is a better State. The State appears to us as a kind of common sense: obviously correct on the surface, for all practical purposes, and therefore value-neutral.

Objectively, it should be possible to look outside the State for solutions and new ways of conceiving human life and community— and many of us do. But time and again, we collectively fall back on the State as the most obvious and obviously powerful force to deal with crisis, be it social and economic inequality, crime, a geopolitical threat, or a pandemic—and we settle for the State's version of a resolution, even though we know the problem isn't solved. No system of social organization has ever covered so much of the globe, exercised

---

* Herzfeld defines a polity as an "ethical space" or "consensus reached by people acting with full awareness of constructing a context in which their actions make moral sense." Michael Herzfeld, "What Is a Polity? Subversive Archaism and the Bureaucratic Nation-State," *HAU: Journal of Ethnographic Theory*, 9, no. 1 (2019): 28.

power so flexibly in so many different ways, or induced acquiescence as adeptly as the modern State does today.

* * *

How each of us judges the results depends on our point of view. But for most of humanity, the State's response to the novel coronavirus pandemic has been a genuine, clear-cut failure, an institutional breakdown that calls into question the State's ability to accomplish one of its principal duties: providing security for its people.

This was a disaster that never should have happened. Governments and scientific and public-health experts had known for a long time that a serious pandemic could and probably would occur, had run through scenarios to gauge their preparedness, and knew what was needed to quell its spread. In the United States, for example, planning began under the Bush administration in 2004 and continued steadily under Obama's presidency. Game plans were developed, prescribing, step by step, the response by government, industry, and the health care system.

But despite the United States having the world's largest and most sophisticated medical and scientific apparatus, its stockpiles were depleted in the years prior to COVID-19's appearance and never replenished, leaving hospitals and other facilities ill equipped. Years of cutbacks in government spending on health care and a profit-driven shrinkage in the number of hospitals had left the country with too little capacity to address a pandemic. In 1978, the United States had 1.5 million hospital beds for some 222 million residents; in 2020, it had 100 million more residents but 575,000 fewer hospital beds.[3]

The country was left terribly unprepared for a major epidemic. Health departments across the United States had seen their budgets shrink by nearly 30 percent over the past dozen years and had cut nearly 23 percent of their workforce.[4] A damning report by the nonprofit Institute of Medicine warned in 1988 that there was no clear coordination between the federal, state, and local governments: "responsibilities have become so fragmented that deliberate action is often difficult if not impossible." Another study fifteen years later by

Trust for America's Health found that some states had no plans for meeting a pandemic; others had plans that had never been tested or discussed with hospitals, fire departments, and other key players. One state refused to say whether it had a plan at all.[5]

"The root of this catastrophe, doctors, scientists and health historians say, is our failure to fully incorporate public health into our understanding of what it means to be a functioning society," a *New York Times* feature on the crisis concluded.[6]

Nevertheless, and contrary to Trump administration claims, scientists knew almost as soon as the coronavirus appeared in China that something extraordinarily dangerous was likely to cross the Pacific. There was time to prepare and to start mobilizing the necessary resources. Instead, the carefully laid-out scenarios were disregarded and the game plans forgotten. The White House ignored the multiple early warnings it had received, well before either China or the World Health Organization (WHO) labeled the outbreak a pandemic; it denied that an emergency existed and then downplayed the problem in the weeks following. With seemingly no deliberation and counter to the assumed procedure, the executive branch decided to leave the response largely to the fifty states, which then entered into competition with one another for personal protective gear, with disastrous results.

With no coordinated program to test for the virus or trace people who had been in contact with the infected, the disease claimed—officially—more than one hundred thousand fatalities by the end of May 2020. Meanwhile, twenty-six million U.S. workers had applied—with varying degrees of success—for unemployment benefits as the economy crashed under the weight of self-isolation orders, layoffs, and business closings.

The folly had begun earlier. A National Security Agency directorate on global health, security, and biodefense established by Obama survived little more than a year before his successor disbanded it in 2018.[7] The Trump administration's 2021 budget, unveiled in February 2020 when the White House already knew about the virus, called for a 9 percent cut in the budget of the Department of Health and Human Services, including a 16 percent cut to the Centers for Disease Control and $3 billion in cuts to global health programs.[8]

Blaming the fiasco on the feckless Donald J. Trump is too easy, however. The roots of the president's mishandling of the greatest pandemic in one hundred years extend back through decades of U.S. economic policymaking that emphasized fiscal austerity, deregulation, and privatization. Plenty of progressive and democratic socialist voices were highlighting this point in the months following the outbreak. But the United States was not alone. Many other governments, including those of Russia and the UK, were also slow to accept the seriousness of the emergency, and the WHO, lacking much ability to act without its donors' support, was reluctant to jump ahead.

But this was to be expected: the virus emerged in China, which had developed possibly the most thorough and minutely controlling state system in the world. As anthropologist Carwil Bjork-James points out, COVID spread initially due to structural defects of hierarchical states: particularly, subordinate leaders' reluctance to pass on bad news to their superiors, even if it means opening the window for a deadly disease to enter and spread. Similarly, the Ebola outbreak in Africa several years earlier was facilitated by the devastating wars, economic exploitation, and decline in health services that had gripped the continent in the decades since it was organized into postcolonial states.[9]

Arguably, China was slow to address the underlying conditions that allowed the virus to spread, increasing the odds of a breakout epidemic; other governments were similarly slow to respond to information coming out of that country and thereby left their people open to the disease. The delays were deadly; according to researchers at Princeton Medical Center, the daily COVID-19 death toll in the United States would have been halved if federal authorities had started recommending self-isolation and the wearing of face masks just four days earlier than they did.[10]

The larger the state, generally, the more likely the authorities were to cover up, delay, and avoid acknowledging the magnitude of the pandemic, at least initially. In the case of the United States and Brazil, for example, federal governments handed responsibility to second-tier state governments that lacked the resources or expertise to cope. Advice from leading scientists—even some on government payrolls—was ignored, and opportunities to coordinate the response globally were spurned or disabled.[11] The atrocious response to the pandemic can be put down to elements of human nature—greed, competitiveness, narrow-mindedness—but it was also a failure of the State, which is supposed to be better at tackling oversized problems and crises than more modest forms of human organization. When the State, including its powerful capitalist economy, fails to properly address a problem like COVID-19, much of its rationale for governing us is called into question.

According to whose criteria, however, has Washington's reaction to the coronavirus calamity been a failure?

From the point of view of the State, which ultimately bears the responsibility for the pandemic, the crisis has been a marvelous opportunity to increase the breadth and depth of its powers, often with broad public support, as was also the case following the September 11, 2001, terrorist attacks. After the 2008 financial collapse and the massive banking rescue operation that followed, the public rebelled against such bailouts; the Dodd-Frank Act was passed to protect financial services consumers and to make sure banks did not overextend themselves in the future. The COVID-19 pandemic has overturned many of those strictures (which were already being not so gradually eaten away) in the name of propping up the flow of credit, vastly increasing the State's ability to dictate the kind of economy we have.

The Coronavirus Aid, Relief, and Economic Security (CARES) Act, which Congress quickly passed to address the COVID-19 crisis, earmarked $1.7 trillion in loans and grants to companies, with few questions asked about their degree of need and only shaky oversight, along with $650 billion in additional business tax cuts. Airlines alone received some $58 billion, half in outright grants rather than loans. The Federal Reserve chipped in $3.3 trillion in cheap loans to banks, corporations, and investors. By contrast, CARES offered only $500 billion—in temporarily expanded unemployment benefits and direct aid—to the rest of the population: only a tenth of business's total take.[12]

Altogether, it was the most comprehensive rescue package ever extended to the capitalist system, demonstrating once again the extent to which the State and its banking complex operate on an invented system of artificial scarcity; when they need to produce mountains of new liquidity, they can always do so. At the same time, the bias in Washington's overall emergency spending made clear that rescuing the capitalist system is always a higher priority for policy makers than are individual households, small businesses, or communities.

By April, Senate Republicans were already pushing to cement capital's increased power by way of a bill that would give companies nearly blanket immunity from lawsuits brought by customers or employees who got sick owing to conditions in their facilities; the senators signaled that they wouldn't support any further aid to state or local governments—which they were reluctant to back anyway—without the bill's passage.[13] Also that month, Trump vowed to craft a rescue package for U.S. oil and gas producers, who were caught in a nosedive as prices for their commodities cratered. Despite abundant evidence that capital-intensive fossil-fuel extraction and consumption are the leading causes of global warming, fossil fuels remained fundamental to the State's strategy for economic growth; the notion of completely replacing them with cheaper renewable energy sources was still unthinkable.

* * *

Just as it did following the 2008 financial crisis, then, the State moved rapidly and in a very focused way to protect the interest group it deems most important to its own survival and success: the capitalist class. We'll examine the relationship between capital and the State in more detail later, but for now we'll note that the modern State's legitimacy is founded on providing three things:

- a degree of personal security;
- a shared identity, including a sense that one's voice is heard; and
- a path to material well-being.

Relentless economic growth is the State's preferred path to power, and so it is also the State's preferred means of delivering material well-being. Capital is the State's essential partner in securing rapid economic growth. A number of needs and preferences flow from this common objective, including the following.

- Both the State and capital engage in social control; both require a pliable human population to serve as instruments of political and economic expansion, as soldiers and security forces and as consumers, and to legitimate them.
- Both need a system of education, training, and cultural attunement geared to produce that population.
- Both need steady revenues and good credit to back their activities and reward their leaders.
- Both need natural resources that can be used to generate tools and products contributing to economic growth.
- Both rely heavily on data and data analytics.
- Both require secrecy, making them prime consumers of surveillance and security tools, both physical and data-related.
- Both require large, tightly controlled physical infrastructure.
- Both derive much of their legitimacy from branding and imagery.
- Both fetishize leadership.*

All of the above make both the State and capital inherently technocratic by inclination: prizing efficiency, impersonality, planning, rational order, and a rigorously analytic approach to governance and management—even if that ideal is never fully attainable and the analysis (usefully) masks value judgments and political deliberation. Capital further requires security of its property and other assets and the backing of the fiscal and monetary power of the State in times of crisis. The State need providers of capital—commercial banks and

* In a Q&A, David De Cremer, founder and director of the Centre on AI Technology for Humankind at the National University of Singapore Business School, said, "We need leaders who are tech savvy enough to optimize their extensive knowledge on business processes to maximize efficiency for the company and for society." ("Artificial Intelligence Will Change How We Think about Leadership," https://knowledge.wharton.upenn.edu/article/artificial-intelligence-will-change-think-leadership/, November 2, 2020.) Substitute "government" for "business" and "the State" for "the company," and De Cremer's assertion would have essentially the same meaning.

other institutions—to extend it credit in order for the government to fund its day-to-day activities as well as its more ambitious projects.

How do their interests intersect? According to free-market ideologues like economist Milton Friedman, the only imperative of business is to create value for its owners. Any other relevant social role is contained in that imperative; otherwise it's not relevant.[14] But this assertion is nothing more than ideology. The fundamental job of capital is to build the State; creating wealth, launching profit-making enterprises, providing needed goods and services, and manufacturing a desire for yet more goods and services are its principal contributions to the project. This often makes for extraordinarily uneven distribution of its benefits and accelerates the destruction of the environment, threatening human life as well, but it also increases the State's sources of taxation, which provides the leverage needed for the State to borrow money and finance its growth. For this reason, capitalism has been a vital part of the State ever since the modern State began.

This relationship is further revealed in the route the State chose for us to address the COVID pandemic. States, like the human community that produces them, aren't solitary creatures; they have composed a System of States almost from the very beginning of their existence. Starting with the first offensive-and-defensive alliances in the early sixteenth century, this system expanded into a process for resolving wars and other major disputes through congresses and, especially in the last one hundred years, a constellation of international agencies, police forces, multilateral financial institutions, rules-setters and enforcers for global trade, and deliberative bodies, from the United Nations to the European Union to the World Trade Organization. While the political Right often views these multilateral organizations as rivals to the national state (the conspiratorial "new world order"), in fact they exist to facilitate the building of the State, extend its influence, and reassure its subjects that the system, if not the individual states, works for their benefit.*

---

* "Free-trade agreements and institutions such as the EU's single market do not reflect a loss but a pooling of sovereignty: control is extended beyond the boundaries of the state." Peter Verovšek, "Brexit and the Misunderstanding of Sovereignty," https://www.socialeurope.eu/brexit-and-the-misunderstanding-of-sovereignty, December 9, 2020.

The System of States includes a number of institutions, including a UN agency, the WHO, charged with coordinating the global response to health risks. But the WHO depends entirely on funding from member states, including the United States, and as a result is generally hesitant to criticize their behavior, even when it contributes to a health crisis. More deeply, the System of States ensures that the vital interests of the State are protected in any globally important strategic matter. One such instance came in 1978, at a conference in Almaty, Kazakhstan, when world health leaders produced a declaration that stated, in the words of science-and-technology scholar Stuart Blume, that "socio-economic development was vital for health and that health care had to be integrated with goals like clean water and safe working conditions."[15]

The Almaty declaration thus prioritized extending good public-health provision to individuals at every level of society as the most important way to forestall epidemics and pandemics. Arguably, a healthy workforce is a more productive workforce and therefore better able to generate the economic growth that capital and the State depend on. But there was a more technological, and more profitable, way to get there. According to Blume, "critics of the declaration—many of them from the United States—argued that its goals were unrealistic and unaffordable. Instead, they said, the emphasis should be on tackling specific diseases for which effective technologies of prevention or control existed—like vaccines. The critics prevailed."

The result was the system that prevailed more than forty years later, emphasizing the staggeringly expensive search for vaccines and even more profitable long-term treatments rather than a more forward-looking and equitable effort to improve public health and make the population less vulnerable to epidemics. Ever since, says Blume, "vaccines and international politics have always been tied together." Vaccines play an important role, but they also represent untold riches to the companies that develop them and a powerful competitive advantage to the sponsoring state. While many governments were slow to launch a public-health response to the coronavirus, they almost immediately began collaborating with pharmaceutical companies on vaccine development. "The rapidly growing vaccine market has become the pharmaceutical industry's major source of growth," says Blume, and a source of "power, profit and national prestige" for the State.*

Even when vaccines exist, the system is geared to turn procurement into a Darwinian struggle that favors bigger developed countries over the impoverished. After the H1N1 influenza outbreak was declared a pandemic in 2009, advance purchase agreements by larger governments with vaccine manufacturers were automatically triggered, hoovering up supplies and leaving poorer countries to wait for months or to rely on donations. The pattern repeated itself with COVID-19. On April 24, 2020, world leaders convened by the WHO said they would ensure equitable distribution of vaccine stocks, but China, the United States, India, and Russia, countries that include most of the biggest vaccine developers as well as the biggest markets for vaccines, did not participate. No authority exists to enforce a more rational, cooperative process globally.

For households and communities ravaged by the pandemic, this amounts to a terrible failure of an international system that's allegedly set up to create a level playing field for public-health provision and alleviate the debilitating effects of poor health care on developing countries. It also provides dramatic evidence that a world system of states with strong command-and-control structures, which ought to be well suited to address massive problems, may actually be no better at it than a more decentralized network of nonhierarchical communities. From the perspective of the State itself, however, this profit-driven melee operated exactly as intended, rapidly ensuring that the solutions being developed to end the pandemic would provide the maximum benefit to powerful states and their capitalist partners.

The pandemic is likely to strengthen the State in numerous other ways, just as the Iraq invasion and the ongoing U.S. wars in the Middle East did. Efforts to build and distribute contact-tracing apps,

---

* Meanwhile, frantic emergency spending on COVID threatened to crowd out efforts to control longer-running health problems that kill even more people in the developing world, such as malaria. (Kaamil Ahmed, "Pandemic Could 'Turn Back the Clock' 20 Years on Malaria Deaths, Warns WHO," *The Guardian*, April 23, 2020.)

notably by Apple and Google, have the potential to create enormous new databases of personal health information on individuals suspected of being exposed to the coronavirus.[16] Similar apps were quickly put into use in China, Israel, South Korea, and Singapore, four of the countries that responded fastest and most aggressively to the pandemic, but the features that Apple and Google outlined would be standard on their phones. While the two tech giants promised that purchasers would be able to opt out, they are practiced at offering such choices but then making them too difficult and time-consuming for most users to take advantage of. These companies' databases will become immensely more valuable, and because their ties to government are dense and mutually supporting, the troves of new data will certainly be available to the State whenever it desires.

Even without these new tools, the effort to get individuals and households to self-isolate in the early stages of pandemic response created a bigger and more broadly accepted surveillance society. In April 2020, it was reported that judges in Louisville, Kentucky, were ordering corrections officers to outfit people who defied COVID quarantine with electronic ankle monitors. Tech companies were falling over themselves to offer new, improved ways to track people's movements. One such company, Attenti, advertised a "quarantine management system" enabling authorities to "easily monitor the location and condition of people under quarantine—anywhere, anytime."[17]

Under the aegis of pandemic social tracing, employers were soon adopting new systems that deepened their ability to monitor their workers—including those working from home.

Software makers such as InterGuard, Time Doctor, Teramind, VeriClock, innerActiv, ActivTrak, and Hubstaff have seen increased demand since the beginning of the pandemic. Each provides minute-by-minute, keystroke-by-keystroke monitoring as workers complete tasks in what should be the privacy of their own homes. Each also provides bosses with "productivity metrics," including how often a worker is sending emails.[18]

"The KGB and Cambridge Analytica suddenly seemed Neolithic," observed former Greek finance minister Yanis Varoufakis.*

Chances are that such measures will never be abandoned or even relaxed; after the terrorist attacks of September 11, 2001, many office buildings beefed up their security and surveillance apparatus, including x-raying briefcases. Large employers and law enforcement routinely share the data they thus acquire, as some Wall Street firms and the New York Police Department did when the Occupy Wall Street protests settled down in the midst of the city's financial district in 2011.

Whistleblower Edward Snowden commented a couple of months after the pandemic exploded, "Do you truly believe that when the first wave, this second wave, the 16th wave of the coronavirus is a long-forgotten memory, that these capabilities will not be kept? That these datasets will not be kept? No matter how it is being used what is being built is the architecture of oppression."[19]

The State relies on both "hard" police and military power (domination) and various "soft" forms of persuasion and inducement (hegemony) to enforce acquiescence. COVID-19 presented a ripe opportunity for governments to widen their exercise of hard power as well. In El Salvador, President Nayib Bukele, a political novice when he entered office in 2019, responded to the pandemic with a military crackdown that included locking in containment centers those who violated social distancing rules. He quickly followed up with a campaign against gangs, authorizing the army to kill gang members if necessary and pack suspects into prisons that were sure to become COVID-19 breeding grounds.[20]

Panama and Peru instituted quarantine rules separating men and women, aggravating discrimination against transgender persons. In Hungary, authoritarian prime minister Viktor Orbán pushed through a law suspending elections and giving him the power to rule by

---

* Yanis Varoufakis, "A Chronicle of a Lost Decade Foretold," https://www.project-syndicate.org/commentary/bleak-preliminary-history-of-2020s-by-yanis-varoufakis-2020-05, May 27, 2020. Cambridge Analytica, a UK political consulting firm, was found to have harvested millions of Facebook users' personal data without their permission; the data was used in 2016 by the Trump presidential campaign and others to create psychographic profiles and customize messages to different groups of voters.

decree. Some proposals went even farther; in Israel in May 2020, just as residents learned that all movements of automobiles in the country and much of the Palestinian West Bank were being tracked by police and saved in an unregulated database called Eagle Eye, prime minister Benjamin Netanyahu proposed "microchipping" students (including kindergartners) when they returned to school so that an alarm would sound whenever they were not sufficiently distanced from each other.[21] In the ostensibly more democratic United States, incidents of police abusing new powers to enforce social distancing surfaced repeatedly in the news.

* * *

"The vast increase in state power has taken place with almost no time for debate," the *Economist* noted in late March.

> The record suggests that crises lead to a permanently bigger state with many more responsibilities and the taxes to pay for them. . . . The most worrying [development] is the dissemination of intrusive surveillance. Invasive data collection and processing will spread because it offers a real edge in managing the disease. But they also require the state to have routine access to citizens' medical and electronic records. The temptation will be to use surveillance after the pandemic, much as anti-terror legislation was extended after 9/11. This might start with tracing TB cases or drug dealers. Nobody knows where it will end.[22]

Surveillance and data collection never happen entirely in secret; the awareness that the State can see more and more of what we do and think reinforces its power by keeping us fearful, befuddled, and off-balance. But would this latest surge in the State's power to pry have happened—in the United States and elsewhere—if governments had responded to the pandemic more competently? Well-thought-through plans were in place for doing so. But had those plans been enacted, there would have been no rationale for turning contact tracing into an exercise in mass surveillance, for beefing up corporate and government data on individuals, for bailing out mismanaged corporate partners, or for handing over extraordinary powers to heads of government. Perhaps most importantly, there would have been no opportunity to induce the public to accept the necessity of such measures.

Was the State's response to the novel coronavirus, then, a failure, at least in Washington? Obama chief of staff Rahm Emanuel famously remarked, in the aftermath of the 2008 financial meltdown, "You never let a serious crisis go to waste. And what I mean by that, it's an opportunity to do things you think you could not do before." That can mean as little as making the best of a bad hand or trying to salvage some modest good from a disaster. But when the State causes a crisis or fails to competently address one, the dynamic is quite different; even when the State is at fault—perhaps all the more so when it is—the solution is an increase in its powers. The answer, in other words, is always more State, and the larger project is always to relegitimize the State, once again ensuring its survival and continued growth.[†]

Such was the case with COVID-19. The pandemic, and the disastrous government response in most of the world's largest countries (China, the United States, Russia, Brazil, and so on) prompted a yearning among a large segment of the public in these countries— and, arguably, an overwhelming percentage of their political and economic elites—for a strong, competent, and professionally managed State. Americans look at the performance of smaller, more homogeneous, easily governed societies like New Zealand, Singapore, and South Korea and wonder, sometimes nostalgically, why their own government—not to mention the private and nonprofit sectors— couldn't muster the same rapid and decisive response to the virus.

But what if the State itself helped to create the problem? If so, do we want the State to succeed or to fail? If the former, how much difference does the State itself make to us? Do we really care whether

---

* Some trace the comment back to Winston Churchill.

† Historian Charles Tilly characterized the State as a protection racket: "Consider the definition of a racketeer as someone who creates a threat and then charges for its reduction." Tilly, "War Making as Organized Crime," in *Bringing the State Back*, ed. Peter Evans, Dietrich Rueschemeyer, and Theda Skocpol (Cambridge: Cambridge University Press, 1985), 171.

it emerges from the COVID pandemic stronger, more trusted and capable of decisive action than it was when the crisis began? Or has this simply become confused with our desire to have a stronger human society that's more resilient in the face of a growing likelihood that more pandemics—and other disasters—will appear?

If our goal is to achieve a stronger human society, with or without the State, then we are free to judge the State more critically as a way of doing so—of providing ourselves the security, identity, and material well-being we need—and we are free to consider alternatives. We can proceed to ask, for example, whether the improvements in the standard of living that we've seen over the last two centuries, at least in the most affluent parts of the world, really could not have come about except in the framework supplied by the State, and whether a framework that favored cooperation over competition, sustainability over growth and consumption, and direct, participatory decision-making over the concentration of power in an elite—elected or otherwise—might have done a better job. Someone, somewhere, has always been asking these questions, ever since the specter of social and economic revolution first loomed more than 250 years ago.

> If our goal is to achieve a stronger human society, and not simply to preserve the State, then we are free to judge the State more critically as a way of doing so—and we are free to consider alternatives.

But the dynamic we've just examined, in the State's tragically disjointed response to a deadly virus, is powerful. It serves to neutralize radical politics, channeling it into reformist projects that, at best, ameliorate some aspects of the economic and social order, but only for as long as the reforms reinforce the State and our elites find it politically expedient to continue them. It induces us to acquiesce to entrenched injustices—based on race, class, and gender, among other forms of human difference—in exchange for a vague hope that they can be addressed, someday, within the system. And it prompts us to wall off the possibility of any social, economic, or political arrangements that can't be controlled or harnessed by the State.

* * *

There was a time—part reality, partly shimmering, nostalgic mirage—when the modern State seemed to provide a serviceable landscape for progressive political action. It could be oppressive, it was corrupt, it was compromised and coopted by capital, but somehow, in many countries, the people were able to make progress toward social justice, greater economic equality, and environmental harmony within the framework of the State.

Not anymore. Instead, the State seems to be taking us backward to our—and the planet's—destruction. Consider three of the biggest challenges facing human society:

Climate change

Thanks to global warming brought about by the seemingly unbreakable marriage of our system of political economy to wasteful and destructive energy sources, life on earth may be threatened within just a few decades—that is, within our lifetimes.

The World Bank has projected that heat levels could rise so high in some regions, such as the Ganges Valley, that they become practically uninhabitable, and high tides could swamp much of Vietnam and Thailand. In just three regions—sub-Saharan Africa, Latin America, and South Asia—as many as 143 million more people could be displaced within their own borders.[23] As water becomes scarce and farmland dries up, regional conflicts will heat up; the civil war in Syria may be a harbinger of this particular future. "Researchers suggest that the annual death toll, globally, from heat alone will eventually rise by 1.5 million," the *New York Times* reported in 2020. "But in this scenario, untold more will also die from starvation, or in the conflicts that arise over tensions that food and water insecurity will bring."[24]

The State, which can make war and dispossess populations almost in an afterthought, appears incapable of reversing course and saving the planet. Much of the trouble stems from structural issues and deliberate decisions that the State itself was responsible for. Almost as quickly as coal, oil, and gas caught on as energy sources, the State gave them a central role in its economic policy. Because they provide energy in a concentrated, highly portable, easy-to-store form, carbon-based fossil fuels were perfectly designed to power industrial manufacturing and an increasingly industrialized military; as long as supplies remain plentiful—new technical advances, like fracking, always seem to keep them that way—the State and the energy industry are strongly motivated to keep producing the stuff.

The State's best collective efforts to wean itself from fossil fuels—the Paris Agreement, for example—fall well short, and even these commitments it walks back almost as soon as it makes them. A 2019 study by the International Monetary Fund (IMF) calculated global post-tax fossil-fuel subsidies in 2017 at a staggering $5.2 trillion, or 6.5 percent of the world's entire gross domestic product. The largest benefactors were China ($1.4 trillion), the United States ($649 billion), Russia ($551 billion), the European Union ($289 billion), and India ($209 billion).*

Rising inequality

In the eyes of the State, inequality is good news; labor costs for businesses are falling, leaving more revenue to be scooped up by owners and managers, in accordance with neoliberal economic policy. A study of fifty-six countries from 1975 to 2012—roughly the period of corporate-friendly, neolioberal economic "reform"—found that the labor share of corporate income fell from roughly 65 percent to about 60 percent. The eight largest economies all experienced significant declines.[25] The working class has been divided and neutralized, meanwhile, leaving the State free to pursue tax and spending policies that further shift the fruits to capital.

---

* "Post-tax subsidies" reflect "differences between actual consumer fuel prices and how much consumers would pay if prices fully reflected supply costs plus the taxes needed to reflect environmental costs and revenue requirements." David Coady, Ian Parry, Nghia-Piotr Le, and Baoping Shang, "Global Fossil Fuel Subsidies Remain Large: An Update Based on Country-Level Estimates" (IMF Working Paper WP/19/89, International Monetary Fund, May 2019), 2, 19–20.

The result is an increasingly stratified society in which people living precariously can be persuaded to blame each other rather than the political-economic system. In the United States, according to economist Emmanuel Saez, the top 0.1 percent of the population by income reaped income almost 200 times the earnings of the bottom 90 percent in 2018, up from 37 times in 1977.[26] With economists and policy makers schooled in neoliberal policy dominating governments and transnational institutions, the direction the United States embarked on some fifty years ago is increasingly being followed elsewhere in the world. The result has been a steadily more violent blame game between nativists and migrants, white folks and Black folks, the middle class and indigents, the educated and the disadvantaged.

Mass migration and dispossession

Together, climate change and policies that aggravate economic inequality are fueling a profound change in the social life of humans. Changing climate conditions contribute to droughts and desertification that combine with disruptive neoliberal economic policy to drive rising numbers of people out of regions they've lived in for hundreds of years, resulting in unprecedented social disruption.* According to the United Nations, the number of international migrants reached 272 million in 2019, an increase of 51 million in less than ten years. International migrants represented 3.5 percent of the global population in 2019, up from 2.8 percent in 2000.

This will continue; according to a 2020 statistical study by the *New York Times Magazine*, the Pulitzer Center, and ProPublica, under the most extreme warming scenarios, more than thirty million migrants will head toward the U.S. border alone in the next thirty years, driven by drought and soil degradation, crop failures, and resulting economic chaos.[27]

---

* "Between 2010 and 2015 the number of migrants from El Salvador, Guatemala and Honduras showing up at the United States' border with Mexico increased fivefold, coinciding with a dry period that left many with not enough food." Christopher Flavelle, "Climate Change Threatens the World's Food Supply, United Nations Warns," *New York Times*, August 8, 2019.

These developments are creating the most diverse societies in human history, including in places that had known little or no in-migration in their past. This enriches cultures and societies everywhere, but states see migrants in only two ways: as a source of cheap labor and as a threat to the dominant ethnic groups in their respective communities. Acting together, these contradictory impulses serve to stigmatize and segregate migrants, stir racial animosities, and make it harder for working people to unite around their class interests to oppose the political and economic elites.

Much the same pattern of ostracization afflicts refugees: persons who have fled collapsing states, collapsing economies, and communities destroyed by invasion, civil war, and freelance violence. The numbers reflect an upward spiral as the State fails to find a solution. At the end of 2019, there were 79.5 million refugees in the world—more than 1 percent of humanity—up from 33.9 million in 2008, according to the UN High Commissioner for Refugees.[28] That includes 45.7 million internally displaced persons, 26 million refugees no longer in their own countries, and 4.2 million asylum seekers, and it considerably exceeds the 60 million who were displaced in World War II, the greatest single conflict the world has ever seen. Research by Brown University's Costs of War Project found that anywhere from 37 million to 59 million of refugees in 2020 were displaced by seven wars the U.S. had helped launch and perpetuate since 2001 as part of its effort to politically manage the rest of the world: in Afghanistan, Iraq, Libya, Pakistan, the Philippines, Somalia, Syria, and Yemen.[29] Rather than address this human disaster, which was largely brought about by the actions of states, governments are closing their doors and leaving these people in a limbo of refugee camps and makeshift settlements.

* * *

If we cannot move to a better method of socioeconomic organization that addresses problems like migration, inequality, and climate change and thereby earns people's confidence, we have no hope of creating a livable society or, indeed, of surviving. Yet, every time the

State appears to have made a fundamental mistake, shot itself in the foot, or done something utterly unforgivable, it finds a way to re-cover and re-cement its control. The State disempowers us. Instead of real change, it offers us a contraption for raising our hopes and dashing them, guaranteeing apathy and disillusion. Politicians replace politics, legislation and lobbying overshadow the streets where power is really won, and bureaucratic institutions take the place of direct organizing and institution-building in our communities and collectivities.

How did we get to this place, where Nietzsche's "people and herds" have been replaced by "the coldest of all cold monsters" or Thomas Hobbes's grim Leviathan? Anarchists and other antiauthoritarians have struggled for many years to understand how the State does this and how it can be effectively challenged and, perhaps, broken. Today, with catastrophic climate change looming, we are fighting for more than a just society; we are fighting for survival. But before we can speak of replacing the State, or even of distinguishing human society from the State in practical terms, we need to push aside the illusions and misdirection that limit our understanding of what this thing is: what its components are and how it enlists us in the work of reproducing itself.

II

Understanding the State

There can be no conception of the State which is not fundamentally a conception of life: philosophy or intuition, system of ideas evolving within the framework of logic or concentrated in a vision or a faith, but always, at least potentially, an organic conception of the world.
—Benito Mussolini, "The Doctrine of Fascism"

In some respects, the State—the idea, the institution—has reached a precarious point in its history. Left and right, Black and white, people express more cynicism and even hostility to government than they have in perhaps centuries. The State's dominant political and economic paradigm, emphasizing markets and wealth accumulation, commands almost no allegiance outside a small global elite. Government is under stress everywhere; in developed countries, "liberal" democracy—supposedly one of the foundations of its popular legitimacy—is being questioned as never before, and in some places where the State only established itself fairly recently, it's literally disintegrating.

People's confidence in government to provide the benefits traditionally expected of it—a degree of personal security, a shared identity, a path to material well-being—is also hitting a low. The gulf between reality as our policy and business elites see it and as perceived by most people has rarely been greater.

As the pandemic took hold, even some leading mainstream economists and pundits were losing much of their faith in the centralized, top-down model of the State. Nassim Nicholas Taleb, the economist who popularized the term "Black Swan" to describe a completely unpredictable, catastrophic event, spoke publicly about the increasing fragility of the global economy and its lack of fail-safes in a time of crisis. An April 2020 profile of Taleb described him as encouraging "the distribution of power among smaller, more local, experimental, and self-sufficient entities—in short, [building] a system that could survive random stresses, rather than break under any particular one. (His word for this beneficial distribution is 'fractal.')"[1]

Taleb was doubtless not advocating the abolition of the State, but his interest in a less centralized, less hierarchical economic order brushes up against anarchism. His thinking also reflects a distinct crisis of confidence. A 2017 poll by Pew Research Center found that only 43 percent of people in the largest western European countries and only 25 percent in the United States had confidence in their representative assemblies to act in the best interests of the public.[2] In 2019, only 17 percent of Americans said they trust the government in Washington to do what's right "just about always" or "most of the time," compared with nearly 80 percent in the mid-1960s (before American intervention in Vietnam went into full swing).[3] The idea of honesty among the people at the top rates an emphatic LOL. In a 2017 poll by Transparency International, almost seven out of ten people in the United States said the government is "failing to fight corruption," and only 28 percent said that voting for a clean candidate or a party committed to fighting corruption was the most effective thing they could do.[4]

But to say that people have lost confidence in the State—that they are no longer loyal to the State—is not accurate either. For some institutions, people make exceptions. The same Pew poll that showed only 25 percent of Americans have confidence in their elected representatives also found that 80 percent have confidence in the military.

A 2019 Gallup poll placed people's confidence in the military somewhat lower, at 73 percent—but that was up drastically from where it stood in 1975, at the end of the Vietnam War. The same Gallup poll found that 54 percent of Americans have quite a bit of confidence or a great deal of confidence in the police, compared with only 37 percent for the presidency or the Supreme Court and a dismal 11 percent for Congress.[5] As we'll see later, people's perceptions of the military and the police are extremely important indicators of their confidence that the State is at least minimally fulfilling its promise to them. Arguably, in the United States and many other countries, this perception is the real bulwark of the State's legitimacy today.

> The modern State is more powerful, more pervasive, more deeply embedded in our collective psyche, and more adept at coopting and neutralizing challenges to its authority than at any time in its history.

Without question, too, the modern State—the form of government and social organization that was born in Europe in the late fifteenth century—is more powerful, more pervasive, more deeply embedded in our collective psyche, and more adept at coopting and neutralizing challenges to its authority than at any time in its history. From a breathtakingly diverse collection of social and political formations during the European Middle Ages, including urban communes, loosely knit feudal monarchies and baronies, tribal and clan enclaves, hunter-gatherer and remote farming communities, and theocratic ministates,* political organization today has narrowed down to only one. Not all states are governed the same way—some are more authoritarian than others—and some diversity still exists at the local level, but even this is disappearing. The modern State is the organizing model of nearly the entire world.

Individual states are bound together as never before. A true global elite is forming itself, with similar if not identical political,

---

* Even medieval states that are sometimes regarded as important predecessors of the modern State, like Norman Sicily, were often thrown-together affairs that combined elements of previous forms of administration in "a mosaic of adaptations and improvisations." Charles Tilly, *Coercion, Capital, and European States, AD 990–1992* (Malden, MA: Blackwell, 1992), 26.

economic, developmental, and social viewpoints; this, too, never really existed in any earlier age. The State's destructive power, including nuclear weapons, missiles capable of hitting targets halfway around the world, and precision drones, outclasses anything humans could have conceived of even one hundred years ago outside of science fiction. In recent decades, it's added remote-controlled drones and crippling economic sanctions that can kill hundreds of thousands of civilians to its repertoire as the "civilized" alternatives to all-out war. Its powers of surveillance, persuasion, and population control far outstrip even the fascist and communist dictatorships of the twentieth century, generally with less outward appearance of coercion.

None of this was true until quite recently. One hundred years ago, much of the world was still governed—if at all—by traditional structures with little connection to the European state model. Today, very few parts of the globe could be described this way, and many of them (such as the Indigenous communities of the Amazon Basin) face annihilation. When the European colonial empires were wound down after World War II, for example, the leadership of the former colonies, without exception, created new modern states rather than building on models suggested by their traditional cultures.

The State also looms larger in economic terms. U.S. government spending as a portion of GDP (the country's total economic output in a given year) was less than 2 percent in 1916; in 2010, it was 45.07 percent, and in many other industrialized countries, the percentage was higher still.[6] Worldwide military expenditure alone was estimated at a record $1.82 trillion for 2018, 76 percent higher than when it reached its post–Cold War low in 1998; close to half the total is accounted for by the United States.[7]

Another useful measure of the State's dominating position is the market for bonds, the debt securities that fund most investment and other activity by governments and corporations in today's world. To take the largest example, the market for government bonds—federal, state, and local bonds, as well as bonds for government agencies— amounted to almost half of *all* debt securities (49.78 percent) issued in the United States in 2017, according to the Securities Industry and Financial Markets Association. Corporate bonds accounted for only

21.75 percent, by comparison. The State is not only the largest economic engine in the world, the debt securities it issues are arguably the most powerful force in the world's financial markets.

The State's influence extends deep into the so-called private sector as well, through the tax breaks and subsidies it supplies to business. The carried-interest tax loophole, which exists to benefit the giant private equity funds that increasingly dominate the corporate sphere, amounts to a $20 billion gift from Washington over the course of a decade.[8] Other tax loopholes, honeycombed betwixt and between the tangle of the world's tax regimes, have enabled corporations, wealthy individuals, and even hospitals and universities to stash anywhere from $8.7 trillion to $36 trillion in offshore tax havens.[9]

When the State wants to address an economic disruption, its power is virtually unlimited. One such crisis hit during the 2008 financial crash, when a critical part of the economic system's basic plumbing, the market for commercial paper—the short-term debt that companies and governments use to fund everyday operating expenses, like payrolls—was on the verge of collapse, raising the possibility of disastrous capital shortfalls at major financial institutions. The U.S. Federal Reserve Bank stepped in, creating the Commercial Paper Funding Facility (CPFF) to backstop the market.

That meant, in effect, that any business or government that issued commercial paper could be confident that it could keep doing so, because if there was any question, the Fed itself would buy it. The commercial paper market at the time was valued at some $1.5 trillion on any given day, and within two months the CPFF owned more than 20 percent of it, or $350 billion.[10] If the commercial paper market had crashed, employers all over the country would have been unable within weeks to make payroll, pay their suppliers, or pay rent, among other things, and the banking system's own vast commercial paper holdings would have become worthless. The entire U.S. economy would have had a collective heart attack and collapsed. The Federal Reserve—a unit of the U.S. government, although essentially run by private bankers—thus held power of economic life and death over every person who lives and works in the United States.

A final example: In March 2020, Congress passed the CARES Act, which included $454 billion in funding provided to the Fed by the U.S. Treasury to support its lending facilities at a time when the COVID crisis was threatening to decimate U.S. businesses. The Fed would use that already large sum to collateralize up to $4 trillion in loans and loan guarantees that banks could extend to companies they decided were worthy of rescue. A month later, in an interview on *60 Minutes*, Fed chair Jerome Powell went even further with this breathtaking statement: "There's really no limit to what we can do with these lending programs that we have."[11]

This statement, and the staggering sums in the examples above—the U.S. budget for 2019 was "only" $4.41 trillion—can be seen as a gift wheedled out of governments by nefarious lobbyists and secured by clever corporate tax strategists. But together, they dramatically underscore the degree of power the Fed—an instrument of the State—has, or that it's believed to have, to impose its will.

The vast majority of the favors that government grants to capital are perfectly legal, a matter of public record, and knowingly enacted into law by the people's representatives, as in the case of a 1995 law that allows oil and gas companies to drill on federal land without paying royalties to the taxpayer. In other words, they constitute spending in pursuit of government policies and therefore should be deemed to expand the role of the State rather than narrow it. It's worth noting, too, that the CARES Act amounted to $2.2 trillion in total, including $500 billion in direct loans to big industries. While Washington often complains that it has no money for social spending, safety-net programs, or old-age pensions, in reality this is nonsense: its power to spend and to support the economic units it values is unlimited. The difference is in who the State deems worthy of support.

* * *

But if we can extend our understanding of state policy to transactions with private businesses that seemingly weaken its control of its own—and our—resources, how do we understand the State's goals? How do we define its boundaries? And how to we define the State itself?

The modern State began as both an idea (in the minds of the educated elite of various European societies) and a necessity (for the rulers of the societies in which it was born). Varieties of states and empires existed for millennia, and the theory and practice of the modern State arguably was gestated in the Italian city-states of the late Middle Ages, with a long look back to classical Greece and Rome.* But the modern State is not the same as the Roman Empire, the Abbasid Caliphate, the successive Persian or Chinese empires, or any other state that we could describe as such; it has a distinct profile and distinct characteristics.

It's fairly uncontroversial that individual states have four things in common: they function as governments, control a defined geographic territory, have a bureaucracy, and have the ability to tax. With these established, a state has jurisdiction over a population and a territory, the means to support its activities, and the personnel to carry them out. But the modern State is very different from those it succeeded.

- Modern states rule directly, rather than relying on local grandees to enforce their edicts and extend their power.
- They create bureaucracies separate from traditional hierarchies built on class, nobility, or religious offices.
- This bureaucracy controls a mechanism of taxation to fund the activities of the modern State, whose predecessors relied more on tribute or rent.
- Modern states focus more intently and systematically on managing and exploiting their populations.
- They rely on standing armies rather than men-at-arms supplied by feudal vassals, semiautonomous militias, or mercenaries. Over time, these become conscripted national armies.
- Over time, they separate armies focused on external threats from police forces focused on maintaining the domestic order.

---

* Dante, the Florentine poet, was one of the first to broach the idea of an overarching "world government" that would command and regulate all the kingdoms and republics of the earth in his early fourteenth-century essay "De Monarchia." See Dante, *On World-Government*, trans. Herbert W. Schneider (Indianapolis: Bobbs-Merrill, 1957).

- Each has a centrally directed foreign policy, managed by elites and largely insulated from popular control, even in representative democracies.
- They forge a network of alliances with other states that, over time, acquires an institutional structure of its own and that provides a major support for the State as a model and system.
- They invent and exploit new technologies—especially weapons, but also sophisticated financial instruments, communications and surveillance systems, transportation networks, and many other innovations—to assert and extend their control more powerfully and efficiently.
- They consciously attempt to penetrate every aspect of their people's lives, taking over much of the social function of religion in earlier times.
- Perhaps most important, they tap into the power of capital to ramp up economic development and secure more of the financial wherewithal they need to extend and deepen their field of control.

When we try to define the modern State more closely, perspectives start to diverge, but we have more from which to pick and choose. Six relatively recent definitions stand out.

According to the German sociologist Max Weber, a state "is any organization that succeeds in holding the exclusive right to use, threaten, or authorize physical force against residents of its territory." In the modern world, such a monopoly must occur via a process of legitimation.[12]

Karl Marx considered the State to be a creature and enforcer of bourgeois economic interest. For his disciple Vladimir Lenin, it was merely a mechanism of power that could be harnessed to achieve the ends of any dominant group, such as those of the bourgeoisie. Once worker control of society was achieved, Lenin expected the State to "wither away."[13]

Kropotkin agreed with Marx's definition, so far as it went, but argued that the State was a more complex arrangement. "It is a society for mutual insurance between the landlord, the military commander, the judge, the priest, and later on the capitalist," Kropotkin wrote, "in order to support each other's authority over the people, and for exploiting the poverty of the masses and getting rich themselves. [Such was] the origin of the State; such was its history; and such is its present essence."[14]

The German anarchist Gustav Landauer defined the State as "a relationship between human beings, a way by which people relate to one another: and one destroys it by entering into other relationships, by behaving differently to one another." Somewhat similarly, French historian and philosopher Michel Foucault said, "The State is a practice, not a thing," that codifies power relations at all levels across the social body and that exists to reproduce itself.[15]

Almost one hundred years after all of the above except Foucault, British scholars Joe Painter and Alex Jeffrey attempted a more detailed definition. For them,

- states have precise boundaries within which they exercise administrative control;
- they occupy large territories, and vest control in organized institutions;
- they have a capital city and are endowed with symbols embodying state power;
- their governments create organizations to monitor, govern, and control the population through surveillance and record-keeping; and
- they increase monitoring over time.[16]

A rough progression emerges in these definitions: the earlier thinkers, like Marx and Weber, focused on what defines power and who wields it through the State; later theorists were more concerned with those over whom it exercises power and control and how that exercise of power affects them. With the exception of Kropotkin and Landauer, the common denominator among the theorists—aside from their maleness and their European nationality—is that they took the State as a given, a fundamental condition of existence in the modern world. Even so, we can glean some useful insights from each.

Weber is still correct that the State's authority is built on a monopoly of force and on the willingness of the population to accept it. Marx was correct that the State acts in the interests of a particular group, caste, or class and is intimately linked to capital, but Kropotkin was right that the ruling elite has a more complex, evolving structure than this suggests. Lenin was right to focus on the State as a mechanism for wielding power. Landauer accurately pointed out that the State is not just an institution but part of our social psychology. Foucault saw rightly that all power relationships within society are regulated, to some extent, by the State; he was also correct that the State's primary activity is reproducing itself. Painter and Jeffrey were right to stress the State's need to surveil and control the population as well as the fact that this activity has a trajectory that has developed and intensified over time.

However, if we're not inclined to accept the State as a given—that it is what there is—then we'll need a more comprehensive and skeptical understanding than most of these writers provide. Weber ignored the question of who controls the State and for what purposes. By his definition, a drug cartel could, in the right circumstances, be a state. Marx defined the groupings that control the State too narrowly, denying that the State has any "will" or trajectory of its own. Kropotkin, likewise, failed to see the State as more than just the sum total of the selfish interests behind it. Lenin effectively canceled out the possibility that any society could function unless it wielded power the same way the State does. Foucault left out any substantial discussion of the State's objectives, other than to reproduce itself. Landauer's definition is too narrow; more than a type of relationship, the State has infrastructure, tools, and symbols of power as well. Painter and Jeffrey left out the economic rationale and underpinnings of the State.

Most important, these definitions omit much of the modern State's complex extensions beyond government, what's essential to it, and what makes it different from other, previous systems of political, social, and economic control. They make a misleading distinction between the State itself and the people who control it and whose interests the State serves. When people on the left talk (as they once did) about the "system" or the "establishment" and people on the right about the "deep state," they use shorthand for a vaguely defined, powerful group who direct the State—and from whom, presumably, it needs to be liberated. Most definitions also assume a distinction that doesn't really exist between the political and the economic realm, even when the economic is said to dominate the political, as in Marxism.

If we think of the State as a machine controlled by a specific group—the landed aristocracy, the bourgeoisie, the capitalist class— we understand only part of it, and we risk assuming that it can be abolished or reformed by abolishing or disempowering these groups. If we think of the State as merely a relationship or a practice, we end up ignoring the details, and we fail to understand its full dimensions. Above all, we fail to understand the magnitude of the task of creating true alternatives and counter-communities—and the opportunity to do so.

* * *

Let's try something different, but also more familiar and contemporary. The State is not synonymous with government, and its borders are not strictly physical (even though establishing and enforcing boundaries is one of the ways it wields power). Nor is it a conspiracy, controlled by some all-powerful clique of politicians, gangsters, or wealthy capitalists; while a great deal of its activity is cloaked in secrecy—and this penchant for secrecy is growing—its pattern of behavior is fairly easy to trace. Instead, the State is a vast operating system for ordering and controlling functions and relations among human society, economy, populations, and the natural world, analogous to a digital operating system like Windows, Linux, or macOS.

An operating system, or OS, is defined by Wikipedia as "system software that manages computer hardware, software resources, and provides common services for computer programs." Like the State, it's one of the defining creations of the modern world; it can trace its lineage back to "analog" classification and

> The State is not a conspiracy, controlled by some all-powerful clique; while a great deal of its activity is cloaked in secrecy, its pattern of behavior is fairly easy to trace.

data analytic schemes developed in the early centuries of the modern State.[17]

The chief characteristic of an operating system is that it enables a computer to operate quickly and efficiently and to multitask; "distributed" operating systems can also network multiple computers together and cause them to function as one. "Time-sharing operating systems schedule tasks for efficient use of the system and may also include accounting software for cost allocation of processor time, mass storage, printing, and other resources." The operating system thus serves "as an intermediary between programs and the computer hardware," directing "hardware functions such as input and output and memory allocation." Operating systems are the backbone of an enormous range of devices, from supercomputers to smartphones to web servers to video game consoles.

Like a state, an operating system "governs" the programs and applications under it and networked with it as well as, to some extent, the individuals who avail themselves of these tools and resources. It defines us in relation to itself, and each other, as "users," and can reward us, reject our requests, or even bar us from access according to its needs. It can also monitor and surveil us. Referring to giant meta-platforms like Android and Apple, the German sociologist Philipp Staab observes, "Their own systems are continuously optimized for maximum convenience, to reduce the need to switch to another system. On the other hand, they make it as difficult as possible for users to use certain services outside their own ecosystem."[18]

This is our starting point for understanding the State. Its central feature is the legal, administrative, and decision-making structure we refer to as government. But the State is a much larger, more complex phenomenon, a comprehensive means of organizing and exercising power that, once it's launched, expands to cover more and more aspects of existence according to a direction and logic of its own. "The state could never be the means for any special or definite end, as liberalism conceived it to be," the German anarchist Rudolf Rocker wrote in his classic, *Nationalism and Culture*; "it was rather, in its highest form, an end in itself, an end sufficient for itself."

At the same time, and again like a computer operating system, the State is not a material object or entity. The various pieces of "hardware" we associate with it—big, imposing neoclassical build-ings fronted by Greco-Roman columns quite often come to mind, along with military bases, roads, and monuments—are merely ma-terial containers and symbols of the immaterial reality. An oper-ating system is *soft*ware, a collection of embedded commands that direct a machine called a computer. The State, too, is "software": a collection of ideas, doctrines, commands, and processes that direct the deployment of human beings and their deployment of physical resources.

The State is at once a political, social-cultural, and economic entity. Like an operating system, it networks together institutions, organizations, and less formal groups including government but also many others: corporations, banks, other financial institutions (state-chartered, as it happens), and other underpinnings of capital-ism; eleemosynary (nonprofit and charitable) institutions; so-called civil society groups and political parties (especially "established" parties like the Democrats and Republicans in the United States, which have evolved into quasi-state institutions); and even basic units like families and households. Other institutions and groupings that form part of the State furnish cultural and even paramilitary support to the social order, strengthen organized religion, and re-inforce racial and gender stratification: for instance, the extreme wings of the nativist Alternative for Germany; the Hindu national-ist Rashtriya Swayamsevak Sangh (RSS) in India; and the American Legion, the Ku Klux Klan, the National Rifle Association, militia groups, the Proud Boys, and the Southern Baptist Convention in the United States.

Any organization recognized and regulated by law is a compo-nent of the State; so are many illegal or extralegal organizations that rely on State institutions and infrastructure in some respect, such as informal or gray markets. The State licenses (or tolerates) these organizations for specific reasons of its own, most importantly that they strengthen and legitimize the State itself; it sets explicit or im-plicit rules for how they can act (laws, regulations, guardrails, tacit boundaries); and it exercises the power to overrule and even termi-nate them if it sees a reason to do so. What these entities have in common is that they all reinforce the State even as they depend on the structure of the State to survive.* This is what makes the State a total operating system, not just a legal or administrative structure.†

Government is, of course, the core institution of the State, but government depends on many of these other institutions and organizations to fulfill vital functions. Government especially depends on private capital as a partner in generating economic growth. Historically, many social and economic functions have shifted back and forth from government to private-sector control while always remaining within the State's power to regulate and legislate—and, in reality, the line between government and the private sector is profoundly blurred.

In the United States, for example, homeschooling is subsidized in many states, which effectively means the State has been enlisted in a project to promote religious education, generally underpinned by a right-wing political ideology. Trump education secretary Betsy DeVos said in early 2020, during the COVID crisis, that she would force public school districts to spend part of the rescue funds they were receiving from Washington on private-school students—even those from affluent families.[19]

Another example emerges from the ongoing right-wing campaign to dismantle the U.S. Social Security system. While shifting some or all of the payroll taxes that fund the national pension system into personal investment accounts is often described as "privatization," in reality it is something else. Under most proposals, workers' payroll taxes would not be refunded or reduced; instead, all or part would

---

* Anything that occupies cracks and corners within the operating system is still part of the State. Urban gangs, drug cartels, and other organized crime couldn't function without the infrastructure of roads, airports, housing, postal systems, identity papers, (corrupt) police, legal loopholes, and so forth that the State provides—and they often collaborate with legal institutions on projects that support certain aims of the State.

† Among Marxist thinkers, Louis Althusser came close to this position, defining civil-society organizations such as churches, schools, and the family as part of an "ideological state apparatus" that complements the "repressive state apparatus" (e.g., police and military) in reproducing social relations. Nicos Poulantzas also came close, with his idea of the "relative autonomy" of the State, to acknowledging that the State has its own particular logic and goals that aren't entirely formed by the capitalist class. But neither made the leap to seeing them as part of the same operating system.

be funneled into a preselected menu of private investment funds. The power of the state bureaucracy would be harnessed to achieve a set of free-market goals, calculated to promote the State's objective of increasing its power through faster economic growth.[20] In both examples, the government does not step aside; instead, it takes an active role, directing outcomes favored by the private sector but that private enterprise could not fully achieve on its own.

Like a computer operating system, the State manages relationships between government, capital, nonprofits, and other entities to make them work together easily and efficiently, many parts operating at the same time. Like an operating system, it lets us do things— make computations, write, communicate, learn, play, create art, make a living—but always within boundaries that it prescribes and manipulates. Like an operating system, it provides a user-friendly interface that makes it much easier for us to conduct our business inside rather than outside its boundaries. Consider citizenship, passports, and other personal identification; it's possible to live in the modern world without them, though barely, and it is extremely inconvenient, to say the least. Or consider the highways, rail lines, and postal systems the State and its private-sector components offer. Or, for businesses, the infrastructure of trade treaties, customs services, and ports that facilitate commerce. There are ways around these, but it's so much easier to use the platform the State provides.

Just like an operating system, too, the State gives us error messages when we do something wrong. It tells us when we've stumbled by inflicting the police on us, hauling us into court, jailing us, declaring us incompetent, or, in the wider reaches of its network, subjecting us to social and peer pressure or economic hardship.

Like an operating system, the State defines us in relation to itself and each other. It defines us, for example, as "citizens" or "residents," "households" and "taxpayers." And these definitions make clear whether the state approves of our behavior: "productive citizens," on the one hand, and "delinquents," "criminals," "illegals," and "burdens," on the other.

* * *

In the foregoing, I'm making an argument by analogy—and analogies have inherent drawbacks. They are never perfect, and they often obscure important aspects of both sides of the comparison. But in the case of the State and the computer operating system, the relationship is deep, because the operating systems we now take for granted on our desktops, laptops, and wireless devices owe their existence to research and development that took place at the heart of the nexus between the State and capitalism.

Federal funding for relational databases helped move that technology out of corporate laboratories to become the basis of a multibillion-dollar U.S. database industry. The graphical user interface, which became commonplace on personal computers in the 1990s, incorporates research conducted at SRI International under a DARPA [Defense Advanced Research Projects Agency, the U.S. Defense Department's research arm] contract some 30 years earlier. . . . Established companies, such as International Business Machines Corporation (IBM) and American Telephone and Telegraph Corporation (AT&T), also commercialized technologies developed with federal sponsorship, such as core memories and time-sharing operating systems.[21]

While it takes private companies to bring these technologies to a wider market, their core capabilities were developed with the needs of the State in mind—especially those related to defense. It would be surprising if today's computer operating systems didn't reflect the logic and ambition of the power structure that devised them and continues to influence its development, directly and indirectly.

Who "controls" the operating system? It's conceived, designed, and built by human beings; once the operating system is launched, however, it begins to mold the individuals who refine and build on it, channeling their efforts and directing them to expand in certain directions according to the guidelines and constraints it imposes. Future developers and designers all have the same job, essentially, however different their specific projects: to build and reproduce the operating system.

Similarly, the State is conceived and set in motion by humans;

once it is established, it absorbs, regulates, and extracts value from more and more of society's activities. The Italian anarchist Errico Malatesta, who generally used "government" and "state" interchangeably, put it this way: "The government, though springing from the bourgeoisie and its servant and protector, tends, as with every servant and every protector, to achieve its own emancipation and to dominate whoever it protects."[22]

While their views differ on matters like war, peace, social welfare, and race relations, a vast array of individuals and social strata, from capitalists and intellectuals to engineers and clerks and laborers, are all engaged in the same task: to build and reproduce the State. To turn a well-worn assertion on its head, if you're not against the State, you're for it.

> A vast array of individuals and social strata, from capitalists and intellectuals to engineers and clerks and laborers, are all engaged in the same task: to build and reproduce the State. To turn a well-worn assertion on its head, if you're not against the State, you're for it.

In the tech world, users are often described as a community; that community and the machine are increasingly regarded as one. Likewise, in the modern world, society (including civil society) and the State are increasingly perceived as one; the State is a vast simulacrum of the entire society, touching, altering, molding, imprinting its preferred pattern onto every dimension and aspect of our being. According to Marx, the State constitutes "the illusory common interest" of a society—also known as the "public interest."[23] Anthropologist David Graeber wrote, "States are the 'imaginary totality' par excellence," a way of "imagining social order as something one can get a grip on, models of control."[24] When a new element or variable enters the social mix, the State must absorb it, assimilate it, and set rules for how it will operate as a component of the State.

While laws, regulations, and customs are sometimes seen as straitjackets, they also confer identity and status within the orbit of the State (as a soldier, a police officer, a licensed driver, a consumer with good credit, a head of household). These designations cement our loyalty to the State or at least our acquiescence to it, but they also exploit our fear that without the State, we would have no identity.

The better it is at replacing reality, the more anxiety the simulacrum creates; if it disappears, won't the corresponding reality disappear as well? If the State disintegrates, surely society will also? Therefore, almost nothing is held to be more important than the security and preservation of the State: a doctrine called "reasons of State." Without the State, any discussion of social or economic justice, cultural expression, health and physical well-being is irrelevant. That's one reason why so much of traditional narrative history, particularly from European and American sources, is really the story of the development of states.

There's something deeply paradoxical about the State as well. While it's not a "thing," it works to create a convincing façade of one in the form of buildings, monuments, roads, border checkpoints, and other physical manifestations. There's nothing organic about a state, but it behaves in some respects like an intelligent being. It's a human creation and consists of human beings—it's an idea acted upon—but it behaves according to a logic of its own and molds people, including those in command, as much as they mold it. Its leadership is essentially self-selecting, but it claims to embody a wider community. It's one and many at the same time, an "it" and a "they." As a result, the State achieves a double deception: it provides cover for the individuals who build their personal power through it ("reasons of state") while its leaders—especially conspicuous ones like kings, presidents, party leaders, and corporate chief executives—provide cover by giving it a relatable human face.

We struggle to work within the State, but it resists fundamental change and remains focused always on preserving itself and extending its reach in every direction.

We also struggle to articulate our understanding of it, as shorthand names like the "system," the "establishment," and the "deep state" underscore. But all or most of us know what it is, in outline. When Democratic presidential candidate Joe Biden named Senator Kamala Harris of California as his vice-presidential running mate in 2020, Bill Daley, head of public affairs at Wells Fargo and former chief of staff to President Obama, told the *Wall Street Journal*, "I think she is a reasonable, rational person who has worked in the system. Is she progressive? Yes. Is she someone who wants to burn the building down? No. I think she wants to strengthen the building."[25]

No one had to be told what "the building" is: it's government, but it's also capitalism and the vast edifice of institutions, identities, and livelihoods grouped under those headings. In this book, we call it the State, but scholars and pundits have been studying aspects of it under various conceptual models for a long time.

Global systems science, for example, aims to "provide scientific evidence and means to engage into a reflective dialogue to support policy-making and public action and to enable civil society to collectively engage in societal action in response to global challenges" such as "epidemics, finance, cities, the Internet, trade systems."[26] A veritable cottage industry has grown up within academia in the last couple of decades that studies how complex global societies decline, lose legitimacy, and fall apart. Cambridge University established its Centre for the Study of Existential Risk in 2012 ("we aim to reduce the risk of human extinction or civilizational collapse"), and Princeton University established a high-profile research program in Global Systemic Risk a year later.[27]

When we examine this literature closely, we find that "systems" and "societies" are nearly synonymous with the State as we're defining it. For instance, the Princeton research program's website tells us that a "massive and accelerating increase in international transactions beginning in the late 1970s" required "the construction of a complex system of global nodes and links providing the channels through which these can flow. The interdependence of massive global interactions and structures has caused systemic risk to increase exponentially in recent times."

Cutting through the jargon, that "complex system of global nodes and links" is the commercial side of the operating system the State molds, embodies, and presides over. When scholars and pundits express concern about the risk of collapse of "systems" or "societies," then, what they're really anxious about is the collapse of the State.

State authority was, of course, founded on physical force, but as it pursued its goals and the society it governed became more complex and sophisticated, legitimacy and acceptance became just as important. The State is a hybrid creature; it exists simultaneously within the community it claims to represent, and over and above that community. By definition, it's a more impersonal institution than religion, the family, an ethnic or geographic community, or an economic class. From the beginning, then, the modern State has struggled to define itself in ways that persuade its inhabitants to give it their loyalty, their love, or at least their acceptance. The importance of this has only increased as populations have grown, denser urban environments absorb more people, and capitalist economies themselves become more complex and more difficult to manage.

III

Versions of the Operating System

The unjust institutions which work so much misery and suffering to the masses have their root in governments, and owe their whole existence to the power derived from government, we cannot help but believe that were every law, every title deed, every court, and every police officer or soldier abolished tomorrow with one sweep, we would be better off than now.
—Lucy Parsons, "The Principles of Anarchism"

The modern State is a constantly evolving operating system, and the composition of the elites at the top of the power structure has evolved with it. Like the designers of a computer operating system, its builders have periodically launched new versions, or upgrades, but according to an internal logic that through-lines from its origins five centuries ago to today. Without a broader understanding of this logic, attempts to reform, restructure, or even overthrow the State always end with the protagonists reproducing the State.

What forms has the modern State assumed over the last five hundred years? Six versions, thus far, have followed each other in ever more rapid succession, each corresponding to changes in states' capabilities and the conditions they encountered at particular times.

Version 1.0: Monarchical or dynastic state

The modern State emerged out of the kaleidoscope of medieval European sociopolitical formations when the quasi-mystical monarch or sovereign began to transform into an authoritarian executive, but it solidified its control through new methods of violence fueled by gunpowder and maintained its legitimacy in part by appealing to traditional and faux-traditional customs. Substantive treatises on effective royal administration and conduct began to appear at the end of the fifteenth century; while Machiavelli's *The Prince* is the most famous, other authors include Erasmus, Martin Luther, the poet John Skelton, and one actual sovereign, King James VI of Scotland (later England's King James I), who wrote *Basilikon Doron* in 1599.

> **The modern State emerged out of the kaleidoscope of medieval European sociopolitical formations when the quasi-mystical monarch or sovereign began to transform into an authoritarian executive.**

Version 2.0: Commercial oligarchy

Many of the earliest modern states were not monarchies, but smaller, urban-centered entities controlled by merchant families. Examples include the republics of Florence, Venice, and Genoa; the free cities of Bremen and Lübeck; the Republic of the Seven United Netherlands (Dutch Republic); and several of the Swiss cantons.

Version 3.0: National state*

The nation is not the cause, but the result of the state. It is the state which creates the nation, not the nation the state.
—Rudolf Rocker, *Nationalism and Culture*

The national state, which replaced the monarch with an equally quasi-mystical entity known as the "nation," defined by traditional and faux-traditional ethnic and linguistic characteristics, took its bow with the American and French revolutions. Premodern European states based their authority on force and dynastic rights rather than any notion of ethnic solidarity, and they could be populated by all or parts of any number of ethnic groups and geographies. National states were founded on a strong personal identification with a given ethnic or cultural group, linguistic type, geographic region, or some combination of these.

National states had a greater aura of legitimacy because they appealed in a powerfully emotional way to individuals' and communities' sense of belonging and camouflaged the State's true nature as an economic engine. Of course, "nation" and "state" have never really been synonymous, and the two frequently clash, as in the case of the United States and the stateless Native American nations it displaced. However, the concept of the national state gives the State the power to decide who and what belongs to the nation and who and what is excluded. And it has the great advantage of inviting the entire population—or at least that portion who "belong"—to participate in building the State.

Manifest Destiny—the nineteenth-century doctrine that the American Empire was ordained to span the North American continent—was one such state-building project. For some members of the Washington policymaking elite, the U.S. "liberation" of Iraq in 2003 represented a renewal of the democratic American state's purpose in the world.[1] The seventeenth-century English generalissimo

* I owe this designation to Charles Tilly in *Coercion, Capital, and European States*, although I define it somewhat differently.

Oliver Cromwell cast the invasion and subjugation of Ireland in similar if more religious terms, describing Ireland as "a clean paper" on which a new and better pattern could be inscribed and hailing his victory at Drogheda as "a righteous judgment of God upon these barbarian wretches."[2] England's colonial expansion into another land was not just a project of the English nation, but a vital part of the building of that nation—and of the English state.

A more contemporary instance is the Israeli policy of expanding into Palestinian Arab lands. Defense Minister Moshe Dayan, in an August 1968 speech to an audience of young kibbutzniks, and referring to the lands Israel seized a year earlier in the Six-Day War, defined this as synonymous with nation-building, and as a project that effectively would never end:

> We are fated to live in a permanent state of fighting against the Arabs. For the hundred years of the Return to Zion we are working for two things: the building of the land and the building of the people. That is a process of expansion, of more Jews and more settlements. That is a process that has not reached the end. We were born here and found our parents, who had come here before us. It is not your duty to reach the end. Your duty is to add your layer to expand the settlement to the best of your ability, during your lifetime . . . [and] not to say: this is the end, up to here, we have finished.[3]

Version 4.0: One-party state

One-party states can be either left or right ideologically and generally emerge during a period of crisis; right-wing regimes are precipitated by fear of revolution from below, left-wing regimes by the need to consolidate power after a revolution. They are generally governed by a single party, conduct a top-down, highly directed economic policy, and aspire to meld the population into an engine in support of an ideology or an economic, social, or political vision. Not surprisingly, they are also more authoritarian, more violent, and more exclusionary than any other model. They exalt their specific vision of the State more overtly than any other version, which makes them less adaptable and less durable as well.

On the other hand, regimes like Nazi Germany, the Soviet Union, and Francoist Spain developed methods of social control and techniques of warfare that survived them and have been copied and advanced by later forms of the State. The one-party state was adopted by numerous newly independent African and Asian nations in the 1960s as a means to cement a national identity within culturally and ethnically diverse societies; the model survives today in mainland China and dictatorships like Assad's Baathist regime in Syria.

Version 5.0: Social-democratic or welfare state

The social-democratic state was supposed to be a color-blind version of the national state, deaccentuating the "nation" and instead defining itself by its capacity to allocate resources to maximize socioeconomic harmony and acceptance while improving economic productivity. Rather than appealing to an emotional sense of belonging, the social-democratic state focused on competently meeting the changing needs of an increasingly complex industrial society, achieving loyalty and acceptance by appealing to a set of liberal values and the universal desire for a good life.

It did so in part by co-opting projects based on mutual aid that many workers adopted during the early industrial period through unions or fraternal organizations, such as old-age, survivors', and unemployment benefits, making them part of the State apparatus and thus cementing a potentially troublesome urban population's loyalty. "Any laws developed from the nucleus of customs useful to human communities," Kropotkin wrote, "have been turned to account by rulers to sanctify their own domination."[4] German chancellor Otto von Bismarck, who instituted the first workers' compensation and old-age pension systems in the industrialized world, acknowledged the relationship even more explicitly:

> That the State . . . should interest itself to a greater degree than hitherto in those of its members who need assistance, is

not only a duty of humanity and Christianity . . . but a duty of state-preserving policy. These classes must . . . be led to regard the state not as an institution contrived for the protection of the better classes of society, but as one serving their own needs and interests. The apprehension that a socialistic element might be introduced into legislation if this end were followed should not check us.[5]

While social-democratic states at least in theory are more humanistic, inclusive, and caring than national states, they often express their rationale in a fairly hard-nosed way. "Today," write political scientists Anton Hemerijck and Robin Huguenot-Noël, "the evidence corroborates the contention that the quality of modern social policy positively affects long-term supply, especially with respect to employment and productivity, and indirectly demand. Central to the financial sustainability of the welfare state are the number (quantity) and productivity (quality) of current and future employees and taxpayers."[6]

While the social-democratic state tends to have more regard for its population as human beings, in the end its goal is the same as that of other forms of the modern State: to mold the population into a productive workforce who can play their part in the building of the State.

Version 6.0: Neoliberal state

But contrast Hemerijck and Huguenot-Noël's assertion with the following, from American constitutional lawyer Philip Bobbitt: "States don't exist to deliver material well-being directly. States exist to maximize people's opportunities to advance themselves, and to get out of the way."[7] No state strictly follows this precept, nor could it; even if the free market is assumed to be the main engine of material progress—a debatable point—it's the State that the people ultimately hold responsible when the economic system fails. But in the era of neoliberalism, it's fashionable in elite circles to frame the State as a network of "limited" governments that outsource as many of their duties as possible to the theoretically more efficient and better-managed private sector and refashion what remains along lean, businesslike lines.

Neoliberalism is an updated version of classical economics, the free-market approach that the United States and the UK adopted in the nineteenth century and proselytized to the rest of the world. It emphasizes lowering barriers to trade and foreign investment; loosening labor regulations to create a more "flexible" workforce; liberalizing markets, such that governments do not protect their economies from foreign ownership or competition; strictly controlling inflation; privatizing state-owned enterprises; and restricting government spending, investment, and social services such that government deficits are eliminated or kept to an absolute minimum.

Together, these policies have three objectives. First, they promote greater competition between companies in the same line of business, between employers and employees, and between workers themselves. This reduces the "reservation wage"—the threshold at which workers feel compelled to take jobs—and thus enables employers to pay lower wages, accumulate more capital for investment, and, presumably, invest that capital in further economic growth.[8] Second, neoliberal policies promote a new, globalized economy with a uniform set of rules that encourage entrepreneurship and technological advancement, discourage inefficient government policies, and remove "friction" (such as protecting "inefficient" local businesses) that prevents different countries from focusing on the goods and services they are best at delivering. Third, and particularly in the United States, neoliberalism recommended itself as a solution to the dangerous political cleavages of the 1960s, when civil rights, the Vietnam War, and disagreements over antipoverty measures threatened to destroy the governing consensus between centrist Democrats and conservative Republicans. If both sides could agree on a return to free-market principles, coupled with some degree of social liberalization, the American state could function more smoothly again.

Under neoliberalism, the market state's objective is to give the people the "opportunity" and inducement to succeed—that is, to build economic value—and the barest minimum of assistance if they fail. The relentless grinding-down of wages is accepted as long as the economy can keep prices of basic goods and amusements low and maintain a flow of credit; consumer credit and abundant cheap stuff equal happy households. Workers, even upper-level ones, are redefined as "human capital," and the system of education is reformed to make sure the State and capital receive the human inputs they need, as in the case of the "STEM" fields (science, technology, engineering, mathematics).*

These policies favor U.S. and western European banks and financial services firms because they ensure that the value of these institutions' government-bond investments won't deteriorate. They also favor multinational corporations, also largely based in the United States and western Europe, that want to exploit the natural resources and cheap labor markets of developing economies. Starting in the 1970s, neoliberalism was packaged into a set of recommendations, commonly known as the Washington Consensus, that the World Bank and the IMF—the big multinational lenders that drive so much of economic policy worldwide—insisted developing countries accept in exchange for loans.

In practice, neoliberalism is an enormously damaging and destructive doctrine, especially for poorer countries, since it places their future development in the hands of multinationals whose principal goal is to extract wealth from them with as little payback as possible and puts their governments on a perpetual debt-repayment treadmill. Developing countries that have been most successful over the past forty years at building economic wealth—South Korea, China, Malaysia, Singapore, Taiwan, Vietnam, among others—did

---

* University of California president Clark Kerr arguably inaugurated this discourse as far back as 1963 in *The Uses of the University*; at the time, Mario Savio, leader of the Berkeley Free Speech Movement, denounced Kerr for wanting to turn the university into a "factory." Marxist theorist Hal Draper, then a librarian at the Berkeley campus, said Kerr wanted to make it a service center for the "military-industrial complex." Seth Rosenfeld, "Clark Kerr's Classic: *The Uses of the University* Turns 50," *California*, Winter 2013. Nevertheless, Kerr's ideas were hugely influential around the world; see Morgan Rodgers Gibson, "Towards a Neoliberal Education System in Queensland: Preliminary Notes on Senior Secondary Schooling Reforms," *Policy Futures in Education* 17, no. 8 (2019): 983–99.

so by consciously rejecting neoliberalism in favor of a more carefully planned economic strategy that focused on investing in their people, nurturing key industries, and avoiding dependence on loans from global financial institutions.[9] Most countries that have submitted to Washington Consensus doctrine—for example, South Africa, Jamaica, Haiti, and Iraq following the U.S. invasion—have fared much worse.

Neoliberalism isn't only a means of prying open developing economies for exploitation, however; it's also actively used to hobble the social-democratic state in the developed world. While western European states still have many of the features of the postwar social compact, over the past thirty years, and especially since the euro's introduction in 1999, pressure from lenders, economists, and technocrats, including many of their own elites who were trained and indoctrinated in neoliberal principles, have pushed them to transform themselves to fit the new model. France, Denmark, and Italy, among others, have "reformed" their labor markets to be more "flexible" (and weaken labor unions); Germany, Italy, France, Sweden, and others have enacted pension "reforms" to reduce state old-age benefits. Trade union membership has declined in nearly every European country, even traditionally highly unionized states like Sweden, since 2000.[10] Neoliberalism was imposed, with tremendous destructive force, across formerly communist eastern Europe almost as soon as the Cold War ended.

The results have often been grim. "Italy's austerity policy led to a dismantling of the healthcare system, which has proved fatal during the Covid-19 crisis," economists Philipp Heimberger and Nikolaus Krowall reported. "Moreover, drastic reductions in public investment have triggered a slowdown in Italy's productivity growth."[11] In Sweden during the COVID-19 pandemic, a switch to a supposedly more efficient, for-profit, voucher-based system for eldercare facilities left them underfunded and understaffed, and it left their workers without personal protective equipment, turning the facilities into breeding grounds for the virus.[12] Yet the economic crisis wrought by the pandemic offered still another opportunity to press the transformation. A proposed €750 billion EU bond issue announced in July 2020, to include grants and loans to the economies hardest hit by the virus, was loaded with stipulations forcing those countries to submit to a crushing regime of fiscal austerity similar to the structural adjustment programs the IMF and World Bank typically recommend for developing economies.

Many developing countries presented a similar picture as the crisis cratered their economies after prices fell for commodities like copper and oil. Faced with steeply declining revenues, states including Ghana and Zambia quickly ran into difficulty making debt payments; over the past fifteen years, advisers from the U.S. government and the IMF and World Bank had encouraged them to shift their borrowing from the multilateral institutions and instead take out loans directly from the financial markets.[13] This put them at the mercy of a far less forgiving group of lenders. After the COVID crisis hit, they faced a real danger of being squeezed by their creditors to either adopt crippling austerity budgets or sell their most valuable assets to keep making debt payments.

The IMF and World Bank themselves were in no hurry to help beleaguered developing countries once the virus reached them; of a comparatively paltry $280 billion the two institutions handed out in the first nine months of the crisis, a bit less than $11 billion went to low-income countries. And the United States, which is the most powerful voice in both institutions, was more concerned about the institutions' shareholders than about low-income economies in a state of emergency. Spouting standard neoliberal doctrine, U.S. Treasury secretary Steven Mnuchin declared, "It is critical that the World Bank manage financial resources judiciously so as not to burden shareholders with premature calls for new financing."[14]

The United States, which is the chief proponent of neoliberalism, since so many of the multinational companies and lenders that benefit from it are based there, itself deviates regularly from neoliberal principles, for example by subsidizing key industries like agribusiness, defense, and oil and gas. But neoliberalism doesn't have to work as advertised to fulfill its real purpose, which is to push governments to scale back restrictions on capital in big states and to eliminate them in states that are less able to resist the demands of the Washington Consensus. So-called libertarian or laissez-faire ideologists and politicians function as part of this dynamic as well, but only as ideological leverage; the political and economic elite of every major country understands that it must have a directed strategy for achieving economic growth and that it couldn't do so if it refused to regulate business, let its currency operate on autopilot, or canceled subsidies to key industries. The same applies more generally. For both the State and capital, ideology is largely a tool for achieving public and elite buy-in to policies moving in a particular direction. That doesn't necessarily mean that those who benefit really want those policies to go all the way in that direction.

* * *

These different versions of the modern State have never been mutually exclusive; earlier forms carry on in certain parts of the world long after they're superseded in other regions, and elements of later forms can crop up long before they become predominant. For instance, commercial oligarchies appeared in Italy, Germany, and the Low Countries centuries before the modern State emerged as a dominant form. The idea of a German "nation" and even its use in official documents ("the Holy Roman Empire of the German Nation") date back to the beginning of the modern State, well before the concept of the national state became commonplace.[15] The era of empire building in nineteenth century Africa and Asia that coincided with the period when the national state was achieving dominance, was supposed to have ended with the dissolution of the European colonial empires following World War II. But it never really did. Palestinians experience empire-building in the forward march of Israeli settlements into the West Bank, Tibetans and Uighurs suffer it as Beijing encourages Han Chinese to establish themselves in Tibet and Xinjiang, and Timorese and West Papuans find themselves dispossessed as the Indonesian government opens their land to natural resource harvesting and encourages Javanese to occupy it.

Nevertheless, we can trace a clear progression as each succeeding form of the State arose to address problems that had bedeviled the preceding one. In the early modern period, the State leaned on the personal authority and prestige of the monarch. But monarchs could be capricious, distracted, and incompetent, which in the worst cases made them a threat to the stability and legitimacy of the State. Europe spent much of the nineteenth and the first half of the twentieth centuries resolving itself into a collection of (supposedly) ethnically homogeneous national states, in part to create a political landscape that was less volatile and prone to warfare. In the process, the informal System of States that was born with the first multilateral alliances in the early sixteenth century acquired firmer underpinnings: everything from Metternich's Concert of Europe to the International Red Cross to the International Criminal Court to, eventually, the UN and the EU. The national state would be the basic building block of this new, more peaceful international order.

Yet, it turned out to be a much more slippery creature than it first appeared. What boundaries were the "correct" ones when more than one state claimed a historical right to a particular piece of territory? How would each state define the "nation" it was supposed to embody? Who belongs, and who doesn't? The states in this new order were never as homogeneous as they presumed themselves to be, and they became even less so as capitalism expanded, superregional economies became more closely knit together, and economic exploitation and ethnic minority oppression (a by-product of the national state model) forced masses of working people to migrate.

The era of the national state was also the period when capitalism achieved maturity as an economic model. Both, in a sense, were built on myths: capital is roughly equivalent to credit, a qualitative notion imperfectly embodied in access to money; the nation is an emotional affinity roughly embodied in a designation of citizenship.

But even before the national state achieved maturity (that is, before most of the developed world had formed states of this type), the State began to redefine itself once again. Out of this period of turmoil grew two new models: the one-party state and the social-democratic state. Both the Soviet Union and the fascistic states of interwar Europe, which together created the one-party-state model, arose out of the wreckage of the reactionary dynastic empires that had persisted into the era of the national state—tsarist Russia, Austria-Hungary, Wilhelmine Germany—and the equally reactionary dynastic monarchies that survived World War I—Savoyard Italy,

Borbón Spain, and the Balkan kingdoms that had succeeded Ottoman Turkey. It began to fade from view once the Cold War ended and the neoliberal consensus took hold globally. The other successor to the national state, the social-democratic or welfare state, was far less rigid and was better able to provide a forum for resolving differences between the various subgroups in society than the monarchical system or the national state. As such, it was a means to counteract working-class discontent, stall the spread of "Bolshevism," and induce anarchists and others organizing outside the State to instead work within it.

> For the middle and working classes, the State is a source of command and a place where complaints are lodged. For the wealthy, the State is a place where transactions are negotiated and carried out.

But here again, there were tensions. For the middle and working classes, the State is a source of command and a place where complaints are lodged. These groups also have a strong need for emotional identification with a larger community. For the wealthy, the State is a place where transactions are negotiated and carried out.* The rich want to know, always, precisely what they are getting in return for their allegiance, and they tend to discount any contribution that the collectivity makes to their own success. In consequence, the social-democratic state couldn't stop an erosion of the sense of community that began at the top. Scholar Mark O'Connell sees the postwar proliferation of suburban fallout shelters and the more recent craze among the superrich for cryogenics, transhumanism, privately owned islands, passport shopping, and schemes to transport themselves to Mars (or at least New Zealand) in the event of a societal collapse—silly as they may sound—as "the logical end of [our] retreat from trust in and responsibility for others."[16]

Since the middle and working classes can't afford to implement such schemes, the result is twofold: support for center-right, neoliberal policies among the political elite, and a readherence to

---

* "The poor have sometimes objected to being governed badly; the rich have always objected to being governed at all." G. K. Chesterton, *The Man Who Was Thursday: A Nightmare* (London: J. W. Arrowsmith, 1908).

nationalism, often rationalized as a defense of freedom, among those with lower incomes.*

That's because the social-democratic state was never able to devise a substitute for the strong emotional appeal that the national state supplied. Since it wasn't able to resolve economic tensions between capitalists and the working class either, whenever economic expansion slowed and standards of living were threatened—a more frequent occurrence under neoliberalism—the social-democratic state was left open to attacks from the nationalist right, turning ethnic and other traditional identities into weapons. We've seen the result in the right-wing populist Trump administration in the United States and the rise of similar authoritarian governments in Hungary, Poland, Russia, and the Philippines. Like the Nazis and other fascist regimes before them, these governments draw support from a deep sense of grievance among middle- and working-class households, yet never really attack the fundamental features of the neoliberal state.

---

* "It is a striking feature of the welfare state that it offers a powerful promise of individual rights, and also demands of its citizens a high measure of mutual engagement. But the self-image that attends the rights cannot sustain the engagement." Michael J. Sandel, *Public Philosophy: Essays on Morality in Politics* (Cambridge, MA: Harvard University Press, 2005), 172.

IV

Characteristics of the System, 1

Ways and Means

*Governments and the ruling classes no longer take their stand on right or
even on the semblance of justice, but on a skillful organization carried to
such a point of perfection by the aid of science that everyone is caught in
the circle of violence and has no chance of escaping from it. . . . Violence
no longer rests on the belief in its utility, but only on the fact of its having
existed so long, and being organized by the ruling classes who profit by it.*
—Lev Tolstoi, *The Kingdom of God Is within You*

The modern State is never entirely one thing at any given time; all but
the first of the six models we just reviewed still exist today in some
form—even the commercial oligarchy, whose approximate descendants we can see in Singapore, Hong Kong, and some small Persian
Gulf states. The State is adaptable, up to a point: able to transplant
itself to regions dramatically different from the continent on which
it originated, in part through economic colonization and in part by
nurturing professional and commercial elites in these places and
imbuing them with much the same worldview and institutional perspective as those in its place of origin.

It couldn't do this successfully if the differences between states
were more numerous and powerful than the similarities. But the
characteristics of the modern State are quite similar everywhere,
as is the logic behind the behavior of individual states, from liberal

free-market democracies to postcommunist regimes to Islamic states to the rising number of quasi-fascist governments. A closer look at these similarities makes clear how thoroughly the State defines and directs our world today.

The State is a relatively new thing in world history

No system quite like this one existed more than five hundred years ago; the State, the "modern age," and capitalism are coterminous with each other. Only in the last hundred years has the State covered virtually the entire globe. What set the State apart almost from the start was that it drew its power not from religious authority, tradition, or personal relationships but from law, bureaucratic efficiency, and an explicit or implied promise to provide economic prosperity and security from internal and external threats. Its ideologists, like Machiavelli, defined its overriding concern as the "public interest," which largely meant preservation of the State's well-being and stability, by any means necessary. Meanwhile, the State has dug itself deeper into societies themselves, saturating more and more aspects of life.

How new is all this? In 1941, less than a century ago, the Austrian author Stefan Zweig wrote in his memoirs, "Before 1914, the earth had belonged to all. It always gives me pleasure to astonish the young by telling them that before 1914 I traveled from Europe to India and to America without a passport and without ever having seen one."[1] This would be impossible today, unless it was done surreptitiously.

The State is European in origin, and remains so culturally

The model of the modern State was created in western Europe in the sixteenth, seventeenth, and eighteenth centuries, at the tail end of the long series of invasions of the European continent that began with the Huns in the mid-fifth century and culminated in the fall of Constantinople to the Ottoman Turks in 1452. Almost immediately afterward, the first modern European states began to project their power beyond the continent.

Arguably, the State is not only Europe's most successful export but the most successful any society has ever produced. Even after they won independence, national liberation movements in developing countries retained or adopted this operating system as their own. Rather than looking back to traditional methods of social organization or trying to envision new ones, the leaders of the new postcolonial societies (re)created some version of the state system that the colonizing power had fastened on them. Every major feature of the State that we'll be exploring in this chapter and the following two was first developed by the European states; every society in the decolonized world that operates as a state adopted them and continues to incorporate them into its system of social organization. Indigenous states that were able to avoid dismemberment and colonization, such as Japan, China, Thailand, Saudi Arabia, and Egypt, nevertheless remodeled themselves in the image of the modern State as their elites sought to guarantee themselves a seat at the table the Europeans were setting.

Arguably, the State is not only Europe's most successful export but the most successful ever. Even after they won independence, national liberation movements in developing countries retained or adopted this operating system as their own.

The result is a remarkable uniformity in at least the formal aspects of how states around the world are organized and governed. Most have three branches of government—executive, legislative, judicial—a federal system in which certain powers are concentrated at the national level and others at local or intermediate levels, and in which certain rights are defined for their citizens, who are registered and counted as such. Most have central banks and treasuries that control most aspects of currency supply and interest-rate policy. Most have private-sector businesses and commercial and investment banking establishments that are intimately connected with government and the global business and financial communities. Most have a national language and a standing national army. And almost all hold elections; even authoritarian states like Egypt and Belarus do so. While there are exceptions even today, notably the absolute monarchies of the Persian Gulf region and quasi-theocratic states like Iran, the pattern holds most everywhere else.

States are "individuals" in the eyes of the law

Just as U.S. law has come to recognize corporations as having many of the rights of individuals, so the Montevideo Convention on the Rights and Duties of States in 1933 provided that the "federal state shall constitute a sole person in the eyes of international law." There is a grain of truth in this; as an operating system, the State isn't so much an administrative unit as an organism, capable of reproducing itself and of creating meaning, expanding, adapting, and absorbing more vital elements, as long as there are people to absorb its logic and tend to it. But that means the State often finds itself in direct if uneven conflict with individuals and communities. In such a fight, the State always wins—unless its adversaries have enormous resources.

The State claims the right to determine who is a person (with legitimate rights and claims on the society)

This authority extends to individuals' right to argue a case before a court of law, to vote, to be free from unreasonable force, and to self-defense. It applies to citizens and noncitizens alike; an individual who is not a citizen or recognized resident of some state, somewhere, is at a serious disadvantage in claiming any kind of consideration from another state in which he or she happens to be located at the time. Indigenous peoples have had this problem for centuries; it is an even bigger issue today given the fast-growing global migrant population.

The State's definition of a person is different from the definitions accepted by many traditional societies. The State prefers to consider the person strictly as an individual, without connection to any larger community, with the occasional exception of the family. "Who has the kind of self that is recognized by the law and the public as worthy of self-defense?" the philosopher Judith Butler asks. "If I think of myself not just as this bounded individual but as fundamentally related to others, then I locate this self in those relations. In that case, the self I am trying to defend is not just me but all those relations that define and sustain me . . . extended beyond local units like family and community."[2] While these extended bonds are sometimes recognized in law, the State generally subordinates them to property rights and other imperatives of economic growth.

The State is an instrument of violence and war

"War is the health of the State," the American radical journalist Randolph Bourne wrote. The modern State came into being in part as a better mechanism for the monarch to conduct war; since then, wars have also provided an opportunity for the State—and capital—to get bigger. Invariably, the State emerges from war with expanded powers; together with capital, it increases its top-down command of its resources, including the lives of its people, and of the economy.

Not surprisingly, then, governments have a habit of treating every crisis—whether an armed conflict, an economic collapse, an epidemic, a cultural deviation, or an uprising of the oppressed—as the "equivalent" of war, requiring a military or police response, a curtailment of liberties, and a total commitment or mobilization of the whole society. ("We're at war, in a true sense we're at war, and we are fighting an invisible enemy," Donald J. Trump said when it finally occurred to him that the COVID-19 pandemic was a serious matter.[3])

War in the era of the modern State is not only about conquest and rivalry between great powers, then; just as often, it's a matter of repression and counterinsurgency, of repelling challenges to individual regimes and the State itself. Among the most dramatic features of the modern era are the dogged resistance of subject populations and the State's efforts to beat them into submission. Starting as early as the Peasants' War in Germany (1524–1525) and the Pilgrimage of Grace in England (1536), these periodic rebellions stretch up through Stenka Razin's uprising in Russia (1671), Tacky's slave revolt in Jamaica (1760), the Whiteboy movement of landless Irish (1761), the revolt of Túpac Amaru II in Peru (1780), Nat Turner's slave rebellion in Virginia (1831), the Mau Mau revolt against British colonial rule in Kenya (1952–1960), and, more recently, the successive Palestinian intifadas, the Free Aceh Movement in Indonesia, and the Tamil Tigers' separatist insurrection in Sri Lanka, not to mention the continuing Zapatista uprising and occupation in Chiapas.

There have been countless others, and likely will be more until the State succeeds in compelling every corner of the earth to conform to its pattern—or conclusively fails to do so. Many of these uprisings pitted Indigenous peoples against the State, others were initiated by poor or working-class people, and many were a combination of the two. Related to these uprisings is the general strike, which anarcho-syndicalists explicitly conceive as a revolutionary action to place workers in command of the means of production and bring about the overthrow of the State.* Whatever rights, benefits, and decently humane treatment the inhabitants of the State have achieved over the past two hundred years have largely been the direct or indirect result of these uprisings and refusals—which, almost by definition, first generate their energy and motivation outside the State. The Movement for Black Lives, for example, with its advocacy of police abolition, is committed to tearing down a vital support of the State, not building it up, and the decentralized, antifascist Antifa movement is inherently anti-State.

While the State aspires to create an encompassing social, cultural, and functional environment for all of humankind, then, it never really succeeds in doing so, and only appears to because it keeps pushing in that direction. But the fact that the State meets violent resistance at nearly every turn compels it to constantly increase its capacity to suppress, occupy, surveil, and, in many cases, liquidate large populations who do not fit in. Often, states cooperate with each other when a rebellion within one state's borders threatens

---

* There have been many general strikes in the past two centuries, including one in Philadelphia (1835), the abandonment of Southern plantations by enslaved African Americans (1862–65), Russia's October General Strike (1905), and strikes in Barcelona (1919), the UK (1926), the U.S. West Coast waterfronts (1934), India (1946), and Cochabamba, Bolivia (2000). Although most were not revolutionary in intention, many were class-based or connected to national liberation movements.

its neighbors' stability or the existence of the State as a form. This occurred in Germany following World War I, for example, when the British, American, and French victors decided to look the other way as the German Army contravened the treaty that ended the war by rearming to suppress the revolutionary uprisings that shook the country. It occurred again in the 1970s, when the military governments of Argentina, Chile, Bolivia, Paraguay, and Uruguay, aided by the CIA, formed Operation Condor, a blood-soaked alliance to suppress leftist dissent in South America.[4]

All of these varieties of rebellion underscore two things: First, the State has always faced strong and determined resistance to its effort to absorb and obliterate other systems and communities as people seek a genuine alternative, not just another reform. Second, internal rebellions compel the State to develop yet more methods of oppression, in turn making economic growth critical to fund these internal wars and absorb the victims into its operating system.

Whether it's internal or external, however, war is presented to us as a virtue; every crisis is another opportunity for the nation to test itself, become tougher, more robust and resilient. War also allows the State to remind us once again that without it, society could not endure a crisis, and so to claim new or expanded powers. The USA PATRIOT Act, passed in the aftermath of the September 11, 2001, terrorist attacks, gave the executive branch unprecedented powers and has been renewed regularly, with bipartisan support, ever since.

One of the primary rationales for the rise and acceptance of the modern State in Europe, initially provided by Thomas Hobbes, is that it guarantees a degree of personal security that was absent in the allegedly chaotic feudal centuries. Yet, the greatest spasms of violence in human history have all occurred during the era of the modern State. Worldwide, deaths from conflict, both in absolute numbers and as a share of world population, rose steadily—and then exploded in the twentieth century, when almost 110 million died, representing more than 4 percent of the entire human population. These include the dead from the nuclear attacks on Hiroshima and Nagasaki, in which the State unveiled one of its most distinctive gifts to humanity—nuclear weapons—and the massive and systematic attempt by the Nazi state to annihilate the European Jews. By comparison, the nineteenth century produced 8 million dead in battle, and the eighteenth, which saw the first conflicts that could arguably be regarded as world wars, a mere 4 million.[5]

War is also the health of capital, however, since military expenditure helps drive the global economy. In 2019, the world's governments spent more than $1.9 trillion on military needs, or 2.2 percent of the entire global GDP, according to the Stockholm International Peace Research Institute. That's close to 20 percent higher than in the final years of the Cold War and 7.2 percent higher than in 2010.[6] Major wars, not to mention the rebuilding that needs to occur afterward, invariably help the financial system to grow and give it a more central role within the State. And while some political parties are regarded as friendlier to the armed forces and the military-industrial complex than others—Republicans over Democrats in the United States, notably—the arms industry and its major investors always have strong ties to both. In the 2020 U.S. presidential campaign, for instance, both the Trump and Biden camps enjoyed generous support from that quarter.[7]

"I think both candidates, at least in my view, appear globally oriented and interested in the defense of our country and I believe they'll support the industries," Dave Calhoun, CEO of Boeing, maker of the Apache helicopter, said on a media call a few months before the election.

One of the hallmarks of the modern State has been the degree to which militarization—the presence of armed forces, "strategic" thinking (which is often synonymous with military thinking), and martial values—has woven itself further and further into our lives. The global emergency that began with the outbreak of World War II and has never really ended has taken this evolution even further; fewer and fewer people are alive who can recall a time before nuclear arms, when the State and its population were not always, effectively, in a condition of high alert.

The mechanization of warfare, which began with the modern State, has accelerated, too, in part because it's thought to render this constant state of conflict or near-conflict more acceptable to the public. It makes killing impersonal and lowers body counts, even as it places civilian populations increasingly in harm's way. The War on

Terror was the fulfillment of a once-impossible dream for the State: a perpetual, never-ending war against a barely defined enemy that can always be redirected and recontextualized.

The State is above the law

If a state is a legal entity, with many of the same rights and privileges as a person, can't it also be held responsible for its misdeeds? Not if it's a state of any size or power. But even smaller states habitually operate outside the rules they set for their citizens, other inhabitants, and even themselves. The French philosopher Gilles Deleuze explained this by distinguishing between "institutions" and "laws." An institution like a state is a "model for action," created to "satisfy [its] tendencies and needs," hence it constantly seeks to free itself from restraints.[8] Laws are created by the State—or by religious authorities or owners of capital—to constrain and cause humans to serve its projects, but for the State itself, they are more fluid and opportunistic.

States take advantage of the extrajudicial status of refugee camps, for example, to illegally warehouse unwanted populations, sometimes for decades. But the criminal activity of the State is actually much broader. Sometimes they partner with criminal networks, as when the EU engaged a vicious Sudanese militia, the Janjaweed, to police migrants attempting to get to Europe through Libya.[9] States have always flouted each other's laws—and their own—to spy on each other, steal valuable physical and intellectual property, meddle in each other's political processes, and carry out sabotage and assassinations beyond their borders.

"The agents of the orderly state can stay within the boundaries of their rewritten laws while the unruly settlers do the work of intimidation and violence to achieve the desired goal," Palestinian civil rights lawyer Raja Shehadeh writes, in reference to the Israeli settlement of the West Bank. "It is all part of the same scheme."[10] As this suggests,

> **Laws are created by the State to constrain and cause humans to serve its projects, but for the State itself, they are more fluid and opportunistic.**

states themselves sometimes exist in two dimensions at once: the legal and the illegal, in the open and sub rosa.

As we noted earlier, following World War I, the German army, or Reichswehr, was limited under the Treaty of Versailles to only one hundred thousand troops. However, it maintained—fairly openly—a much larger "Black Reichswehr," which it used partly to put down uprisings and which included an assassination squad known as the Feme. North Korea maintains an elaborate smuggling and black-market network to circumvent the U.S.-led sanctions against its regime. The U.S. Central Intelligence Agency (CIA) in the years after the 9/11 attacks maintained a chain of secret "black site" prisons around the world, with the knowledge of the White House and the cooperation of host countries, where detainees were interrogated, tortured, and held without any but the most convoluted legal authority.

Arrangements such as these reveal perhaps more than any other characteristic the true workings of the State. One of the most detailed and revealing documents exploring this side of state institutions is the Sasson Report, a 2005 study that Ariel Sharon's government agreed to undertake as part of a political deal with left-wing Israeli parties. Conducted by Talia Sasson, former head of the State Prosecution Criminal Department, it detailed how numerous agencies of the state had covertly spent millions of dollars to finance the building of illegal settlements and outposts in the occupied territories. According to Sasson's summary,

> The "engine" behind a decision to establish outposts are probably regional councils in Judea, Samaria and Gaza [the West Bank], settlers and activists, imbued with ideology and motivation to increase Israeli settlement in the Judea, Samaria and Gaza territories. Some of the officials working in the Settlement Division of the World Zionist Organization, and in the Ministry of Construction & Housing, cooperated with them to promote the unauthorized outposts phenomenon. After the mid-nineties, these actions were apparently inspired by different Ministers of Housing, either by overlooking or by actual encouragement and support, with additional support from other Ministries, initiated either by officials or by the political echelon of each Ministry.

The Settlement Division is supposed to be an executive echelon, implementing decisions made by the political echelon. In this case it was the other way around, and the executive echelon became partners with the political one, contrary to its role.[11]

In simple language, the report revealed a network of officials within several powerful ministries and agencies who either secretly or quietly funded and directed resources to illegal settlements and outposts. Elected officials and cabinet members who should have been exercising control instead were complicit in diverting funds or failed to provide oversight, thus freeing individuals who reported to them to redirect resources. Among other findings were the following:

- The Housing Ministry supplied four hundred mobile homes for outposts on private Palestinian land.
- The Defense Ministry approved the positioning of trailers to begin new outposts.
- The Education Ministry paid for nurseries and their teachers.
- The Energy Ministry connected outposts to the electricity grid.
- Roads to outposts were paid for with taxpayers' money.[12]

In other words, a shadow government, operating with the tacit consent of the legal state and commanding large amounts of money, directed the settlements project, independent of any democratic control. In the eyes of international law and even of much relevant Israeli law, the state was conducting an illegal enterprise. Sasson recommended the prime minister pursue criminal investigations, some political leaders spoke in favor of change, and Palestinian leaders expressed outrage, but the report was effectively shelved and the settlement movement continued. As Israeli lawmakers surely understood, the arrangements that Sasson uncovered were no aberration; legal or not, they were a necessary part of the state's long-term project of occupation and settlement.

Nothing in the Sasson report's findings was anomalous in the context of the longer history of the State. Much the same thing occurred, only more openly, in the United States in the late nineteenth century, when the United States Army was employed to defend settlers on the Great Plains in the face of binding treaties with Native American nations inhabiting the land. A century later, officials in the Reagan administration financed and conducted an illegal, shadow foreign policy that included arming and supporting right-wing insurgents in Nicaragua and paying off Iran to release U.S. hostages.

When the State needs to operate out of sight and outside the law, and wants greater deniability, satellites like white-supremacist militias and vigilantes, the KKK and the RSS, take over the dirtier side of the business. If these groups threaten to become a destabilizing force, as the Klan did in the 1960s and the violent boogaloo bois in the U.S. and armed settler militias in the West Bank have done more recently, the State sometimes—reluctantly—steps in.

Such was the case in January 2021, when thousands of Trump supporters burst into the Capitol in Washington in search of lawmakers in the process of certifying their hero's loss in the November presidential election. The riot resulted in vandalism, the evacuation of the House and Senate chambers, and five deaths, and federal authorities were forced to initiate a national dragnet after most of the perpetrators were simply allowed to leave by Capitol Police. Biden, Democratic and Republican lawmakers, and leaders of finance like JPMorgan Chase chair Jamie Dimon, many of whom had long abetted Trump, quickly protested that this violent outpouring of grievance by the extreme right did not represent America. But as author Roxane Gay pointed out in the *New York Times*, "This is America. This has always been America. If this were not America, this would not have happened."[13]

This propensity to toggle between official and unofficial, legal and illegal means, and collude with violent reactionaries, extends to partnerships between states. Governments often aid and abet each other in conducting these shadow operations, and learn from each other in the process. Operation Condor was a secretive, U.S.-backed campaign of political repression and state terror organized by six South American military dictatorships from the early 1970s into the mid-1980s. Many Argentine military personnel who carried out human rights abuses as a matter of state policy during this period had been trained in counterinsurgency by the French forces in Algeria during France's bloody war of repression against that country's independence movement.[14]

In any given situation, such actions can be chalked up to abuse of power and bad behavior by bad elements in leadership or dismissed as the behavior only of "rogue" states, but in reality, they are not aberrations; they are the State in action. Since no value is higher to the State than its own preservation and reproduction, no action in pursuit of these goals can, practically speaking, be regarded as off-limits. Any individual, group, or community that comes between the State and its primary objective must therefore understand that the State will respond in any way it decides is most effective, regardless of legality.

V

Characteristics of the System, 2

Motivations and Drivers

Economics is the mother tongue of public policy. It dominates our decision-making for the future, guides multi-billion-dollar investments, and shapes our responses to climate change, inequality, and other environmental and social challenges that define our times.
—Kate Raworth, *Doughnut Economics: 7 Ways to Think Like a 21st Century Economist*

The State is first and foremost an economic endeavor

This may be the most powerful and consistent through line in the State's five-hundred-year development. The drive to construct more public policy around economistic rationales, and likewise to understand more of human activity and motivation as propelled by some form of cost-benefit analysis, has reached its highest pitch ever in recent decades. Today, through its control of monetary and fiscal policy, the State holds the commanding heights of the economy. It can make or break any enterprise, any rival political authority, and any attempt to create an alternative economic order, thanks to its mastery of these tools. But this has been the goal of the State from the beginning of the modern era. It grew out of the desire of political and dynastic leaders in the late Middle Ages to amass economic wealth as a means of stabilizing, deepening, and extending their power and, if possible, making it permanent.

For example, the revival of slavery by western European elites and the reenergizing of serfdom by their eastern European counterparts at the dawn of the modern State in the sixteenth and seventeenth centuries stemmed from the need to marshal economic forces—in this case, captive human labor—to build economic power. While slavery and serfdom are no longer widespread, they have not disappeared: low-wage and unpaid "human capital" are critical elements of the global economy, and components of the State like corporations still think of workers primarily as productive units.*

This way of thinking about human beings has become so commonplace that we have to make an effort to notice it as such. But sometimes it sticks out too conspicuously. "Compulsory slave labour . . . was in its time, a progressive phenomenon," Trotsky told a 1920 Russian trades union conference.[1] A century later, in May 2020, when asked whether COVID-period unemployment numbers were likely to remain in double digits at election time in November, Trump economic adviser Kevin Hassett replied, "Our capital stock hasn't been destroyed, our human capital stock is ready to get back to work," thus reducing human beings, with their multifarious lives, to anonymous inputs in a political-economic equation.[2] Similarly, when Amazon's Jeff Bezos described a futuristic project to send surplus human beings into space, where they would have unlimited room to reproduce, he exulted, "we'd have a thousand Mozarts and a thousand Einsteins," reducing genius itself to a factor of production.[3]

Such thinking would seem outlandish enough, except that the State—and people with Bezos's level of wealth—have the means to materialize it. According to an item in the *Wall Street Journal* in 2020,

* In the United States, "guest workers" brought in under the fast-growing H2 visa program are recruited directly by industries like agribusiness and meat-processing, have few if any rights, and are widely subject to discrimination, sexual harassment, and wage theft; the Southern Poverty Law Center has compared them to "modern-day indentured servants," only "today's guest workers have no prospect of becoming U.S. citizens." Maurizio Guerrero, "How Trump Is Privatizing the US Immigration System," *In These Times*, September 26, 2020.

researchers were working on "brain boost-ers," drugs that might help athletes "play smarter," as well as "non-invasive magnetic and electrical fields that might temporarily affect brain activity to boost performance. Some of these techniques have already been tried out on bicyclists."[4]

The motivation, then as now, was much the same. By adopting policies that raised productivity and held down labor costs, early modern states hoped to encourage economic growth that would boost taxes and other revenues, in turn allowing them to field more formidable armies, expand their geographic reach, and establish more pervasive control over their lands and populations.

> The State was the original capitalist, and it remains the greatest. It aspires to incorporate every inch, every corner of the society over which it presides into a vast wealth-producing machine.

A long line of political theorists, beginning with Machiavelli, provided an ideological (and sometimes idealistic) rationale for this power-centric project. Trotsky takes his place in this pantheon with this succinct definition of the role of labor in the State, which would be difficult for the most hardened, anticommunist capitalist to disagree with: "The only solution to economic difficulties that is correct from the point of view both of principle and of practice is to treat the population of the whole country as the reservoir of the necessary labour power—an almost inexhaustible reservoir—and to introduce strict order into the work of its registration, mobilization and utilization."[5]

The State therefore was the original capitalist, and it remains the greatest. Its fundamental aspiration is to incorporate every inch, every corner of the society over which it presides into a vast wealth-producing machine. The capitalist class (that is, the class of owners of property and other forms of capital) steadily emerged as its critical component because it served the State's need to marshal resources for economic growth. This prompted states to charter trading companies, explore the world for essential resources and seize them, and nurture the growth of banking and financial systems that could help them leverage these assets for even greater growth. It also led the State to support the development of science and technology in its search for new and better ways to solidify its material dominance, and to shape the society and culture to generate more growth.

"The elimination of internal rivals and development of the capacity to extract resources is the process of statemaking," wrote sociologist-historian Charles Tilly.[6] "In the long run, the quest inevitably involved them in establishing regular access to capitalists who could supply and arrange credit and in imposing one form of regular taxation or another on the people and activities within their sphere of control."[7] Today, this system, in which the political and the economic are tightly woven together, is even more intricate and closely managed, starting with the U.S. dollar's regime as the world's reserve currency and the related petrodollar system, in which oil, the world's key commodity, is priced, bought, and sold in U.S. dollars.

A feedback loop emerges: the State's demand for capital to grow the economy catalyzes and accelerates economic change, which makes the society as a whole more complex and in greater need of management, which makes the administrative and security apparatus of the State larger and more essential, which increases its demand for capital. The solidification of this pattern corresponds to the period of the most rapid technological and scientific development in human history. How the State navigates this journey has always been highly contentious; for roughly the past four hundred years, almost every major state at any given time has subscribed to a specific economic doctrine—mercantilism, free trade, classical liberalism, protectionism, social democracy, Marxist-Leninism, Keynesianism, neoliberalism—which has generated a great deal of argument and not a little violence. But all of these doctrines serve the same goal: the reproduction of the State and the deepening and expansion of its overall power.

That's why the State is always on the side of "progress," defined strictly as economic growth and innovation, and the professed enemy of inefficiencies, bottlenecks, waste, and needless expenses. A century ago, the State promoted and justified eugenics as a way to save households and government the expense of supporting and caring for individuals who could not contribute productively to their society or economy; arguments for their value as human beings were dismissed as unscientific. The practice of culling "mentally defective" and other persons thought to have "undesirable" traits and encouraging the "breeding" of supposedly superior stock began in the UK and the United States, but quickly spread to Belgium, Brazil, Canada, Sweden, France, and, most devastatingly, Germany.[8] Even the new Soviet Union hosted an influential Russian Eugenics Society in the 1920s.

Supposedly discredited after the Nazi period, aspects of eugenics continue to find advocates, including longtime Singapore prime minister and strongman Lee Kuan Yew and philosopher John Rawls, and some practices related to eugenics continue into our time.[9] It's been reported that from 2006 to 2010, at least 148 women received tubal ligations in violation of prison rules at the hands of doctors under contract with the California Department of Corrections and Rehabilitation; perhaps 100 were sterilized during the previous ten years.[10]

Questions about U.S. Immigration and Customs Enforcement's (ICE's) treatment of women in its custody exploded in 2020 when a whistleblower at ICE's Irwin County detention center in Georgia claimed that women there had their uteruses removed without their understanding and consent. ICE later admitted that two women at the facility, which was run by a private prison company, LaSalle Corrections, had been given full hysterectomies, but more than forty others later alleged that they, too, had been subjected to invasive gynecological procedures.[11] "When I met all these women who had had surgeries, I thought this was like an experimental concentration camp," said one investigator. "It was like they're experimenting with their bodies."[12]

Practices like these appear to come out of nowhere, or to be summoned up from the depths of the Nazi past, but they make perfect sense as part of the State's job of regulating and cultivating the populations under its control. As long as the modern State exists, some form of eugenics is likely to be at least a temptation, if not a practice, to its leaders and ideologues.

More recently, techno-optimism has mounted as quickly in government as it has in business. We've been assured, for example, that algorithms, artificial intelligence, and machine learning, combined with technologies like facial recognition,* can remove human inefficiency and bias from decision-making in any number of fields, including the justice system, help us to predict the future more accurately, and even quantify our socioeconomic worthiness. In reality, these tools bend in the direction of the biases and prejudices of the ethnocultural group from which the State draws it leadership, but this hasn't stopped the State from forging ahead. China's nascent social credit program, which collects data to grade individuals on everything from financial fraud and no-show restaurant reservations to blood donations and volunteer work, can lead to blacklisting for "untrustworthy" persons. While the program is perhaps the highest-profile effort of this sort, it's merely the latest elaboration of the actuarial science that's been developed over many decades in Europe and the United States by insurance companies, motor vehicle registrars, and other elements of the State.

Thanks to its single-minded focus on squeezing out "value" for capital and the State, economics comes to be seen in elite circles as the organizing discipline of (practically) all life. That which has no economic justification has no justification at all.

Linking today's high-tech analytics to old-fashioned green-eyeshade practices like insurance underwriting is the State's drive to pigeonhole individuals and communities, not to mention nature in general, as economic assets or liabilities and assign a value to them as such. As a result, the State has little motivation to grapple with issues like climate change, racism, abusive labor practices, or gender inequality, nor does it have any incentive to promote truly sustainable economic solutions. Ignoring or minimizing the significance of these problems enables it to rationalize extracting energy from fossil fuels and maintaining a low-wage system for women and people of color. Thanks to this single-minded focus on

---

* The market for facial recognition technologies was valued at $5 billion in 2020 and projected to double by 2025. Daniel E. Ho, Emily Black, Maneesh Agrawala, and Fei-Fei Lee, "How Regulators Can Get Facial Recognition Technology Right," Brookings Institution, November 17, 2020.

squeezing out "value" for capital and the State, economics comes to be seen in elite circles as the organizing discipline of (practically) all life. That which has no economic justification has no justification at all.

This begins with property. When early modern European states began turning feudal lines of obligation into landed property—a form of direct ownership—the modern economy was born. Property ownership is a central principle of the State, a safeguard of authority and social order, and every state devotes a significant measure of its resources to defending property against almost any other moral or economic consideration. "Private property and contract make possible the variety of personality, the wealth, the leisure, and the fertility of invention that sustain civilization," wrote the American conservative political theorist Russell Kirk. Property is "the highest among the social rights of mankind [sic]."[13]

A distinction is always made between public and private property, but this is less significant than it sometimes appears; the State regards public property, too, as a productive asset, and frequently makes it available for private use—for example, for oil and gas and timber leasing. And while in libertarian-capitalist circles property ownership is often framed as a matter of individual liberty that must be defended against the State, in fact, property is one of the most important arenas in which the interests of capital and the State come together. In early modern Europe, the appropriation of common lands helped create agribusinesses that in turn facilitated faster economic growth and the expansion of the State. In more recent centuries, the private real estate market, and the lenders that service it, cater to a largely white, affluent audience and thus help maintain the privileges of the State's most important constituency. Zoning and commercially directed urban planning prop up property values for the biggest landlords and investors while driving out smaller homeowners and small businesses, enabling those landlords to optimize their investment for more "productive" use. Tax breaks and loopholes further accelerate this process.

This confluence of interests highlights the slipperiness of the distinction between the political and economic realms. Beginning in the nineteenth century, the State came to define the two as distinct and to define the economy as a closed system. This shift was useful because it allowed classical economics, focused exclusively on growth, to be presented as an objective, scientific area of study, and anyone who took issue with growth as an overriding goal to be stigmatized as scientifically unsound or a dangerous radical.

But the distinction is false. The State is an economic entity, just as much as a corporation or a company or a cooperative. It runs on revenues (taxes) and borrowed capital, just as a private company does. The two big differences are that a state can create money and, because it is assumed to be perpetual, its credit is less open to question (although there are exceptions). When Hitler wrote, in *Mein Kampf*, "the state is a racial organism and not an economic organization," he was not only making a statement of breathtaking bigotry; he was completely and perhaps deliberately misunderstanding the nature of the State. It's highly unlikely that any of the bankers, investors, and industrial tycoons who partnered with his regime had the same misapprehension.

The conjunction of interests between capitalists and the State (although not necessarily any one state) is profound. Both need steady, perpetual economic growth to remain viable and to legitimate themselves. Both are concerned with marshaling resources—animal, vegetable, inanimate, and human—for this purpose. Both therefore have an insatiable need (which we'll explore more closely later) to track, record, evaluate, and make these resources more exploitable. Both play to mass audiences: citizens and other longtime residents, in the case of the State, and consumers, in the case of capital, the two groups largely overlapping.

Capitalism already existed in the activities of bankers and lenders in the cities of medieval Germany and Italy, but the formation of the modern State in the late fifteenth century supercharged it, giving capital a primary client with far greater resources. That client could coin and later print its own money, could open up vast new territories for capital to explore and exploit, and would always need capital's services as it grew and became more ambitious. Just like the State, modern capitalism isn't something that arose "naturally"; it had to be constructed, subsidized, and directed, and it still does. It couldn't exist without the State to supply the rules, enforcement, guardrails, and social acceptance that enable it to function—and, crucially, the credit backstop and subsidies needed to keep it profitable.

As an example, let's briefly examine limited liability laws, which shield shareholders from responsibility when corporations inflict harm on others. While disasters—like the deadly gas leak at the Union Carbide plant in Bhopal, India, in 1984; the massive oil spill from British Petroleum's Deepwater Horizon drilling platform in 2010; Purdue Pharma's promotion of highly addictive opioids; and the negligence that resulted in two Boeing 737 Max jets crashing and killing 346 people in 2019—may result in fines and loss of reputation for companies, their shareholders suffer only minimally or not at all. As Katharina Pistor, a professor at Columbia University Law School, points out, Boeing was required to set up a disaster fund of only $50 million to compensate the families of the victims of its design failings—about $144,500 per victim—despite the fact that the manufacturer's shareholders made $43 billion from share repurchases in the six years before the two disasters.[14]

Limited liability laws make no economic sense, Pistor argues. They encourage owners to disregard companies' misbehavior because often the owners benefit from it; because owners are shielded from responsibility for their actions, markets don't adequately incorporate risk into their valuation of companies. But without these laws in place, many companies, including some of the very largest, would not be able to survive; no one would want to own their shares or lend to them. They remain in business because the State allows them to.

Likewise, the State couldn't exist without capitalism, since it's the fastest driver of the economic expansion states work to promote. Without the one, we would not have the other. The result is an intensely close alliance that has defined the modern world. "Enrichissez-vous, messieurs!" François Guizot, minister to French king Louis Philippe I, allegedly said to his majesty's wealthier subjects, underscoring a conviction that what's good for the capitalist is good for the State. If capitalism did not exist, the State would have to invent some other mechanism that fulfills more or less the same function; the "state capitalism" once practiced in the Soviet Union and Mao's China offers an example.

While promoting economic growth is the principal reason it fosters capitalism, the State has other motivations as well. As an accelerating cycle of hurricanes, floods, and wildfires grew to become a seminormal part of modern life throughout the world in the early twenty-first century, numerous government policies that promoted growth were revealed to be wasteful and counterproductive. In the United States, the National Flood Insurance Program, for example, encouraged people to build and rebuild homes in flood-prone areas since they could recoup their losses in a disaster, and at taxpayers' expense. Even when private insurers tried to discontinue policies or raise rates, states imposed regulations to stop them, ostensibly to protect vulnerable poor communities but mostly to benefit wealthy ones (as of 2020, thirty of the fifty states had such regulations in place).[15]

Propping up the property values of the rich is not the only reason for such irrational policies, however, or even the most important. They are the latest in a succession of laws and other measures that were designed to encourage white Americans to occupy every portion of the country's continental territory, starting with the Homestead Act of 1862 and the generous subsidies supplied to railroads in the same era. As a colonial society with a vast and vulnerable landmass, the United States was committed to spend whatever it took to make its title to the land real, principally by settling it with people. Today, it still subsidizes human occupancy even of inhospitable regions to maintain its control. The UK subsidizes its tiny colony in the Falkland Islands, and China underwrites Han Chinese colonization of Xinjiang for similar reasons; economic rationales come later.

The private sector also serves as a convenient place for the State to reroute and cover up activities the public doesn't approve of. The United States outsources much of its security and other military activities in far-flung places like Afghanistan and Iraq so that those activities escape public scrutiny; the CIA and other agencies have been known to camouflage their work by setting up import-export or other front businesses. When Congress investigated the CIA's covert operations in the mid-1970s, it found that "a 'Who's Who' of business and finance" spanning "petroleum, rubber products, heavy manufacturing, banking, consumer products and services, travel, advertising, publishing [e.g., Fodor's Travel Guides, Inc.], public relations and the import-export trade" had "commercial cover agreements" that placed CIA agents in their overseas offices.[16]

More recently, the Trump administration was found to have created "a largely unregulated shadow system of detention and swift expulsions" of migrant children "without the safeguards that are intended to protect the most vulnerable" by stashing them in hotels and motels like Best Western and Hampton Inn, guarded by private security personnel, where they didn't have to be registered or extended legal protections.[17] Here again, the private sector acted as cover when the State wanted to sidestep its own laws and norms.

Even the web of tax incentives the State typically provides to encourage charitable giving has an economic and state-building rationale. "Sponsorship of the arts is not charity," observes UK art historian Gavin Grindon; "it is a strategic expenditure. To conduct their business, companies must build a web of influence and operation through many of the institutions that are often clustered in cities. . . . Cultural institutions are a key part of this infrastructure into which businesses must insinuate themselves to establish an air of social legitimacy and acceptability for practices that might otherwise risk coming into question."[18] Legitimacy, opportunities for profitable networking, and tax breaks to boot: museums, libraries, and performing arts are very much a component of capital and the State's drive for economic growth.

A distinct trajectory marks the relationship between a private enterprise and the State. Once an enterprise reaches a certain size, it becomes visible to the State and is obliged to operate according to rules the State sets forth. As it continues to grow, it acquires greater influence within the State, becoming a more powerful component of the whole. Capitalists and entrepreneurs consciously pursue partnerships with government as the highest level of their (and their chief executives') ambitions. A recent example is the intimate cooperation between the federal government, military, and police forces and the high-tech sector to produce better means of tracking, surveilling, and managing the population. This alliance began with the Pentagon subsidizing the computer industry in the years following World War II and has only become more central to U.S. military planning.

Exemplary in this respect is the career of Google chairman Eric Schmidt. As a graduate student at the University of California, Berkeley, in the mid-1970s, Schmidt did research on distributed computing that was funded by DARPA. In 2009, he was a tech adviser to the Obama administration. Three years later, he participated in classified briefings on cybersecurity as part of a Pentagon program called Enduring Security Framework. His venture capital fund, Innovative Endeavors, later invested in start-ups that sold satellite imagery to defense and intelligence agencies. In 2016, he became chairman of the Defense Innovation Board, a civilian advisory panel that brings new technology to the Pentagon's attention. Until three thousand Google employees signed a letter complaining about it in 2018, the company had a contract with the Pentagon to build systems using drone imagery to pinpoint particular objects and people.[19] Along the way, of course, Schmidt and his partners created one of the biggest private enterprises ever to roam the earth, one of whose biggest customers was the U.S. government.

Another example of this blurring between State and capital is China's Belt and Road Initiative, which aims to knit Eurasia into a vast commercial web. Beijing facilitates this undertaking with soft loans to Chinese companies, vast infrastructure projects in participant states from Spain to Indonesia, and a conscious attempt to make Chinese technology, economic, and administrative practices the standard wherever possible. Not so incidentally, Beijing's cross-border investments "are increasingly protected by Chinese private security companies, charged with defending Chinese infrastructure and workers abroad," note political scientists Andrew Phillips and J. C. Sharman. "Nominally private, for-profit entities, these companies have strong ties to the Chinese state and are typically staffed by veterans of the People's Liberation Army."[20]

Note that in this instance, the State supplies capital to business to pursue its geopolitical ends, and that those businesses, aside from making money, serve as an autonomous, quasi-colonial administration in the countries to which they carry their operations. Similar arrangements go back a long way: to the first century of the modern State, when, as Phillips and Sharman note, great trading companies "were founded under royal or parliamentary charters to undertake the long-distance trade and colonization that rulers were too poor to finance themselves." The British and Dutch East India companies, the Hudson's Bay Company, and the Royal African Company (which funded and coordinated the African slave trade for Britain) not only built capitalism but began the work of spreading European dominion—and the apparatus of the State—into new parts of the world.

The immediate interests of the State and capital are not always congruent—and when they are not, usually it is the State that determines the agenda. For example, in 1834 the British Parliament downgraded the rich and politically powerful East India Company into a managing agency for the British government in India and in 1873 dissolved it (after a final dividend payment and stock redemption). The European carve-up of the developing world into colonies and protectorates, at around the same time, which in reality was sparked by political ambitions, territorial rivalries, and proxy warfare, not to mention the need to supply military and civil posts to members of polite families, was rationalized as a business proposition. But European capitalists and businesses underinvested in these territories, which served primarily to extend the State's military and political control. Commercial exploitation took place mainly in other parts of the developing world, such as the Americas, that Europe did not politically control, and later in the former European colonies after they (re)gained independence.

More recently, the U.S. government for strategic reasons has forbidden American companies from doing business in post-revolutionary Cuba, despite the fact that other governments have allowed their businesspeople to pursue opportunities there—and U.S. companies have largely accepted the edict. In 2020, the Chinese government shut down the initial public offering of Ant Group, the enormous Internet finance firm, when its controlling shareholder criticized Chinese regulators.[21] Meanwhile, the Trump administration pursued a damaging trade war with Beijing, regardless of the preferences of major corporations and agricultural interests that by then were intimately and profitably connected with China.

Likewise, when the United States returned Shah Mohammad Reza Pahlavi to the throne of Iran in 1953 and replaced the UK as his government's dominant foreign partner, it took over 40 percent of what had been Britain's stake in Iranian oil production. U.S. oil companies initially weren't interested, preferring cheaper Saudi Arabian oil, and had to be persuaded to participate in an enterprise that was primarily about extending Washington's influence in the Middle East. But they understood their role to be, in part, as agents of Washington's foreign policy in the region, and so, of course, they went along. A further instance occurred during the post–Cold War period in the 1990s, when the U.S. defense budget shrank—temporarily, as it happened—in the wake of the Soviet Union's collapse, and the Defense Department forced the merger of dozens of American military contractors into three giants: Boeing Company, Raytheon Company, and Lockheed Martin Corporation.[22] Finally, there is the close cooperation Washington has exacted from high-tech and communications companies since 9/11 in its effort to expand its surveillance capabilities.

These examples underscore the State's knack for taking the long view and the willingness of capital and big business to follow its direction, knowing that in the end, they all contribute to the same project. Lacking both the leadership and the protection (from itself) extended by the State, capital would either destroy itself or be quickly brought down. More fundamentally, the State dictates the environment in which capital functions, and unless a regime is directly hostile to capital itself, business and financial interests will play ball. Following months of street protests against Beijing's increasing encroachment on Hong Kong's autonomy, for example, many large foreign-owned banks, trading houses, and other enterprises were expected to relocate from the island city to other parts of East Asia, perhaps crippling the territory's economy. But it quickly became clear that wasn't going to happen.

"Global financial institutions that are deeply rooted in Hong Kong . . . have already been adapting to a changing business environment," the *Wall Street Journal* reported weeks after a repressive new national security law was imposed. "They have ramped up hires of Mandarin speakers and Chinese professionals [Hong Kong residents' principal language is Cantonese] and positioned themselves to win more deals and attract more money from Chinese companies and investors. . . . Western banks . . . have been careful not to say anything critical of Chinese policy or the national-security law."

Just as the law was coming into effect, Hong Kong "played host to a blizzard of stock sales," the *Journal* noted, and "the city's famously expensive real-estate market has been resilient." To bolster confidence, regulators announced new rules making it easier to move money across China's borders.[23] If Beijing wanted to crack down on civil liberties in Hong Kong, multinationals were not going to let that get in the way of business.

Capitalism, then, is not a closed or all-encompassing operating system; it needs the State to function. But the State needs capital to realize its goals.

The Left tends to see this relationship quite differently, if it sees the relationship at all. "Capitalism is not the solution to urban America's problems," anthropologist and geographer David Harvey wrote in response to the economic collapse during the COVID crisis; "capitalism itself is the problem." "Unless we address the root causes of those problems in the structure of our economic system," he declared, "we'll never be able to solve them."[24]

This is true so far as it goes, but unless we first understand the capitalist system as a component of the larger system of the State, any attempt to move beyond capitalism will only lead to a further buildup of the State and, in the end, the reproduction of capitalism in some form. This was precisely the outcome at the end of the "socialist decades" following the Russian Revolution and the heyday of social-democratic governments in Europe and elsewhere. The more that social movements and collective and cooperative practices were integrated into the State, the more likely they were to be displaced by practices that relied on capital. To get rid of capitalism *requires* getting rid of the State.

The State encourages bigness and uniformity

One of the principal commonalities between the State and capital is their propensity to "go big" or, in business parlance, to "scale": to centralize, to eliminate competition, to expand exponentially, to promote a social and cultural uniformity determined from the top. For capital, the objective is to create markets that are as large and uniform as possible, since this makes them more predictable and easier to extract maximum profits from. For the State, this makes them easier to govern and tax.

In many facets of society, the State leads the way in this: for example, by nurturing a select number of very large defense contractors to guarantee its supply of weaponry and technical resources or by favoring and working closely with high-tech and communications companies that provide it with necessary tools and services for surveillance, data gathering, and analysis. These companies become privy to state plans and secrets and thus become ever more deeply embedded in the State itself.

It's easy to lose sight of this aspect of the State because neoliberal economists and pundits like to extol business entrepreneurialism and small businesses as innovators and job creators. In reality, whatever the ideological cast of its present leadership, the State always tends to the needs of the biggest commercial and financial enterprises first because they are its closest partners in directing the society under its control. All too often, government projects ostensibly designed to aid small businesses and farmers—like the COVID-period Paycheck Protection Program—mostly benefit their larger rivals (and their investors).

The State is a system of cultural hegemony

If violence is the State's first and last method of control, it relies day-to-day on complex methods of cultural hegemony to keep the population loyal or at least acquiescent. The key audience for this system is always the Core Identity Group: the ethno-cultural group that the State regards as its primary constituency, critical to its legitimacy and security. This key constituency, with the assistance of the State, seeks to absorb other groups, eliminate them, or else maintain them in a subordinate position.

Marx and Engels held that "the ideas of the ruling class are in every epoch the ruling ideas."[25] This is correct as such, but the elite's ideas are always strongly affected by its origins in the Core Identity Group, and what it thinks it has to do to retain that group's loyalty. This group models what's socially and culturally normal; is given access to education, opportunities, and influence in political decision-making; and is the reservoir from which the elite selects new members and leaders. Its definition of itself leans heavily on ethnicity and nationality—"nationalism expropriates the logic of ethnic belonging and turns it into an instrument of exclusion,"

> If violence is the State's first and last method of control, it relies day-to-day on complex methods of cultural hegemony to keep the population loyal or at least acquiescent.

Michael Herzfeld observes—but can stir in other ingredients, like religion, occupation, and even loyalty to certain sports teams.[26]

These dominant groups "are surrounded by images of themselves," writes American social historian Isabel Wilkerson, "from cereal commercials to sitcoms, as deserving, hardworking and superior in most aspects of American life, and it would be the rare person who would not absorb the constructed centrality of the dominant group [or] would go out of their way to experience the world from the perspective of those considered below them."[27]

On the other hand, the State also has a significant degree of power to designate or construct the Core Identity Group; every state does so almost from the moment it consciously exists. In the United States, it's people of European stock and Judeo-Christian religious background; in China, Han Chinese; in Indonesia, Javanese; in the Russian Federation, ethnic Russians; in India, Hindus. In early modern France, the Core Identity Group was quickly established as white Roman Catholics who spoke *moyen français*, which became the legal language of the kingdom with the Ordinance of Villers-Cotterêts in 1539, and then modern French. The closer one conforms to these groups, the more easily one can access education, opportunities, and, above all, the trust of the regime.

Members of the Core Identity Group believe implicitly that the national state belongs to them and must serve to perpetuate their cultural dominance, and are conditioned to do so; they can be easily mobilized politically when they perceive some other group or groups to be challenging this belief. However, the Core Identity Group is also a perpetual work in transition; new populations are admitted as needed, new cultural features bolted on and old ones shed or downplayed, although the original group always retains a certain cultural prestige. The State enforces the cultural norms typified by the Core Identity Group through governmental institutions like law enforcement and schools as well as other components including organized religion, groups focused on cultural indoctrination (like the Boy Scouts or military academies), and fringe groups like citizen militias and (sometimes xenophobic) cultural heritage organizations.

The Core Identity Group is vital to the State's existence, reinforcing an "illusion of fixity" by associating it with a certain group of ethnic and cultural traits and identifiers that it presents as eternal. "Nation-state logic attempts to freeze the passage of time," Herzfeld writes, "to turn its historiography into a machine for the production of timeless truths" that it embodies in nation-day celebrations, national museums, and cultural centers, among other things. The story of a "preordained march to national perfection,"[28] with the Core Identity Group at its center, is always a distortion, covering over the complex ways that different communities intersect within and between states and the violence that regulates them, but the State works ceaselessly to make that story seem true and timeless.

Of course, the Core Identity Group also form a bedrock of loyal citizens who invest their consciousness in the symbols, inspiration, and sense of mission the State provides; the State works hard to nurture this group, and loses sleep—figuratively speaking—when it appears to be in decline. So, for instance, the State becomes concerned when birthrates fall among the Core Identity Group, typically responding by boosting benefits for families and even paying indirect subsidies to them to have more children. (Minority groups, of course, are generally stigmatized as "irresponsibly" having too many children.) In the United States in the early twenty-first century, the state finally began to treat drug addiction as a public-health emergency rather than just a law enforcement problem when it began to affect white working-class households significantly.

The State also works hard to create a common culture that can satisfy the emotional needs of the Core Identity Group, which in turn fortifies it with security and legitimacy. Capital plays a role in this process, since capitalist economies grow by creating new needs and desires: for new technology, new forms of entertainment, new ways to feel part of the favored community through dress, other personal preferences, and forms of consumption. Capital and the market have a keen eye for the balancing act that people in an expanding economy constantly negotiate between fitting in and asserting their individuality, and they take pains to make their offerings dovetail with the messages the State sends to the Core Identity Group.

Capital is never the primary mover in this dynamic, however. Historian Peter Fritzsche notes that the Nazi Party seduced Germans not just by giving them permission to hate the Jews, communists, and other suspect parties who had supposedly "betrayed" the nation at Versailles, but by promising them a rejuvenated national identity, a *Volksgemeinschaft*, or "people's community." After the party came to power, for example, it recast May Day as a Day of National Labor celebrating not class struggle but national unity.[29] Capital made sure the messages implicit in its consumer offerings fit the new project.

But it's the State that leads the way here, and capital that endeavors to stay in line. One reason is that a capitalist economy's appeal to the people—to the worker and the consumer—is always essentially optimistic: urging them to embrace a utopia of opportunity, variety, and gratification. The State has something more powerful and primal at its command.

In a review of *Mein Kampf*, George Orwell cautioned that those fighting fascism ought not "to underrate its emotional appeal." "Fascism and Nazism are psychologically far sounder than any hedonistic conception of life," he argued, because "human beings don't only want comfort, safety, short working-hours, hygiene, birth-control and, in general, common sense; they also, at least intermittently, want struggle and self-sacrifice, not to mention drums, flags and loyalty-parades. . . . Hitler has said to [the Germans] 'I offer you struggle, danger and death,' and as a result a whole nation flings itself at his feet."[30]

The French anarchist Daniel Guérin, who visited Germany in the early days of the Nazi regime, argued that Marxists "interested only in the material factors . . . understand absolutely nothing of the way in which privations suffered by the masses are transmuted into a religious aspiration."[31] But even democratic and social-democratic states must offer some form of quasi-spiritual ideal that appeals to the Core Identity Group—otherwise, the State lacks any emotionally loyal population.

One element of the Core Identity Group whose allegiance the State has little trouble retaining is the capitalist class, given how critical the State is to its survival. Even in aggressively capitalist societies, the State exerts enormous cultural sway over the conduct and values of the wealthiest members of the society, with surprisingly little pushback.

A prime example is German finance and industry under the Nazis. Responding to a 2020 book commissioned by the big German auto parts maker Continental about its conduct during Hitler's regime, Ariane Reinhart, Continental's chief of human relations, said, "It shows me how fragile company cultures are. In the 1920s, Continental was an open, international, liberal company. Within a few years, the Nazi system was able to smother all of these qualities." While Reinhart may have been exaggerating the company's virtues, Continental was founded in 1871 by a group of Jewish bankers and had always included Jews in high-ranking positions; by 1938, all had been forced out and the company continued to profit from Hitler's rearmament program, even testing out a new rubber-soled shoe on prisoners in the Sachsenhausen concentration camp near Berlin.[32]

The State is always hierarchical

States are, almost by definition, class-based societies—although, given the pivotal position of the Core Identity Group, class distinctions are always braided together with race, ethnicity, cultural profile, and religion. Making the matter even more complicated, class structures are never firmly set in place. Workerist and autonomist Marxists began to note in the 1970s that class relations "are not eternal but are constantly shifting fields of power that are determined not by the autonomous force of capital, but rather by capital's need to integrate forms of working-class insurgency into its working," writes anarchist scholar and activist Stevphen Shukaitis.[33]

The early centuries of the modern State in Europe witnessed the scrapping of the feudal vassal system, which was gradually replaced by a system of direct landed property ownership by an aristocratic upper class, under which were smallholders and tenant farmers. As the economy grew, deployment of financial capital became more important, trade and manufacturing expanded, and a parallel urban class system formed. A proletariat began to develop as the medieval guilds declined and, eventually, modern industrial production commenced. In the past century, the mix has become even more dynamic as trade and industrial unions—Marx's "aristocracy of labor"—weakened, manufacturing was shipped out to less "developed" countries, various forms of creative and "knowledge work" were commodified, and more and more occupations lost whatever insulation they once had from economic precarity.

Hierarchy in the modern State is never simply defined by the kind of work one does, the amount of money one is paid, or even the amount of capital or wealth one manages to accumulate. In other words, modern "meritocratic" society is always something of a myth. Family ties, cultural background and connections, education, race and ethnicity, and assumptions about gender scramble the equation in ways that provide great advantages to some groups and push others further down the ladder. The result is a complex caste system that is of tremendous value to the State, which can use it to drive wedges between groups that would be natural allies in a strictly income-driven class war and to keep some from attaining the earnings or degree of wealth their skills would otherwise indicate—that is, to maintain them as cheap labor.

Here's an example of how this works, from American journalist Nikole Hannah-Jones:

> Black families earning $75,000 or more a year live in poorer neighborhoods than white Americans earning less than $40,000 a year, research by John Logan, a Brown University sociologist, shows. According to another study, by the Stanford sociologist Sean Reardon and his colleagues, the average black family earning $100,000 a year lives in a neighborhood with an average annual income of $54,000. . . .

[A 2018 study by Duke University's Samuel DuBois Cook Center on Social Equity and the Insight Center for Community Economic Development] shows that the racial wealth gap is not about poverty. Poor white families earning less than $27,000 a year hold nearly the same amount of wealth as black families earning between $48,000 and $76,000 annually. It's not because of black spending habits. Black Americans have lower incomes over all but save at a slightly higher rate than white Americans with similar incomes. It's not that black people need to value education more. Black parents, when controlling for household type and socioeconomic status, actually offer more financial support for their children's higher education than white parents do, according to the study. And some studies have shown that black youths, when compared with white youths whose parents have similar incomes and education levels, are actually more likely to go to college and earn additional credentials.[34]

At the top of the State hierarchy is an elite composed of capitalists (including both inherited wealth and new wealth), technocrats and administrators, lawyers, military brass, politicians, influence peddlers, and other policy influencers, such as think-tank denizens. These categories are often very fluid; former senator Phil Gramm of Texas, for example, moved during his career between the roles of technocrat (academic), politician, corporate executive, influence peddler (lobbyist), and think-tanker. Elites are self-selecting: many are born into the elite, others work their way in by dint of education, savvy, and connections built up along the route. Top military figures, for example, typically move to jobs in the defense industry, technocrats and politicians move up to executive positions in the industries they regulate or into lobbying jobs, and lobbyists take up top positions with the regulatory agencies they seek to influence. Traffic moves ceaselessly in all directions at once.

Members of the elite are treated differently by the State from other members of the Core Identity Group, and the advantages have only expanded in recent years. In the United States, for example, the Treasury Inspector General for Tax Administration released a report in 2020 finding that 879,415 high-income individuals didn't file tax returns from 2014 to 2016 and owed the Internal Revenue Service $45.7 billion in taxes for those years. More than three hundred thousand people from this group were never put into the IRS's enforcement system, more than forty-two thousand cases were closed without any work being done on them, and the remainder—more than five hundred thousand—"will likely not be pursued as resources decline."

That's because the IRS, in the face of political attacks by Republican lawmakers, had seen its budget slashed and lost 19 percent of its collections staff in recent years. Yet, some 1,890 individuals who hadn't paid their taxes owed the IRS more than $1 million each, according to the report. The average U.S. household pays an annual surtax of more than $3,000 to subsidize these deadbeats, the IRS's Taxpayer Advocate Service reported.[35]

There are many other examples of how members of the capitalist and policymaking elites and their acolytes are subsidized by the State. The most important is access to credit. During financial crises like the 2008 meltdown, the Wall Street elite, who had spectacularly mismanaged some of the most powerful firms in the world of capital, were propped up by the U.S. Treasury Department and the Federal Reserve, largely through access to credit on outrageously easy terms. Millions of homeowners who had dutifully paid their mortgages for years, meanwhile, were either forced to sell at a loss or else had their homes foreclosed.

Just because one is born into the Core Identity Group doesn't make one creditworthy, or even not poor, although it's a strong indicator of both. What it suggests is that you have a chance, however slim, of rising into the elite. This life passage is what's called "opportunity," and individuals have been known to approach it via some unlikely routes: revolutionary and convict (Lenin and Stalin), homeless street artist (Hitler), failed haberdasher (Harry S. Truman), impoverished minor gentry (Napoleon Bonaparte), Zapotec peasant (Benito Juárez), chemist (Margaret Thatcher and Angela Merkel), broadcaster (Ronald Reagan and Jesse Helms). Once established, however, each, in his or her own fashion, pursued the same mission: to build and reproduce the State.

"All political power inevitably creates a privileged position for those who exercise it," wrote the Russian anarchist revolutionary

Volin.[36] The structure and practical requirements of the State itself also inform the composition of the elite, conditioning new members to perceive the society in ways that dovetail with the State's needs and to act accordingly. For anyone who wants a career and is ambitious, the rewards of toeing the line are overwhelming.

How are people selected for these charmed careers? As an aristocracy of birth, rooted in agricultural production, faded, education became the primary portal into the ruling elite at both the national and global levels. Top-tier universities, business schools, and law schools mold leaders in law, politics, and commerce. In the neoliberal era, the ideology and worldview that underpins the education they dispense is remarkably uniform, regardless of geography; a student at Harvard Business School receives essentially the same indoctrination as one attending INSEAD in France, for example.

Often, too, this process occurs in schools specifically designed to manufacture a power elite. After the Paris Commune tried and failed to topple the French state in 1871, a group of intellectuals founded the École Libre des Sciences Politiques, or Sciences Po, which would supply the nation with a meritocratic elite. Émile Boutmy, the institution's founder, explained the need for a switch from a hereditary elite to one built on talent as follows: "Obliged to submit to the rule of the majority, the classes that call themselves the upper classes can preserve their political hegemony only by invoking the rights of the most capable. As traditional upper-class prerogatives crumble, the wave of democracy will encounter a second rampart, built on eminently useful talents, superiority that commends prestige, and abilities of which society cannot sanely deprive itself."[37]

Sciences Po has continued to turn out presidents, diplomats, technocrats, and many, many top corporate executives down to this day. But it merely regularized a process that was born in early modern Europe, when the monarchical state began recruiting advisers and administrators from the middle classes, who were presumed to be more loyal to the sovereign than the frequently rebellious nobility and to better understand the newly central role of economic growth. Likewise, institutions like Sciences Po ensure that aspiring members of the elite are properly indoctrinated: that they understand the role of the State and the role of the economy within the State and that they are committed reflexively to working within it.

China fashioned the prototype of this system centuries before the modern era when it instituted an exam process to select the most promising candidates to become mandarins, or high civil servants. In 2005, resurgent China established the China Executive Leadership Academy in Pudong, whose mission is to "significantly improve the quality of our leaders." Instruction is pragmatic in the contemporary, neoliberal, business-inflected sense; the talk is "of leveraging your skills, strengthening your global mind-set, and improving your presentation abilities," according to a recent account.[38]

In other places, these high-level institutions of leadership indoctrination are less centralized, although they seldom fail to place people with business, political, or administrative ambitions close together. Everywhere, they form a tight cultural affinity group based to a great extent on where and how much the members were educated and the occupations they then adopted.* Barack Obama's political rise dates from his years at Harvard Law School, where he developed connections and learned the language and mode of thought of the elite; the majority of current members of the U.S. Supreme Court attended law school at either Harvard or Yale. In one-party states like China, the party selects each new generation of the elite; this was also true of earlier European states like Nazi Germany, fascist Italy, and the Eastern Bloc countries.

Whatever their avowed political orientation, members of each state's meritocracy adopt similar cultural markers and trappings; republics are headed by presidents who live in executive mansions, elect members to representative assemblies, choose high courts, and appoint corps of diplomats attached to the executive branch. Most visibly, they govern from a traditional seat of power. This is true even in postimperial and postcolonial states. For example, the Bolshevik governments after 1917 ruled from the Winter Palace and then the Kremlin, the seats of tsarist power; the newly independent Irish Free

---

* "They may denounce racism and sexism, but they are unapologetic about their negative attitudes toward the less educated." Michael J. Sandel, "The Consequences of the Diploma Divide," *New York Times*, September 6, 2020.

State governed from Dublin, the traditional hub of English colonial power on the island (but which had never been an Irish capital before the conquest); and the revolutionary Chinese Communist government after 1949 ruled from Beijing, the ancient imperial capital with its Forbidden City.

Likewise, the new(ish), postcolonial Indian and Indonesian empires are governed from the old colonial capitals of New Delhi and Jakarta (Batavia), denoting deep institutional, strategic, and even cultural continuity with the European-controlled empires that preceded them.* Even in Haiti, a relatively small state, the new local elite, after independence from France, quickly set themselves up to rule from Port-au-Prince, as the colonial masters had, and even tried to preserve the old economic model based around sugar plantations and forced labor; some early leaders after independence adopted royal titles in imitation of their European exemplars. In each of these cases, the seat itself was taken over by very different people—but the seat of power, fashioned by European colonialists, remained.

This extends to more substantive matters as well. For example, when the Irish Free State came into existence in 1922, it retained the legal code the island had followed under English rule rather than creating its own, perhaps one modeled after Brehon Law, the well-developed Indigenous Irish code that had prevailed in Gaelic-speaking areas up to the seventeenth century.[39] This despite the Irish having endured a fearfully bloody, atrocity-ridden insurgent war of independence for the right to be able to make just such choices and the highly nationalistic outlook of the new state's leadership. More often than not, the watchword following a political revolution is continuity, not root-and-branch upheaval, whatever the rhetoric might indicate.

---

* Postcolonial regimes are also intent on erasing cultural markers other than those of the Core Identity Group. China's campaign of cultural erasure against its Uighur minority has included demolishing some 8,500 mosques in the northwestern region of Xinjiang and damaging 7,500 more, according to the Australian Strategic Policy Institute. Chao Deng, "China Razed Thousands of Xinjiang Mosques in Assimilation Push, Report Says," *Wall Street Journal*, September 25, 2020.

VI

Characteristics of the System, 3

Distinguishing Features and Preferences

*For nation-states, boundaries are not spaces of ambiguity or reciprocity;
they are walls, both forbidding and concealing transgressions of moral
sovereignty.*
—Michael Herzfeld, "Boundaries, Embarrassments, and
Social Injustice: Fredrik Barth and the Nation-State"

The State has borders

A border is not a simple physical boundary or line in the ground
(or in the rivers, seas, and oceans). It's a system of enforcement and
exclusion. While the direct authority of every state stops at its legal
boundaries, it claims the right to protect its citizens wherever they
might be and to intervene in the internal affairs of any other state
that does something to offend it. Borders are a flexible concept that
states can leverage to achieve greater control over sections of their
population—and, sometimes, the populations of other states. Borders are defined as much by drones, by internal police surveillance
and data-gathering on noncitizens, by national police forces like ICE
in the United States, by jails built to house noncitizens, and by the
heightened degree of force the State can exercise over these persons,
as they are by actual lines of demarcation.

Borders are present whenever and wherever an undesired individual comes in contact with an agent of the State. This in turn means that the State really has no spatial limits.

Borders are present whenever and wherever an undesired individual comes in contact with an agent of the State. This in turn means that the State really has no spatial limits. Agents of particular states enjoy the cooperation of governments in other countries with which they have agreements to return dissidents and other accused to their control. Even when this is not the case, they routinely snatch and grab their targets, who they then spirit away inside their own borders.

Customs and naturalization agencies have become increasingly militarized in the past century; today in the United States, ICE has a largely free hand to apprehend and dispose of any undocumented person, no matter where they reside. In the EU, borders are being beefed up as waves of refugees pour in from regions destabilized by neoliberalism and devastated by civil wars. Israel exploits its own ambiguous borders with the Palestinian Authority to hold its population of noncitizens in the open-air prison of Gaza, complete with walls, guard towers, and sophisticated electronic sensors that can track nearly everything that happens there. Australia, notoriously, confines migrants in detention centers rife with human rights abuses.

The State is fundamentally opposed to any identity that competes with it

Almost every modern state is built on an injustice: the dispossession or shunting aside—the ethnic cleansing—of one or more Indigenous or other groups by the Core Identity Group. This can take the form of expulsion (as in the "Trail of Tears" removal of Native American peoples from the eastern United States in the 1830s or the dispossession of the native Irish in the sixteenth and seventeenth centuries), confinement to ever-shrinking reserves (as in the case of the Sami in Norway and Sweden), or attempted extermination (of Jews and Roma at various times in Europe). In colonial societies, European rulers generally replicated this pattern by favoring one group over the rest (Hindus over Muslims in India, Tutsi over Hutu in Rwanda and Burundi), and enlisting this Core Identity Group as bureaucrats, soldiers, and clerks to help build the new state that they would eventually run.

The treatment of those with nonmainstream identities is much the same today, as the native-born elites in contemporary, postcolonial states continue to subordinate populations that do not fit into the Core Identity Group: for example, the Javanese cultural imperialism practiced in the Indonesian archipelago against the Timorese, Achenese, and Papuans and the increasing repression of Muslim rights and self-expression in India. Virtually all states practice these ethnic policies to some extent, and this pattern applies regardless of state ideology. For example, the Soviet Union fully abolished the semifeudal states of Central Asia that the tsarist state had tolerated and continued the old regime's campaign of Russification while Maoist and post-Maoist China has worked to complete the imperial project of the preceding dynasties by eradicating the cultures of the ethnically distinct Uighurs and Tibetans, in both cases using revolution and modernization as a rationale. Elsewhere, we see vigorous forms of ethnic cleansing in the suppression of Mapuche identity in Chile, of Ndebele in Zimbabwe, of Rohingya in Myanmar, of Bedouin in Israel, of Roma and Travellers in many European states, and in the continuing encroachment on the rights and lands of Native Americans and First Nations by the United States and Canada.

The State is totalizing

The State is driven to inhabit and control every aspect of the lives and territories over which its power extends, leaving no room for any other form of social-political organization.*

---

* *Nineteen Eighty-Four* is in some ways a warning, in some ways an extrapolation of elements that already existed in the State in Orwell's time.

Political scientists have always claimed primacy over social theory; David Graeber noted that the very first works of social theory—in China, Persia, and Greece—were all framed as theories of statecraft. One "disastrous" result of this, he wrote, is that "we tend to assume that states, and social order, even societies, largely correspond."[1] But if this conflation was a disaster for humanity, it was done quite deliberately as a way to induce us to accept as natural the State's overweening presence.

"The Fascist conception of the State is all-embracing," Benito Mussolini declared in 1919; "outside of it no human or spiritual values can exist, much less have value." If he had left out the reference to fascism, his statement would apply perfectly to the world every state strives to create. Over the centuries, functions that local communities, religious establishments, and systems of mutual aid used to serve have gradually been absorbed into the State and transformed into agencies, nonprofit institutions, or businesses, all operating subject to law: in other words, as quasi-arms of the State. The boundaries of the State are theoretically limitless, and once it acquires a certain set of powers or resources, it does not give them up.

Here again, the State and the digital operating system resemble each other.

The developers of operating systems like Windows or macOS started with an idea. They envisioned systems that could establish a comprehensive platform for executing any and every task that could possibly be carried out on a computer and then could scale up, creating a total environment that was versatile enough to absorb more and more of the activities we carry out in daily life and that could be refashioned as action via software.

The State's drive for totalization aims for something similar when, for example, it encounters a people or population who practice a different form of economic organization. The result in most cases is an ongoing war of the State and its dominant groups against Indigenous and migrant peoples and against labor. For instance, Germany's right-wing power brokers, and then Hitler, spent the years between the world wars doing everything they could to break the country's left working-class culture, which they regarded as a permanent revolutionary threat. Forty years later, Prime Minister Margaret Thatcher declared war on Britain's radical mine workers because they similarly represented an obstacle to her plans to remake the economy along neoliberal lines.

The aspirations of the modern State in all its varieties include a drive for cultural and economic uniformity, which it achieves through three basic tools: surveillance, control of public spaces, and deception. The history of the State is in part the history of its use of these tools against countervailing social formations—such as Indigenous societies, traditional cultural or social patterns of governance, organized religion, organized labor, and organized crime. The State tries to assimilate or suppress them, push them to the margins, or eliminate them by more violent means. A very recent example is the 2020 decision of the U.S. Bureau of Indian Affairs to revoke the reservation status of the Mashpee Wampanoag, established only thirteen years earlier, which meant that a portion of their lands was no longer held in trust for the tribe.[2]

In any state, a great deal of law is concerned with preserving the State itself, which effectively gives it the power to override other laws meant to hold it in check. Democratic processes and a constitution theoretically act as a brake, since they are the institutional foundation of the State's legitimacy. But because the State, paradoxically, exists at once among the people and above them, it has tremendous flexibility in justifying its actions. Dictators, for example, claim to derive their authority directly from the democratic masses as embodiments of the people's will, placing them above any elected or other responsible body. But states with a more functionally democratic governmental structure can still assume a position above the people to outlaw political activity by certain groups of actors—or expel dangerous "aliens"—by invoking the need for internal defense of the state.

Social provision is another aspect of the totalizing State. As we've noted, in the nineteenth and twentieth centuries, the State absorbed into government and the nonprofit sector most of the social provision once supplied through traditional community-rooted systems and mutual aid groups. As societies grew larger and more complex, these social supports became more critical; the desire to preserve and, if possible, improve them, tied people more strongly to the State.

Many of those on the left—or at least those who are left-of-center—still feel loyalty to the State based on its social policy accomplishments, which undoubtedly improved the lives of large sections of the working class. Progressives and social democrats tend to understand contemporary politics as a contest between conservative "antigovernment" forces and people like themselves who believe in an expansive government that serves society's needs. They believe strongly—emotionally—that social progress is only possible within the context of the State. This is how the State retains the loyalty of women, ethnic minorities, sexual minorities, and much of the working class, who often see capturing the State as the most powerful means of securing equality. It's also how the State retains the support of white liberals, who have a deep desire for social reconciliation and unity and tend to believe the only way to achieve a resolution of social conflicts is through the State.

All of these means—cultural assimilation, careful control of its relationship with the masses, provision of social services—enable the State to construct an organism that saturates every part of our lives with the meaning it creates while subsuming or remaking our social relations in its image to render us useful to its purposes. Growth fueled by capital is perhaps the most important element of these, but it can only be achieved as part of, and in harmony with, the larger operating system of the State. This totalizing urge disempowers us and blocks the development of a sense of mutual interdependence because the State sets itself up as the filter through which we must think about our relations with each other. Any time we attempt to tighten our community (through cooperatives, social insurance, or social welfare programs, for example), it must be done through channels recognized, controlled, or presided over by the State and subject to standard budgeting.

The task of the State is to create a cultural context in which this outcome feels inevitable, even without specific commands and directives. Addressing the controversy surrounding the State's response to COVID in 2020, the anarchist collective CrimethInc. observed, "Fundamentally, the problem is that we lack a discourse about health that is not premised on centralized control. Across the political spectrum, every metaphor we have for safety and health is predicated on the exclusion of difference (for example, borders, isolation, protection) rather than the aim of developing a positive relationship with difference (for example, extending health-care resources to all, including those outside the borders of the US)."[3] The result is a great narrowing of our perceived political, economic, and cultural options.

The State spins its web, but, of course, the operating system neither operates perfectly nor perfectly realizes its creators' aspirations. Social movements and political and labor revolts, riots, and insurrections bedevil it, forcing it to make economic and political accommodations, admit new parties to the Core Identity Group, and rethink its means of control. But it has been astonishingly successful at subsuming dissenting movements and co-opting insurgents because, thanks to the modes of thinking it forces us into, we accept that it's there—even those of us who hate the inequality, oppression, and environmental destruction that come with it.

This process is one reason the mass appeal of (state) socialism of various types surpassed that of anarchism in the early twentieth century. Thanks to the rise of the technocratic Progressive movement in the United States, the success of the Russian Revolution and the achievements of the New Deal, and the social-democratic governments that took power in much of western Europe after World War II, the State seemed to emerge as *the* locus of political activity; if you were outside the State—outside of politics as defined and organized by the State—you consigned yourself to irrelevancy. This argument continues to recommend itself as a political fact of life.

The State is fundamentally technocratic

Data replicates systems of power.
—Mona Chalabi[4]

The State is devoted not just to economic expansion in general but also to a particular kind powered by technological analysis and innovation. Its go-to response to every material problem is to devise a technological solution, since this is generally the way to promote further economic expansion as well. Power in any society has always been founded on arcane forms of knowledge; in the modern State, these become increasingly technical and "scientific," more fully geared to deliver economic growth.

The result is that the State becomes ever more closely wedded to the Machine: the ideal of a form of human organization that comes as close as possible to the perfection of an efficiently functioning mechanical device.* One of the first manifestations of the modern State in human life was a terrific expansion in techniques of warfare, many of which were later adapted for civil and commercial purposes, a pattern that continues to this day. Each new version of the State has enhanced its ability to make war, from gunpowder (a foundation of the monarchical state) to conscript armies (central to the national state) to drones and cyberwarfare (preferred by the neoliberal state). But the connection between the State and the Machine is much broader. The convergence of technologies demanded by the State— for warfare and to coax economic growth out of the population and the territory—was what historian Lewis Mumford called the "mega-machine": "the convergence of science, economy, technics and po-litical power as a unified community of interpretation rendering useless and eccentric life-enhancing values."[5]

Mumford explained that in the twentieth century, and espec-ially after World War II, "the economic center of gravity shifted to the State, that is, the national megamachine: and between repairing the destructions of the war itself, and inventing and manufacturing new weapons of destruction, more complex and costlier than ever, the necessary condition for full employment, full production, full 'research and development,' and full consumption was for the first time approached."[6]

The process continues, even if the State has removed full

* "Under the new scientific dispensation it was the organic world, not least man himself [sic], that . . . must be brought into harmony with the mechanical world by being melted down, so to say, and molded anew to conform to a more perfect mechanical model." Lewis Mumford, *The Myth of the Machine*, vol. 2, *The Pentagon of Power* (New York: Harcourt Brace Jovanovich, 1970), 58.

employment from the mix. After World War II, the aerospace industry, the U.S. government, and a cohort of universities, research institutes, and wealthy "private individuals" set up the Rand Corporation, a technocratic think tank that, perhaps better than any other single institution, embodies the thinking and direction of the State. In 1999, former Lockheed Martin CEO Norm Augustine and Gilman Louie, a venture capitalist, set up In-Q-Tel, a nonprofit venture capital firm, which received a charter from the CIA to support the intelligence community's information technology needs. In-Q-Tel is a central player in the dense web of relationships between the government's intelligence arms and high tech; reportedly, a $1 investment by In-Q-Tel in 2012 attracted, on average, $9 of investment from other companies.[7]

Artificial intelligence and machine learning, which are being eagerly adopted today by both business and government, had their origin in state-sponsored research programs dating back to the 1990s. Larry Page and Sergey Brin, later the founders of Google, did much of the original research that is at the core of their search engine while at Stanford University, under grants from DARPA, the National Science Foundation, and a working group within the intelligence community called Massive Digital Data Systems (MDDS). MDDS sought to harness the staggering lode of nonclassified information that the Internet was bringing together online. An important part of the goal, according to research by Jeff Nesbit, former director of legislative and public affairs at the National Science Foundation, was to give the Pentagon and the intelligence agencies the ability to pick out like-minded groups of people online—"birds of a feather"—and identify them: an exceedingly ambitious vision of total surveillance that, after 9/11, began to turn into reality.

Google's subsequent overwhelming commercial success was very much a part of its government sponsors' plan. The more users it pulled in, the more data for the intelligence community to track. Thanks to the latitude they enjoy under the various iterations of the USA PATRIOT Act, government authorities issued almost twenty-four thousand subpoenas, search warrants, and court orders to Google in 2016 and 2017 alone, turning the world's favorite search engine into a priceless resource for the national security state.[8]

The financial connections run deeper still: Google Earth, the search engine provider's satellite mapping program, was originally developed by another firm, Keyhole, Inc., with support from In-Q-Tel; Keyhole was acquired by Google in 2004, giving In-Q-Tel 5,636 shares of Google, which it sold a year later for over $2.2 million.[9] The other common thread between Silicon Valley, the military, and the intelligence community is less transactional, however: it's a desire to break down the boundaries between humans and machines, bestowing more of the latter's virtues on the former, and vice versa, something that has been a continuing objective of the State. Other ideas bubbling out of the military-industrial nexus, like the powered exoskeleton suit, reflect this.[10]

The Pentagon has even mapped out plans for creating a "Joint All Domain Command and Control (JADC2)," a system-of-systems that connects sensors from all of the military services—Air Force, Army, Marine Corps, Navy, and Space Force—into a single network.[11] That network would use algorithms to present commanders with "a menu of viable courses of action . . . enabling faster adaptation to complex events." In other words, commanders would be selecting decisions preformulated by machines.[12] But the desire to strike faster, harder, and with minimal human error (or discretion) dates back to the introduction of hypersonic missiles during the Cold War, to Germany's blitzkrieg ("lightning war"), and even further back to the logistical feats of Napoleon's French armies.

What the State does and what it knows is "privileged"

The State jealously guards its knowledge: its history, decision-making, and "sources and methods." While it generally gives lip service to the importance of transparency, in practice it fights to keep as many of its activities secret as possible—and it has only become more insistent on this in the decades since World War II, when warfare became more technological and capitalism more tightly enmeshed with the war machine. Secrecy is necessary for the State to meet three objectives:

- to protect the elites from being held responsible for their actions;
- to keep the State's decision-making opaque, which keeps the public befuddled and prey to distracting conspiracy theories; and
- to control the State's own narrative: the "story" the public receives of what the State does and why it does it.

The State, as a result, operates increasingly behind closed doors. More and more of the data and other documentation it amasses—its "paper trail"—is kept secret from the public in the name of national security, protecting the privacy of State officials, or defending intellectual property. The State began asserting its right to do so early in the modern era; in the English-speaking world, government secrecy developed in parallel with (and limiting) an independent judiciary. Under Charles I in the 1620s, Crown privilege began to be extended to British state secrets that the sovereign claimed had to be kept from public view to protect the public interest; today in the UK, crown privilege is known as public-interest immunity. As a component of English common law, the concept transferred to the United States and was solidified there in a series of nineteenth century court rulings.[13] Since then, states have consistently used emergencies or perceived threats to increase their power to resist transparency: in the United States, for example, following the acquisition of nuclear arms in 1945,[14] the hardening of the Cold War a few years later, and the inauguration of the War on Terror in 2001.* Many

> The State operates increasingly behind closed doors. More and more of the data and documentation it amasses is kept secret from the public in the name of national security, protecting the privacy of State officials, or defending intellectual property.

---

* As early as 1956, the Defense Department estimated that 90 percent of its classified documents could be publicly disclosed without harming national security. Monte Reel, *A Brotherhood of Spies: The U-2 and the CIA's Secret War* (New York: Anchor Books, 2019), 71.

public officials in the United States, beginning with Richard Nixon, have fought tooth and nail to avoid handing their papers over to public archives once they leave office. Businesses, too, have become far more secretive under cover of laws protecting intellectual property.

Tracking down and punishing leakers and whistleblowers has become an obsession of both government and business, even as they narrow the public's options for using the legal system to examine their doings. Exposure of company secrets can be stymied in the courts for years. Declassification of government secrets, too, can take years, even after the expiry of a secrecy rule.

Often, sensitive records are simply deep-sixed. The National Archives and Records Administration announced in 2020 that ICE would be permitted to start destroying records from the first year of the Trump administration, including detainees' complaints about civil rights abuses and poor treatment in custody. Another agency, Customs and Border Protection, petitioned to be allowed to designate thousands of its internal records documenting abuse as "temporary," meaning they could be destroyed in as little as four years, according to the *Intercept*.[15] Meanwhile, writes historian Matthew Connelly, "the Department of the Interior and the National Archives have decided to delete files on endangered species, offshore drilling inspections and the safety of drinking water. The Interior Department even claimed that papers from a case where it mismanaged Native American land and assets—resulting in a multibillion-dollar legal settlement—would be of no interest to future historians (or anyone else)."[16]

Efforts to force transparency on the State are often a tug-of-war between bureaucrats (and their political-appointee bosses) and the citizenry. "The National Archives has pending at least one FOIA [Freedom of Information Act] request that is twenty-five years old," notes author Nicholson Baker in *Baseless*, his book about the FOIA process. In the U.S. system, when documents are finally produced they often are blacked out to the point of being useless. "Redaction is a form of psychological warfare directed against historians and journalists," writes Baker.[17]

Either way, the objective is to wear down and discourage the petitioner while permitting the State to claim a degree of transparency. Secrecy extends to scandals and failures involving the elites themselves. It's been argued, for example, that the impeachment of Trump in 2019 was limited narrowly to his abuse of power and obstruction of Congress—even though the House Democratic leadership might have been on firmer ground with more serious charges such as violation of the Constitution's war-making and appropriations clauses—because politicians of both parties have routinely committed similar violations, and prosecuting Trump would have made it harder to protect his successor of either party. Howard Zinn argued similarly regarding Congress's decision not to include Richard Nixon's war crimes in its bill of charges against him in 1974.[18]

Such deliberate omissions are closely related to what Reagan national security adviser John Poindexter famously called "plausible deniability": making sure high-level officials—for example, the U.S. president—don't have to personally sign off on dubious policies. Those high officials can then plausibly claim not to have ordered or even been aware of those policies. This happened when Poindexter and others attempted to insulate their boss, President Reagan, from responsibility for illegal arms sales to Iran, the proceeds funding the Nicaraguan Contras, even though the policy was his.[19]

Increased secrecy and more thorough insulation decrease the need for officials to tell the truth. The State therefore lies routinely in the service of constructing the reality it asserts is best for the rest of us. Here's how one historian, Martin Jay, rationalizes this behavior:

> Politicians often have responsibilities, which allow them, at times, to delay the truth. Or, especially when they're representing us in an adversarial relationship with another country, they may be very sparing with the truth. Certainly in diplomatic circumstances, and obviously in wartime, politicians who are responsible for protecting us can withhold the truth. We had no obligation to tell the Nazis where we were going to land on D-Day. Having said that, there are many examples of politicians who hide behind those justifications as an excuse not to tell us truths that we are indeed owed, and those politicians often do pay a price. My argument certainly is not a defense of politics as inherently hypocritical. I think the default position of politics, as in life, has to be telling the truth, simply because lies don't work unless they're

told against the backdrop of the assumption that people are, in fact, telling truths.[20]

Governments have an arsenal of euphemisms for lying—"delaying" or "withholding" the truth, being "sparing" with it—and they understand the need to create an aura of truth-telling (or "truthiness," as Stephen Colbert usefully put it) in order to lie effectively. Interestingly, Jay picks D-Day as an example of successful "withholding" of the truth, yet World War II was replete with examples of ill-judged and reckless decisions—such as the Allied assault on Arnhem, the carpet-bombing of Dresden, the choice not to destroy railroad lines transporting Jewish prisoners to the death camps, the top-secret development of an atomic weapon and its detonation above two Japanese cities—that might have been made differently if daylight and some dissenting opinions had been let into the proceedings.

The State has developed lying into a sophisticated art form, a repertoire that blurs the lines between truth and fiction. The more obvious of these techniques are actual lies, such as the rationales offered—and widely accepted—for the 2003 U.S. invasion of Iraq, and spin, such as cherry-picking facts and issuing "nondenial apologies." Misdirection—for example, Trump's repeated insistence that there was "no collusion" when confronted with the possibility that Russia attempted to influence the 2016 U.S. presidential election on his behalf—is more subtle.

"A magic performance," says Jim Steinmeyer, a historian of magic, "consists of a collection of tiny lies, in words and deeds, that are stacked and arranged ingeniously to form the battlement for an illusion." "Trump isn't trying to distract us; he's misdirecting us," wrote sociologist and practicing magician Barry Glassner. "Trump's supporters know he lies, but like fans of magic, they accept his lying as part of the deal."[21]

This is the core of what states often do to protect their favored practices and policies in the face of significant public opposition: use sleight of hand to keep the public's attention focused elsewhere. When multiple states do it, the result is a funhouse-mirror effect that makes it nearly impossible to grasp and assess their actions, especially when combined with their practice of secrecy. For instance, unidentified U.S. intelligence sources in 2020 accused Russia of having offered bounties to Taliban fighters in Afghanistan for the killing of American troops. The reports were widely disseminated in the mainstream media and framed in such a way as to imply they had somehow been "confirmed." Russian officials denied the claim, the intelligence sources offered only circumstantial evidence, and some critics questioned why Russia would have felt the Taliban needed any additional incentive to kill American troops to begin with.

Yet there was also no reason to presume that Russia would *not* launch such a program; after all, the United States had fairly openly funded the mujahideen campaign against the Soviet occupation of Afghanistan in the 1970s and 1980s. The facts about what happened may never be known, which works well for both sides; each gets to denounce the other and champion its own commitment to the truth. The State, in the abstract, is defended. Likewise, when the Mayak nuclear disaster occurred in the Soviet Union in 1957, Soviet authorities, as was typical, covered up the explosion at the reactor site and the contamination of an area the size of West Virginia, including the homes of some 270,000 people. But so did the United States government, which learned of the accident a few years later—arguably, according to some critics, to forestall concerns about its own nuclear programs.[22] Nuclear armaments and nuclear energy were by that time a major component of the State's military and economic power in a growing number of countries; Moscow and Washington, despite their differences, essentially cooperated to prevent any challenge on that score.

When governments rationalize lying, it's for reasons of state. As we saw earlier, these reasons really boil down to just one: the preservation of the State itself. When governments lie, then, it's quite often out of fear that any discussion of certain choices they make would encourage a larger debate over how much primacy the State's interests ought to have over other considerations—and whether the State's interests might be opposed to legitimate human needs. Beyond that, the lies underscore the antidemocratic nature of all states, however representative their outward form of government; the implicit assumption, going back to the "noble lie" of Plato's *Republic*, is that the masses will not and cannot understand the actions being taken in their interest. The State, therefore, must be placed in the hands of a capable elite, whose duties include persuading the people to go along with their decisions through slogans, propaganda, emotional manipulation—and lies.

The State wants to know everything so it can predict the future

Thanks to the State's mania for secrecy, on one hand, and the vast communications landscape of the digital age, including the huge expansion of both government surveillance and Silicon Valley–style "surveillance capitalism," on the other, there's a growing asymmetry between the State's knowledge of us and our knowledge of the State. This places the State at a critical advantage in conveying its story and making it stick, pointing the way to what sociologist Shoshana Zuboff calls "the shift from monitoring to actuation, in which a critical mass of knowledge about a machine system enables the remote control of the system. Now people have become targets for remote control."[23]

As this suggests, the State has always been obsessed with data; as a totalizing entity, its consistent desire over time has been to know everything that happens within its purview, including, as far as possible, what everyone is thinking and feeling. Here, again, it has an interest in common with capital and frequently partners with private enterprise in pursuit of that interest. Corporations, for example, have taken to monitoring "data exhaust" from email, text messages, laptop cameras, and other devices, enabling them to track employee morale.[24] Microsoft thinks it has found a way to go even deeper, gearing workers' pay to how fully engaged their brains are with the work assigned to them. In 2019, it filed a patent application for a "Cryptocurrency System Using Body Activity Data" that would "pay" workers in cryptocurrency based on "body activity" detected by a sensor "communicatively coupled to the server." Presumably, the individual would be "paid" only if their body activity indicates they are actually problem-solving, rather than, say, browsing social media.[25]

Other digital tools enable companies to track their customers and every participant in their supply chain. More often than not, they willingly share this data with government—which itself pursues massive data-mining projects through DARPA.

The State's obsession with turning knowledge and data into control is most visible in police work, because that's where it's applied to anticipating and containing "discontent" among the masses. In the years after 9/11, an anthropologist at the University of California, Los Angeles, named P. Jeffrey Brantingham started marketing PredPol, an algorithm that crunches crime data to predict when and where crimes are likely to take place next. "Predictive policing" was all the rage, but Brantingham insisted that his tool was nothing like the futuristic system depicted in the novel and movie *Minority Report*, which enabled the State to know who was contemplating a crime, track them down, and punish the prospective perpetrators ahead of time. "*Minority Report* is about predicting who will commit a crime before they commit it," he said. "This is about predicting where and when crime is most likely to occur, not who will commit it."[26]

That wasn't what a lot of police understood. A few months after the interview in which Brantingham attempted to brush the dystopian aura from his product, New York police chief William Bratton participated in a panel hosted by the *New York Times* titled "Data Mining the Modern City." "The *Minority Report* of 2002 is the reality of today," he enthused. Bratton, who had long been a proponent of more data-driven police work, said the NYPD would be a leader in amassing "huge amounts of information" and developing "algorithms that will effectively mine that data in a way that the human brain cannot."[27]

The State's aspirations are often as important to grasp as its actual capabilities. Nothing in its arsenal can yet predict the future—so far as we know—but its near-obsessive desire to do so may be matched only by the passion that drove rulers of the early modern State to bankroll alchemists claiming to be able to turn base metals into gold. In a recent book, historian Jill Lepore tells the story of Simulmatics, an early predecessor of today's data analytics providers. Started by a dubious team of hucksters, Simulmatics claimed it could predict where urban riots would happen next and fine-tune the United States' counterinsurgency campaigns in Vietnam. DARPA found itself supplying 70 percent of Simulmatics' budget before concluding it was a "sham."

But, as Lepore writes, this comic-opera enterprise and its gullible government sponsors "helped invent the data-mad and near-totalitarian twenty-first century, in which the only knowledge that counts is prediction and corporations extract wealth by way of the collection of data and the manipulation of attention and the profit of prophecy. . . . Simulmatics . . . helped invent a future obsessed with the future and yet unable to prove it."[28]

The State's desire to get as close as possible to the Holy Grail of prophecy also tells us a great deal about the relationship it wishes to have with its subjects. In particular, it has no use for personal privacy—for the masses, at least—seeing it mainly as an obstacle to be evaded. The more the State works to build its powers of prediction, the less privacy remains for the rest of us.

When states network together each other's databases, the scenario becomes even more forbidding: a 24/7, real-time dragnet that spans continents. The EU in 2019 was considering legislation that would interconnect the national police facial recognition databases of every country in the union. This would expand an existing EU-wide network called Prüm, which connects DNA, fingerprint, and vehicle registration databases for mutual searching and shares access with other countries that are part of the U.S. Visa Waiver Program. The EU was already studying how to effect an expansion to include facial recognition.[29]

Prior to 9/11, this welding-together of state resources would have been unthinkable, both for technical reasons and because of concerns for privacy and civil liberties. But the State's desire to be all-seeing and to predict the future dates as far back as monarchs' employment of court astrologers during the Renaissance (a practice continued in later centuries by leaders including Hitler and Reagan). The society depicted in *Minority Report* is one the State has always aspired to create. In our time, we've come closer than any tyrant ever did. And while big data, artificial intelligence, and machine learning may never coax trustworthy forecasts from recent events and actions under consideration, the State's ambition to do so will continue to grow.

The State fetishizes leadership

States come in a variety of ideological furnishings, from liberal democracy to autocracy to fascism, but the deep concern cutting across all of them is always the same: the State's ability to generate strong, wise leadership. Politicians and theorists tacitly agree that while the people may do an acceptable job of choosing their leaders—when capably directed to the right group of candidates—they have no capacity to actually govern themselves. Government as such must be supplied by leaders selected from an elite that understands and can act as stewards of the public interest.

Whether the state in question is a free-market democracy (the United States or western Europe), a Stalinist dictatorship (North Korea), or a latter-day theocracy (Iran), the quality of leadership is assumed to be critical to its success. "All the political parties of the 'left'—whether social democratic or Bolshevik—oppose the present order only by offering 'better' leaders, more 'experienced' and more capable of solving the problems of society than those who mismanage the world today," the British libertarian socialist Maurice Brinton wrote in 1961.[30] This reduces to a game: Will we get a Chamberlain or a Churchill? A Kennedy or a Nixon? A Gorbachev or a Yeltsin? A Trump or a Biden?

"Where can we find the leadership to save us?" *New York Times* columnist Thomas L. Friedman lamented in a column about the United States under Trump.[31] "We are witnessing the consequences of three years without mature leadership," former defense secretary James Mattis wrote on June 3, 2020, reacting to his former boss's conduct toward peaceful protesters outside the White House and the previous three and a half years of maladministration.

"Leadership matters. Competence matters. Preparation matters," wrote another member of the extended Beltway circle, Steven M. Lieberman, a nonresident fellow in economic studies at the Brookings Institution and longtime White House and congressional staffer.

> Above all, organized action by a capable government matters. . . .
> Leadership organizes our responses to a crisis, enabling effective
> action and inspiring heroic contributions. . . . Having missed the

opportunity to contain COVID-19, our leaders must act to mitigate its spread and devastation. Effective action requires clear, consistent communication dictated by public health and science, not public relations. All levels of government must work together seamlessly, driven by the mission, not worries about bureaucratic turf. Action must be immediate and overwhelming. Continuing failures to fully mobilize all available federal resources and powers will add immeasurably to the human and economic toll.[32]

Leaving unexamined the possibility that overreliance on leaders is itself part of the problem, Lieberman in this passage connects leadership with a larger, romantic vision of the State: as a catalyst for "heroic" action, "mobilization," commitment to a "mission," a clear vision of what actions need to be taken, and a determination to execute them in "overwhelming" fashion. This had echoes in the months leading up to the 2003 Iraq invasion, when a group of influential "liberal hawks" exhorted the Left to solidify with the Bush administration over its plans to liberate Saddam Hussein's subjects. One of their key rationales was that a crusade to free an oppressed Middle Eastern people was just what Americans needed to heal the bitter partisanship of the Vietnam years and beyond—and, implicitly, to reignite their love of the State.

Rarely do our pundits and political scientists consider how profoundly undemocratic this type of thinking really is. What if the system proves incapable of producing a wise leader and must settle for one who is merely strong: a Hitler, a Mussolini, a Trump? Leadership, to the acolytes of the State, is always the magic ingredient that determines whether a particular state will succeed or fail, but that failure is never seen as a failure of the State itself. When a bad leader is finally expelled or liquidated—for example, in the defeat of Hitler's Germany—it's regarded as proof of the State system's ability to reform itself, even though the same system elevated that person to begin with.

There's no doubt that bad leaders can lead their countries to catastrophe and wreak horrific crimes on human beings, not to mention the planet. But so can presumably good leaders, such as Theodore Roosevelt (the long war to suppress the Philippine rebellion), Franklin Delano Roosevelt (the wartime internment of Japanese-Americans),

Harry S. Truman (the dropping of the atomic bomb and the inauguration of the Cold War), Barack Obama (the flourishing of drone warfare), and Tony Blair (aiding and abetting the 2003 Iraq invasion).

If there's a genuine need for leadership, it's generated by the practices of the State and the problems the State creates, not by anything more fundamental to human society. Russia's desire to reassert itself as a great power made Vladimir Putin necessary; earlier, the advent of nuclear weapons and the United States' desire to mobilize the so-called free world against communism created the "imperial presidency." The growing list of military and economic challenges to United States global hegemony makes it necessary for the president "to assert more political control over sensitive matters like Justice Department investigations of foreign-owned firms," for example, wrote the conservative foreign-policy pundit Walter Russell Mead in 2020. "The new shape of world politics is conspiring to make the U.S. presidency more powerful."[33] It's doubtful, however, that there has ever been a period in the history of the modern State when the same claim couldn't have been made on behalf of one or another form of leadership.

Good or bad, then, a system founded on leadership always reinforces the need for leaders—or, generically, for "strong leadership"—by producing crises that leaders can then respond to. This dynamic operates on a psychological level in the world the State constructs for us, as the English biologist and anarchist Alex Comfort explained:

Crowds, like bullocks, are most easily directed by loud noises. The modern citizen lives under a barrage of threats directed at his [*sic*] security, his independence, his sexual powers, and his desire to maintain a competitive status. This continual uproar blends with the inherent insecurity of asocial life, and with its phenomenal speed and congestion, to play a large part in the production of individual anxiety states, and in their counterpart, the chronic political, social or economic crises which the powerholders maintain to dramatize themselves.[34]

Without the drama the State constantly generates, we might come to see our leaders as a distraction rather than a necessity, and the State itself as the core problem in social organization.

Without the drama the State constantly generates, of course, we might come to see our leaders—our powerholders—as a distraction rather than a necessity, and the State itself as the core problem in social organization. Instead of celebrating the demise of another deeply damaging political figure—say, the electoral defeat of Donald Trump—we might want to consider why the State repeatedly elevates such individuals to power to begin with.

The State is male

One of the alleged achievements of the State over the past two centuries is a great improvement in the condition and status of women. At least in the developed economies—in Europe, North America, Australasia—that are widely taken to be the aspirational model of the modern State, women have indeed made dramatic progress: securing legal rights as autonomous persons and broader rights to work outside the home, gaining greater control over their bodies and their sexuality, and forcing men to accept them in positions of authority, among other important advances.

But even in the most liberal societies, all of these remain highly contested. Women are still underrepresented in public office and representative bodies, in corporate boardrooms, and in the highest levels of academia. The #MeToo movement has highlighted the appalling extent to which women are routinely subjected to sexual exploitation, harassment, and physical abuse at home and in the workplace, even in conspicuous fields like popular entertainment. Legal protections in most countries are inadequate, and cultural norms, even in Europe and North America, militate against women getting justice for sexual abuse and harassment. Across the industrially developed economies that make up the Organisation for Economic Co-operation and Development (OECD), female workers in 2015 earned almost 15 percent less than their male counterparts, on average, and did far more unpaid work than men.[35]

The further down the income scale one travels—and the deeper into communities of color—the worse it gets. In 2012 in the United States, the National Women's Law Center found, women were more likely to live in poverty than men across all age groups—and especially past age sixty-five. But while 33.1 percent of non-Hispanic white female-headed households with children lived in poverty, the percentage rose to 46.7 percent for similar Black households and an appalling 56.9 percent for similar Native American households.[36]

Admittedly, conditions have improved from the time when, even in comparatively progressive states, women were expected to stay in the home and often were treated as their family's or husband's property. Sexism and gender discrimination did not begin with the State, and some of the pushback against these forces was led by women in public life who have pursued changes in laws and norms through the State. But the social structure of the State was responsible for many of the inequities under which women suffer.

In her groundbreaking 2004 book, *Caliban and the Witch*, Silvia Federici argues that during the European witch hunts of the sixteenth and seventeenth centuries—which were a purposeful part of the transition from feudalism to the modern State—women who took part in popular resistance to the new order were cast as forces of evil to be contained. "Witches" embodied everything "that capitalism had to destroy," Federici writes: "the heretic, the healer, the disobedient wife, the woman who dared to live alone, the *obeha* woman who poisoned the master's food and inspired the slaves to revolt."[37]

The change in women's status occurred in both subtle and unsubtle ways. For instance, as ale-brewing—traditionally a female occupation—became men's work, women were increasingly forbidden to walk alone outside the home, and the term "gossip" (family and familiars—originally "god-sib[ling]") acquired a more negative meaning. "The witch-hunt grew in a social environment where the 'better sorts' were living in constant fear of the 'lower classes,'" Federici writes.[38]

Specifically, the destruction of the commons in the early modern era and the conversion of once-fluid, personalized feudal relationships into impersonal connections founded on property ownership (thus creating "haves" and "have-nots") coincided with a new ordering of domestic society in which women were subordinate, a structure that persists to this day. The modern State's economic order privileges households made up of a nuclear family headed by a male worker; accordingly, the male head of household becomes the primary figure in the Core Identity Group, the one to whom the State primarily addresses itself. Likewise, the institutions that mold the State's elite—including prestigious educational institutions, the military, organizations like the Boy Scouts and Guides, professional associations, and exclusive gentlemen's clubs—are the products of a male tradition of leadership and learning. These institutions retain this culture even after women are admitted, and when ambitious women make the upward career pilgrimage in business, politics, and other traditionally masculine pursuits, they must constantly prove that they fit into the fraternity.[39]

In some ways, the progress that white, middle-class women have made in the decades since the advent of second-wave feminism has widened the cultural gap between them and lower-income and nonwhite women, making progress through lower tiers of the pay scale more difficult and making it harder to connect women's rights to other social movements. Those who make it to the top generally are not interested in changing the culture to make it less masculine, or else are unable to do so without undermining the position they have achieved among their male colleagues. Less privileged women find their status little changed and become alienated from a women's movement that often seems uninterested in addressing the problems they and their communities face.

States are (inter)connected and mutually reinforcing

In modern times there have never been just "states"; almost from the beginning there has been a network or System of States that legitimize each other by recognizing their neighbors, respecting each other's boundaries and rights, and cooperating and forming alliances on projects of common interest. Once a new state is established in any part of the world, it qualifies for membership in a wide variety of international organizations as well as the global financial and trade structure. The new state becomes eligible for loans and other aid from private banks, multilateral lending institutions, and other nongovernmental organizations—indeed, these resources are one of the main practical reasons for setting up a state. "Development," for better or worse, is made easier and more accessible.

Together, states form a web of mutually supportive relationships, bolstered by treaties—which by definition have the force of domestic law—and a wide range of transnational institutions, such as the International Red Cross, World Trade Organization, International Monetary Fund, World Bank, the EU, the UN, INTERPOL, and NATO. These relationships also extend to elite convocations like the Group of Seven (G7), the annual World Economic Forum meeting in Davos, Switzerland, and the annual Jackson Hole Economic Symposium, along with other treaties, conventions, and convocations.

The overarching aim of this global network is to extend the reach of the State as an operating system. A prime example is the so-called Five Eyes, the intelligence-sharing alliance between the United States, the UK, Canada, Australia, and New Zealand. Beginning as a Cold War program to share information about the Soviet Union and the Eastern Bloc, the Five Eyes later monitored communications from a host of public and private sources, including each other's citizens; in the words of Edward Snowden, it "does not answer to the known laws of its own countries."[40]

At one time, multilateral institutions like the Red Cross were viewed (by Kropotkin, among others) as a potential replacement for the State and even as examples of nonstate cooperation. Although they demonstrate that it's possible to organize essential services outside the direct control of the State or capital, they also reinforce the State and even provide ways for individual states, often in cooperation with each other, to perform an end run around their own democratic institutions. When the people pressure their representatives to reject legislation favored by capital, a multilateral treaty, which has the authority of domestic law, can be a way to recontextualize the proposal and push it through as a matter of national interest. We've seen this, for example, with the North American Free Trade Agreement (later superseded by the United States-Mexico-Canada Agreement), which enabled Canadian mining companies to challenge U.S. state and local laws regulating or restricting natural resource extraction as illegal violations of the treaty.

As this suggests, every state needs a high degree of cooperation from every other state to fulfill its goals—or just to function routinely. Systems of borders, identity papers, and protocols that military units of one state observe when they encounter those of another are all essential; so are laws and regulations that allow capital to flow between states, that recognize property rights across borders, and, not incidentally, that recognize and respect arrest warrants and other police activities of various jurisdictions. These forms of cooperation are essential to preserving every state's integrity, which even the most powerful, including the United States, can never secure entirely on their own. As such, they are vital to the continued construction of the modern State itself.

The System of States enables the operating system to extend itself over every space on earth and deep into every aspect of life—even into geographic areas that aren't controlled by one specific state but which the "family" of states collectively claim common control over, such as the poles and the oceans. Common regulations, standards, and protocols that all states accept also enable them to cooperate, emulate, and reinforce each other, reinforcing each other by sharing technology, intelligence, and techniques of governance and control. New states automatically become engaged in the same game of catch-up and mimicry. Chinese high-tech companies, for example, produce tools for government surveillance that Beijing first adopts, then sells to other countries that want to harness the Chinese model of population management and control. Other countries, like the United States, then encourage the production of similar or competing tools in order to counter the spread of China's influence. Either way, the result is a more powerful and pervasive state in all countries sharing the same or very similar tools and techniques.

Underpinning this pattern of mutual support, imitation, and close parallel institutional and practical development is the formation of the global elite of capitalists, businesspeople, technocrats, politicians, and intellectuals, or thought leaders. They not only form the brain trust of individual states but also facilitate the spread of the latest ideas about how the State should be built, reproduced, and managed through multilateral institutions, informal groups, and gatherings.

The latter-day career of Tony Blair, former UK prime minister, offers an instructive example. Since leaving office, Blair has been an adviser to JPMorgan Chase and Zurich Financial Services (now Zurich Insurance Group) on climate change; head of Tony Blair Associates, which provides "strategic advice on a commercial and pro bono basis, on political and economic trends and governmental reform"; and a Middle East envoy for the UN, the EU, the United States, and Russia. He also taught a course on issues of "faith and globalization" at the Yale School of Management and Yale Divinity School, and he created the Tony Blair Institute to promote global outlooks by governments and organizations. No surprise, then, when it was reported that in 2010 the ex-PM's personal security guards were paid £250,000 salaries apiece by the British taxpayer.[41]

Many others, trained at the same elite schools and nurtured at the IMF, the World Bank, and high-end consultancies ranging from Kissinger Associates to McKinsey & Company, serve as foot soldiers to the likes of Blair. None of this is exactly new; even in the eighteenth century, French, Italian, and British diplomats likely had a more equivalent view of how the world worked than they shared with their countrypeople. But the global elite today is larger, farther-flung, and more tightly bonded intellectually than at any other time in human history. It's still possible to speak of one country—the United States, most powerfully—imposing its values and interests on the rest of the world, but an increasingly uniform mandarin class, spanning the public and private sectors and both conservative and allegedly liberal parties, supplies the infrastructure. While some scholars see in this a dissolution of the West and its cultural hegemony in a more multicultural world,[42] the reality is that the State, with its very European cultural and institutional origins, has effectively taken over the world and molded the new global elite to solidify its control; multiculturalism, in this context, is mostly window dressing.

The powerful role of the System of States underscores a couple of paradoxes in our political discourse. Some American conservatives grumble that the "world government" represented by organizations like the World Bank and the UN threatens to diminish the sovereignty of the United States, and European right-wing populists regularly accuse "Brussels" (that is, the EU) of doing more or less the same. In reality, these organizations are there to augment the power of the State, which has always been as much a cooperative venture as a collection of competing nations, despite the emphasis in mainstream political theory on the conflicts and rivalry between them.

That being the case, multilateral institutions and treaties like the EU and the World Bank or the Universal Declaration of Human Rights and the Geneva Conventions are unlikely to fulfill the hopes that self-described progressives sometimes place in them to give birth to an enlightened "world government"—because they were never meant to do so. Often, we can learn more about the State from the ways individual states cooperate than from the ways they quarrel—and cooperation between states can serve many purposes, from mapping the human genome to engineering the destruction of Libya as a functioning society.

The State is an ideal

Every state is, to a degree, utopian: an attempt to build the perfect society or community, with the perfect method of government, the perfect set of economic arrangements, the perfect territory, and the perfect populace. This applies as much to allegedly democratic states, like the United States and western European countries, as it does to authoritarian, one-party China, an absolute monarchy like Saudi Arabia, or an attempted theocracy like the Islamic State (ISIS). Education, policing, economic policymaking and planning, revenue raising, and the design of cities and other infrastructure are all established with a view to achieving this ideal.

This being the case, every state in the modern era is the expression of an ideology, be it the divine right of kings, liberal democracy, Leninism, democratic socialism, national unity expressed through a one-party system, or the paternalistic model of Singapore's Lee Kuan Yew. And even at a time when faith in government and the State as such runs low, this idealistic element—the notion of a society perfected through the State—is deeply embedded in our thinking and can manifest itself at crucial moments.

A story ran in the *New York Times* during the COVID-19 pandemic about an explosion in the use of drones, both to enforce and to relieve social isolation. It mentioned a drone called the "Anti-COVID-19 Volunteer Drone Task Force" that flew one day along the East River, admonishing strollers to "please maintain a social distance of at least six feet." The vehicle wasn't launched by law enforcement—although police in many cities were using such devices—but was the project of "a Queens drone enthusiast."[43]

> "Robots are so often cast as the bad guys," said Daniel H. Wilson, a former roboticist and author of the 2011 science fiction novel *Robopocalypse.* "But what's happening now is weirdly utopic, as opposed to dystopic.... Now we have a sudden global emergency in which the machines we're used to fearing are uniquely well suited to swoop in and save the day."

The State hasn't only conquered the world; it's colonized our imaginations, inducing us to see its trappings and tools—even menacing ones like drones—as cool or romantic. This is one of the deepest and strongest supports of the system itself. While reproducing the State is first and foremost the task of the elite, millions more people yearn to embody it. White militias and border patrols, the "Invisible Empire" of the KKK, mainstream volunteer organizations, even revolutionary organizations like the Black Panther Party reflect a desire to transfigure or purify the State, or else to replace the existing version with a more perfect one.

Something similar lies behind the nine hundred or so artificial languages that have been created over the past three hundred years* as well as today's proliferating assortment of games that allow users

---

* Artificial languages, often created by amateur linguists and philologists, embody almost perfectly the State's aspiration to streamline human society, rationalize it, and make it submit to a firm logic. John Quijada, creator of Ithkuil, wrote that he wanted to fashion "an idealized language whose aim is the highest degree of logic, efficiency, detail, and accuracy . . . while minimizing the ambiguity, vagueness, illogic, redundancy, polysemy (multiple meanings) and overall arbitrariness that is seemingly ubiquitous in natural human language." Cited in Joshua Foer, "Utopian for Beginners," *New Yorker*, December 24 and 31, 2012.

to create and rule their own states: "NationStates is a nation simulation game. Create a nation according to your political ideals and care for its people. Or deliberately oppress them. It's up to you."* But these join a long history of imaginative realms, from Sir Thomas More's *Utopia* to the Space Federation in *Star Trek*, the Republic of *Star Wars*, Wakanda in the comic and film *Black Panther*, the cavalry in any number of American Western novels and films, and any number of police departments in any number of police procedurals: each of them a Dream State, as we wish it could be in real life.† Sometimes reality, too, slides over into the comical, as when capitalists whose wealth is matched only by their desire to avoid taxes and community accountability establish micronations: for example, when the chairman of Pepsi-Cola Company established a "Principality of Outer Baldonia" on an island off the coast of Nova Scotia in 1945.

The State, in other words, doesn't exist only in our human community or the territory it inhabits. We re-create it constantly in our imaginations, and, in so doing, we prepare ourselves for our common task of reproducing the State as it actually exists. In this sense, the State is an addiction.

The State has a sense of destiny

Just as we dream about the State, it dreams about itself—and us. Intellectually, the modern State in Europe was born in a burst of protoromantic idealization of ancient Rome, jumbling together the alleged perfection of its republic and the power and majesty of its later emperors. Beginning in the fifteenth century, Roman-style

---

* NationStates, https://www.nationstates.net/. Then there's Simcountry: "The war game in Simcountry has many features. You can setup [sic] your own army, conquer countries and build a large empire," Simcountry–Virtual Worlds Strategy Game, https://www.simcountry.com/cgi-bincgip?plogplay&miDesktopTab=2.

† There are also plenty of comic-opera satires of the State, including Gilbert and Sullivan's *Utopia Ltd* (1893), Klopstokia in the W. C. Fields comedy *Million Dollar Legs* (1932), and Freedonia in the Marx Brothers film *Duck Soup* (1933).

architecture was revived in the Italian city-states; later, it was used by the increasingly imperial sovereigns of England, France, Spain, and the Habsburg monarchy to provide an imposing visual counterpart to their ambitions to consolidate, centralize, and project power.

From dreams come not only concrete symbols but also a sense of destiny. Every modern State has to have a mission, a reason for being that goes beyond its particular interests. Without such a mission, holding the State together, especially in a more materialistic age, would be impossible. In a recent book on the leadership style of her grandfather, Susan Eisenhower, a "Washington strategy consultant," notes that General Dwight Eisenhower, then the military head of NATO, decided to run for president in 1951 because he feared the Republican Party would otherwise nominate Senator Robert Taft, an "isolationist" who was skeptical of the Cold War and the American crusade against communism. With the Republicans likely to win the White House in 1952, Eisenhower feared that under a Taft presidency, the United States would back away from its assigned role as leader of the free (market) world.

Against such extremism, Eisenhower "believed there was a middle way that could draw Americans into a moderate center that could serve as a gathering place for compromise and conciliation, a place to coalesce around a national unity of purpose."[44]

Eisenhower was right; building that "moderate center"—which made possible civil rights but also the fossil-fuel economy, development of the American nuclear arsenal, the Cold War, the Vietnam War, and numerous bipartisan foreign-policy crimes and disasters since then—was his greatest accomplishment after defeating Nazi Germany. Were these great projects failures? Not if they brought the nation together behind the State.

That's because they help the State to assert its universality, its indispensable, exceptional nature; to be a state is, automatically, to be more than just a political unit. The modern State's mission is carried forward in vast, visionary projects to remake the earth and remold societies, often with little real input from the people who are directly affected. Some are feats of engineering, some of conquest and settlement, some of economic and industrial policy; some have been beneficial, some disastrous, some out-and-out murderous, many a mix of both.

The first great mission of the United States as a state was built on the dream shorthanded as "Manifest Destiny." The Soviet Union's mission was to knit back together the tsarist empire that collapsed during World War I and, ultimately, complete its project of Russification of the minorities within its borders. Communist China's mission has been to extend its dominion over all the territories once claimed by imperial China—even those over which it never really exercised effective control—and to impose Han culture on them. Israel's ongoing project is to secure an exclusively Jewish state occupying all the territory west of the Jordan River. These aspirations only occasionally, if ever, appear explicitly in public documents, but it's impossible to understand the history of the respective states without taking them into account.

Other relatively recent manifestations include:

- Britain's assembly of India into a new South Asian empire
- The Netherlands' knitting together of the Malay Archipelago into the empire that would become Indonesia
- The Soviet Five-Year Plans
- The Nazi project to create a racially pure, German-dominated Europe
- The building of the U.S. federal highway system
- Maoist China's Great Leap Forward
- Xi-era China's Belt and Road Initiative
- The neoliberal drive for a uniform global market economy

Earlier states accomplished similarly ambitious, culture-defining projects: the pyramids of Egypt, Rome's network of roads and aqueducts, China's and Persia's astonishing irrigation systems. But projects such as these proliferated under the modern State; they typify it perhaps more than any other visible feature because whatever their immediate purpose, they are all fundamentally about building the State. A mere act of government could never bring any of them about. To succeed, they must activate every element of the State: a people organized around a single aim, all of the society's material resources at the disposal of the cause (no matter the expense), and opposition firmly neutralized.

What's interesting about these projects, too, is that they are just as likely to be carried out by representative democracies as they are by authoritarian states. Anthropologist James C. Scott argues that state-initiated social engineering needs four elements to succeed: the administrative ordering of nature and society, a "high-modernist" ideology focused on scientific and technical progress, an authoritarian state, and a "prostrate civil society."[45] The Great Leap Forward and the Five-Year Plans were brutal exercises in forced economic development, yet the subjugation and settlement of the American West and the neoliberal makeover of the world economy were far more ambitious projects—and the states that directed them were not authoritarian and had lively civil societies.

But the other two common features—the administrative ordering of nature and society and an ideology focused on scientific and technological progress—are central to the idealism of the modern State, whatever its political profile. For example, the U.S. crusade against Saddam Hussein and the invasion of Iraq, before it was actually launched and then fizzled into a quagmire, was cast in part as one of these great projects: a way to bring the American nation together again behind a noble cause, comparable to the crusade against Nazi Germany. Neoliberalism is perhaps the greatest of these projects or crusades: an attempt to shoehorn every economy in the world into a uniform model with common rules and laws, perfectly free flows of goods and services, an elite meritocracy, and no "friction" to stand in the way of efficient wealth-building.

The State also dreams of the ideal State—in this case, the State that knows everything, has decisive influence over what the population knows and thinks, and thus can formulate and execute its plans in full confidence of the outcome. Earlier, we looked at some of the ways it attempts to achieve this: through surveillance, data analysis, and the increasingly technological, networked culture it has encouraged us to adopt. In reality, it can never succeed, no matter how sophisticated and pervasive its efforts become. But the State's desire to attain "total information awareness," as the Pentagon once termed it, is a fact of our lives, an aspiration it has pursued ever since the time of the first spymasters during the Renaissance.

Its efforts to reach that goal—sometimes successful, sometimes not, often terribly destructive of lives and communities—will continue as long as there's a State. In a moment of candor during the months leading up to the U.S. invasion of Iraq, Defense Secretary Donald Rumsfeld lectured a reporter who asked about the short-lived Office of Strategic Influence, which the Pentagon had set up to carry out disinformation and psychological operations in targeted countries:

> And then there was the office of strategic influence. You may recall that. And "oh my goodness gracious isn't that terrible, Henny Penny the sky is going to fall." I went down that next day and said fine, if you want to savage this thing fine I'll give you the corpse. There's the name. You can have the name, but I'm gonna keep doing every single thing that needs to be done and I have.[46]

VII

Why Are We against the State?

The master's tools will never dismantle the master's house. They may allow us temporarily to beat him at his own game, but they will never enable us to bring about genuine change.
—Audre Lorde, *Sister Outsider*

The State communicates strength; fundamentally, this is what many if not most defenses of the State boil down to. "It is a popular misconception that liberal democracies necessarily have weak governments because they have to respect popular choice and legal procedure," writes the neo-Hegelian political scientist Francis Fukuyama. "All modern governments have developed a powerful executive branch, because no society can survive without one. They need a strong, effective, modern state that can concentrate and deploy power when necessary to protect the community, keep public order, and provide essential public services."[1]

The State isn't just a barrier to the kind of world we want to have—it's what we have instead. The State has trained us to think of it as a substitute or perhaps a shorthand for the collective or the community, as the vehicle through which we work together and make decisions as a society, the provider of our common education and culture, our mechanism for caring for the less fortunate, our defense against violence. Any group or organization that attempts to compete or offer an alternative therefore must be absorbed or superseded or else be tagged as an enemy and destroyed by the State. The message is simple: the State is what we have, the only viable way to achieve the goals of community. Imperfect as it may be in many respects, it's what there is.

Why, then, do we need the State? In theory, because it is the most effective means of achieving the three things it promises:

- a degree of personal security,
- a shared identity, including a sense that one's voice is being heard; and
- a path to material well-being.

Let's look at the case for the modern State in a nutshell. A state with a strong executive is better able to exercise leadership, the argument goes, both in periods of stress and in other times, when society needs farsighted planning. Otherwise, the society and the polity— the society as political organization—fall apart. The State creates a framework and means for rapid economic growth, which raises standards of living and opens up opportunities for more people to rise.

One of the ways it does this is by providing security—freedom from fear, disruption, and dispossession—and a high degree of certainty that this will continue. To this end, it monopolizes the right to use violence, making war a matter of considered policy, subject to rules and limits, rather than a free-for-all, and placing local security in the hands of a trained, competent police force; better that, the argument goes, than unregulated, ad hoc militias. The State acts as the lender of last resort in an economic crisis, making sure the vital pillars of the economy— banks, the money supply, markets, social safety nets—do not collapse. It promotes scientific and technological progress,

The State isn't just a barrier to the kind of world we want to have—it's what we have instead.

which fuels economic growth. And it molds a farsighted meritocratic elite that makes wise choices according to the public interest and knows how to put difficult decisions into effect.

The State is uniquely able to forge a common identity from culturally disparate ethnic and doctrinal groups. Switzerland, the United States, Australia, and Canada are examples of how a collection of white ethnic groups can be brought to function together and share a common identity, even if people of color are often excluded. Independent India was founded as a secular democratic republic offering equal status to its diverse multiethnic, multilinguistic, multifaith peoples. Later, it began fashioning itself into a sharply Hindu-centric national state in which Muslims face increasing discrimination. But India's initial success suggests that when the State wants to offer a more expansive definition of the nation, it can.

The State is also more efficient than any decentralized or patchwork system of governance; it settles on uniform standards for everything from currency to regulation of commerce to weights and measures, providing a common set of assumptions that make life more predictable and therefore easier to navigate. And it's better able than less rigid structures at scaling: building out its institutions and practices to cover larger populations and larger territories and extending the benefits of security and economic progress to greater numbers of people. By creating a common political culture—liberal democracy, communism, fascism, Islamism, and so forth—it instills in the population a sense of belonging to a common enterprise or ideal, which brings them together and minimizes particularist sentiments. Combining all of this, the State forges great national cultures—French, German, English, Italian, Eqyptian, Russian, Chinese, Japanese, Indian, Korean, and many more—out of a collection of disparate local and tribal communities, enriching the world with their philosophies and their artistic and other material accomplishments and nurturing vibrant urban cultures.

Another argument in favor of the State is that it is getting better at what it does. Over the years, it has refined its techniques for controlling territories and populations to be less brutal, less dictatorial, and more reliant on soft methods like education, monitoring and analyzing trends among the public, more sophisticated design of housing and public spaces, and propaganda through popular culture and entertainment. While these can often be criticized for their banality, monotony, and crudeness, they fulfill people's need for strong sensory experience and help to create a unified and accessible common culture through largely peaceful methods.

Voting, at least in nonauthoritarian states, offers citizens the opportunity to participate indirectly in decision-making and to organize behind candidates who represent their views, interests, and general outlook. More importantly, voting cements the population's loyalty to the State; each time we vote, we signify our assent to the present system, which is why voter turnout is considered such an important indicator of public feeling about government in general.

Politics itself is better managed than ever, thanks in part to the stabilizing element known as the two-party system. Democratic practice in countries like the United States, the UK, Germany, Ireland, Canada, Spain, and the Nordic countries is channeled through two political parties, roughly one of the Left and one of the Right, although the range of views they actually represent is carefully restricted. Within these limits, the two parties allow citizens to channel their preferences into effective vehicles for competition and governance, give them opportunities to participate indirectly, and are adept at co-opting ideas from more ideological third parties when the time is ripe for them to be brought into the mainstream. The two-party system also makes for smoother governance and lawmaking, since one or the other party generally holds the legislative upper hand.

Finally, the modern State has more checks and balances than powerful institutions have ever seen in human history, including elections that hold officials publicly accountable, independent judiciaries, a free and often highly critical media reflecting multiple points of view (especially in the Internet age), and community-based activists who know how to expose state abuses and press for change. These elements, along with regulatory bodies, are also effective at policing capital and business, setting limits and enforcing codes of conduct that keep them from sacrificing the public good in their pursuit of growth, and updating the rules to keep abreast of new developments in the economy and markets.

Certainly, many states fail in just about all of these respects; they brutalize or murder their people, allow capital to operate without effective controls, squash the opposition, muzzle the press, and exploit racial and other divisions to cement their power. But even these regimes face pressure from the System of States when they don't follow accepted norms, such as those embodied in the UN Charter and the Universal Declaration of Human Rights. The System of States may impose trade and travel restrictions and other economic sanctions; it may apply military pressure or cut off military and other aid. The Marcos regime in the Philippines, many of the Latin American dictatorships of the 1970s, and the apartheid regime in South Africa finally fell in part due to quiet and not-so-quiet pressure from other governments.

But the capstone of the argument for the State is the simple assertion that it can be improved. Living under the modern State is nothing like the hopeless condition George Orwell described in *Nineteen Eighty-Four*; when it misbehaves, abuses its power, and commits atrocities, there are ways and means to stop it and put it on a better path without doing away with it and risking chaos. One only has to look at the nearly universal acceptance of democratic elections as the correct way to transfer power within the State: even dictatorships generally honor the form if not the substance of the exercise. Masses of people have fought and died over the past three centuries for the right to elect their leaders; their success demonstrates powerfully that the State is reformable.

* * *

In reality, the State has never performed up to the expectations it creates. It provides degrees of security for the Core Identity Group, but not so much for others; the shared identity it creates necessarily excludes much of the population; and the path to material well-being through economic growth is paved with the bones of exploited working people all over the world.

Democracy, which most countries profess to practice, has always been a carefully managed affair, and not only in countries with authoritarian governments. Elections provide a regular outlet for people's political energies, channeling them into personality-driven competitions that address the most serious issues—if at all—only in simplistic and distorted ways and that divert grassroots movements away from effective organizing. In recent decades, electoral campaign cycles have lengthened, and elected officials treat the time in between as extensions of their campaigns, further narrowing the window for substantive discussion and organizing.

This is all by design. "Western countries almost invariably introduced the mass franchise only after they had already introduced sophisticated political regimes with powerful legal systems and entrenched constitutional rights," journalist-historians John Micklethwait and Adrian Wooldridge point out, "and they did so in cultures that cherished notions of individual rights."*

The apparatus of the State very much includes voting and the two-party system, which in the United States, for example, has become a quasi-official feature of government; the Republican and Democratic parties are both directly and indirectly subsidized and otherwise advantaged in order to keep others from challenging them.[2] The two-party system may make electoral democracy more stable, but its real purpose is to block anticapitalist and anti-State movements by keeping the "Overton window" of acceptable political discourse as narrow as possible.

Voting is not an exercise of popular will but a surrender of our power as equal members of a human community. It keeps us hoping against hope that the next statesperson-hero is just around the corner if we go to the polling place, play our assigned role, and pull the lever. It maneuvers potentially revolutionary social movements into unthreatening political channels. It nudges us to blame specific policies and politicians for society's ills, rather than take a desperately needed hard look at the State itself. It sets us up for disillusionment and apathy when yet another candidate disappoints us once in office. And it aggravates the caste system by dividing citizens from noncitizens, thus creating an arrangement in which elected lawmakers and

---

* John Micklethwait and Adrian Wooldridge, *The Fourth Revolution: The Global Race to Reinvent the State* (New York: Penguin, 2014), 262. "Only a completely ready state can permit the luxury of a liberal government," Bismarck said in a speech to the North German Reichstag, March 11, 1867, when he was assembling the German Empire.

governors make decisions that directly affect many people who had no opportunity to vote for or against them.

When we vote, we also give up the ability to say no. States, governments, and socioeconomic orders crave legitimacy. When we don't vote, we're refusing to recognize a system that claims to express our interests and aspirations but does not. Voting, on the other hand, confers legitimacy on the State—just for today, perhaps, but if we do it over and over, it becomes forever. We may not see it this way when we enter and leave a polling place or drop our ballot in the mail, but this is how people and governments see it when they look at elections in any country other than their own.[3]

With legitimacy secured through our participation in the election process, the State and its political leadership, collectively, have wide latitude in the policies they decide to pursue, even if those policies go against the will or interests of the people who elected them. It's largely democratic governments, not authoritarian ones, that have carried out the neoliberal overhaul of the global economy, for example, moving it away from the social-democratic reforms of the mid-twentieth century.*

In the decades since the State pushed to jump-start economic growth and capital formation following the commodity shocks and inflation of the 1970s, a new economy built on cheap labor, automation, low taxes on wealth, and few if any barriers to mixing and matching these features across national boundaries has created a world of breathtaking inequality and wealth concentration. Barriers to resource extraction and the exploitation of human populations have been torn down, and concerns about racial and gender discrimination brushed aside or explained away. These changes came about not simply because capital and business asked (and paid) for them, but as matters of national policy, adopted by the State as the best, most up-to-date path to economic dynamism.

"Progress and catastrophe are the opposite faces of the same coin," Hannah Arendt wrote.[4] As the imperative for rapid economic growth has gripped the State harder and seized more of the globe,

---

* The United States above all, the UK, and the EU collectively have been the principal drivers of neoliberalism while more authoritarian governments have generally been less eager to embrace it.

we've become accustomed to living with a succession of catastrophes, atrocities, and accidents. The list is almost too long to recount: nuclear disasters and near-disasters like Three Mile Island and Chernobyl; industrial accidents like Bhopal; airliner, railroad, and tanker-truck crashes; "natural" disasters including forest fires of unprecedented size, droughts, typhoons, and hurricanes; terrorist attacks like those on the World Trade Center that exploit the many weak spots in our hyperefficient, intricately networked artificial environment; electrical overloads and communications breakdowns, including the crashing of computer networks; and the explosion of landmines, bombs, and other ordnance left over from the wars that have always been going on somewhere for more than one hundred years. In 2020, pandemics—which, depending on who you talked to, were either entirely predictable or absolutely impossible to predict—jumped to the top of the list.

"The unprecedented growth in catastrophes between the beginning of the twentieth century and our own day when, for the first time, there are more 'man-made' [sic] accidents than 'natural' ones, faces each of us with a choice: we must each opt to one version or the other of a current tragic event," the French urbanist Paul Virilio wrote as the political impact of the 9/11 attacks was still sinking in.[5] To the disasters mentioned above can be added coups, the collapse of states like Somalia and Yemen, and the drive to obliterate the remaining "unincorporated" populations in Amazonia, the Philippine jungles, central Africa, and east-central Asia. Risk management has become a high-priced practice as businesses and governments—the State—struggle to understand where and when the next Black Swan event will hit.

Much of the blame for the "natural" disasters that have beset us falls to the State and its unceasing push for growth, in particular its drive to exploit more and more of the natural world and situate more of its communities and productive facilities in places that previous generations were sensible enough to avoid. "We invade tropical forests and other wild landscapes, which harbor so many species of animals and plants—and within those creatures, so many unknown viruses," author and environmentalist David Quammen writes. "We cut the trees; we kill the animals or cage them and send them to markets. We disrupt ecosystems, and we shake viruses loose from their natural hosts. When that happens, they need a new host. Often, we are it."[6]

In the wake of Hurricane Maria in 2018, Puerto Rico discovered just how dangerous it was to depend almost entirely on imported fossil fuel for energy, most of it arriving through the single port of San Juan; with much of the city destroyed, beleaguered communities in the interior were left without power for months.[7] Likewise, after COVID-19 hit, Amazon.com, because of its overweening position in online sales, became a choke point in the effort to get essentials from surgical masks to toilet paper to communities across the United States; the online sales giant sucked up such a large chunk of these products that not enough was left to stock local retail outlets, and Amazon itself couldn't fill orders quickly enough. Puerto Rico's logistical map and Amazon's position in the consumer supply chain both stem from State policies that favor them on the grounds of scale and efficiency. Experts in think tanks, consultancies, business schools, and university economics departments developed those policies and then formed an echo chamber propagating them. But in a time of emergency, they made the society they serve far less responsive and resilient.

"American supremacy in logistics has been a calling card for decades," the *New York Times* commented in the months after the pandemic; "the country is flunking a curriculum that it basically wrote."[8] But the issue of how to respond to the coronavirus revealed more fundamental defects in the entire, finely tuned global socioeconomic system the State and capital have constructed over the past half century, according to Friends of the Earth campaigner Meadhbh Bolger: "Our economies have . . . created the ideal conditions for the virus to spread. They have required the workforce to be highly mobile and to aggregate in densely populated cities— and to depend on ever-growing overconsumption of products from fast-moving complex global supply chains, which quickly and efficiently spread the virus."[9]

Far from providing greater security in the face of these problems, the State's penchant for bigness, rationalization, regimentation, and monopolization of decision-making actually aggravates them. Think local, think small is not just an anarchist ideal, perhaps; it's also a better path to human survival than the road the State has picked out for us.

The State, however, is happy to help us "understand" what is happening—the catastrophes, the logistical failures in their wake—with a string of rationalizations: the earth's climate is changing, but it runs in cycles and there's nothing to be done about it except hunker down; terrorists are responsible for the violence, and only a victorious War on Terror will end it; nuclear energy, air travel, and logistics are becoming safer and more efficient, not less, despite appearances to the contrary; and the answer to forest fires is to cut down more of the forests.

Even public figures who are more willing to face the seriousness of these problems seldom question the State's drive for growth through the creation of a global neoliberal economic monolith—even though the increasing chaos in both the human and natural worlds traces back to this transformation. Political leaders struggling and failing to square the circle wrought by increasing inequality and unrest, on the one hand, and the demands of the State and capital, on the other, give way to Trump and other right-wing populists who thrive on chaos and have mastered the trick of misdirection.

Yet the State's answer is always more growth, more centralization, more rationalization—because that way lies greater power for the State itself. "Globalisation provides the 'state of emergency,' that foreclosure which transforms, or will soon transform, every state into a police state, every army into a police force and every community into a ghetto," Virilio writes. "The effect of the closed field of globalisation is, then, simply the progressive asphyxia of the constitutional state of representative democracy, with 'control' society replacing the society of local confinement."[10]

The State, which was supposed to provide a measure of security to the public, is increasingly unable—and far less motivated—to do so, except for sections it considers strategically important. The history of the last hundred years in the United States offers a quick illustration.

In the depths of the Great Depression, the Roosevelt administration rescued capitalism by creating social provisions that assisted white, urban, industrial working-class households headed by male breadwinners, because it feared they could be radicalized by the socialist and communist Left, destabilizing the State and the capitalist economic order. Ten years of progress in American civil rights, beginning with the Supreme Court's decision in *Brown v. Board of Education*, stemmed from Washington's desire to present itself as a champion of freedom and democracy in the face of what it viewed as a global rivalry with the Soviet Union. The Great Society programs of the 1960s were propelled by the Johnson administration's "guns and butter" strategy to shore up support for its war in Vietnam and its desire to contain the urban uprisings of the period.

Today, no other superpower provides a countervailing force; labor unions and erstwhile social-democratic parties like the Labour Party in the UK, Germany's Social Democrats, France's Socialists, and—marginally—the Democratic Party in the United States have been co-opted and driven into a defensive posture; and an ever more precarious economy has forced individuals to focus ever more intently on keeping themselves afloat materially. The pattern has become predictable: parties of the Left are raised into power by the support of the working class and the precarious middle class; as their operatives become more professional and technocratic and the parties themselves acquire more hierarchical power structures, they move to the right. Eventually, we find them implementing milder versions of the same policies pursued by the Right, from promoting the corporate global trade agenda to "reforming" social services, generally in the name of achieving political consensus.

Thus, the Left lends its hand to the reproduction of the State, which is then free to bail out the financial sector, deregulate the extractive industries, and encourage property speculation at the expense of the urban poor and middle class. To insulate the propertied class's investments, the State facilitates, or at least turns a blind eye to, the sheltering of assets in offshore tax havens and condones a fast-growing, ancillary market in citizenships and residencies for the rich.[11]

Since the neoliberal revolution that began in the 1970s, "real" wealth—the kind that mints billionaires—has been built on a foundation of cheap labor, minimal social provision, and enormous household debt coupled with vast direct and indirect subsidies to favored industries and finance. Of the features that characterized the postwar "golden age," only mass consumption remains. The exhaustion that accompanies physically demanding minimum-wage work, often with no benefits but supplemented by two or three side hustles, leaves workers feeling resentful but powerless. The State is adept at safely channeling their disgruntlement into popular entertainment, cheap consumer goods, and—especially for white male workers—resentment of other ethnic groups, women in the workplace, and immigrants.

Such a system can't be maintained without some measure of force, however. Accordingly, spending on police is beefed up, and the cops themselves increasingly operate as a quasi-military unit, insulated from accountability to the public. Policing of impoverished communities and those with nonwhite populations becomes more punitive; counterinsurgency measures are applied to activists, to undocumented persons, and to petty criminals as a constant reminder of who's in charge; and the feedback loop between military (including counterinsurgency and occupation forces) and domestic police forces intensifies, such that they come to resemble each other more and more in equipment, training, and outlook.˙

From the point of view of the State, this blurring of the lines makes perfect sense.

"When your job is defending the status quo at all costs," says American sociologist Brendan McQuade, "it isn't a ridiculous overreach to apply a theory for defeating an armed movement in a developing country that has been in a civil war for decades against a protest movement in a country that isn't at civil war."[12] Protest movements appear especially dangerous and in need of repression during periods that the American political analyst Thomas Frank calls "democracy scares," when "society's high-status groups come

---

* "Every overseas war has reshaped policing in the United States, including by filling the ranks of police departments with veterans and pushing surplus materials into their hands. But many campaigns abroad have also entailed policing civilian populations, with US experts advising other governments while also learning lessons to repatriate in the process." Stuart Schrader, "Yes, American Police Act Like Occupying Armies. They Literally Studied Their Tactics," *Guardian UK*, June 9, 2020.

to believe that their privileges have been placed in mortal danger by the actions of the vast, seething multitude."[13] In North America, such occasions include the populist political uprising of the 1890s in the United States, Franklin Delano Roosevelt's campaign for reelection as U.S. president in 1936, and the Co-operative Commonwealth Federation's drive to institute universal health care in Saskatchewan, Canada, in 1962.

In more recent decades, acts of mass resistance have been more firmly blocked and contained, and policing of public spaces has tightened in nearly all countries. Spaces like Fifth Avenue and Times Square in New York City that, half a century ago, were open to public displays of opposition no longer are. Marches and demonstrations are bottled up and routed to out-of-the-way locations, and participants are prevented from achieving too much interaction with passers-by or proximity to their targets.

The State is testing the limits of how much violence it can employ to control public spaces. In Hong Kong in 2019, the Chinese government threw unprecedented force at large but peaceful prodemocracy demonstrations, firing tear-gas canisters, rubber bullets, and beanbag rounds and chasing protesters into subway stations and other shelters. The crackdown hasn't ended as of this writing, and Beijing has proceeded to impose draconian laws intended to squelch any further opposition or questioning of its authority, even purely verbal expressions.[14]

Some months into the Hong Kong uprising, as Black Lives Matter protests mushroomed on the other side of the Pacific, the Trump administration launched a very similar response, sending marshals and other federal agents into the streets of Portland, Oregon—and, it promised, other cities—to battle against what acting Homeland Security secretary Chad Wolf called "lawless anarchists."[15] Tear gas and rubber bullets were fired against peaceful demonstrators. The feds outfitted their virtual army in camouflage without name tags or insignia to indicate who they were or precisely what agency they belonged to—just as the police had done in Hong Kong.

That tactic made it difficult for victims to figure out who to complain to or take action against, but it also blurred the line between the military and law enforcement. Arguably, Hong Kong and Portland represented extraordinary situations, but in the period of the neoliberal state, such confrontations are becoming more frequent. The succession of events in both cases fit into a familiar trajectory of increasing State authoritarianism, one that's not confined to expected offenders like Russia, mainland China, and Saudi Arabia. Police reform, which the State could surely carry out if it really wanted to, never goes so far as to alter this pattern in any significant way; a 2020 study found that not one of the twenty largest U.S. cities was in compliance with minimum human rights standards.[16] The end result is less security for populations that aren't part of the Core Identity Group, though security is precisely what police—and the State as a whole—are supposed to provide.

None of this is new, just more technologically and organizationally sophisticated than in earlier periods of the modern State and now sold to the public in a slicker, more reassuring package. But very few states are so democratic and noncoercive that they're willing to abandon statutes like the Insurrection Act, the 1807 law that empowers the U.S. government to deploy the military and federalize the National Guard under certain circumstances. It's been used repeatedly to beat back challenges to the socioeconomic order: during Nat Turner's Rebellion, the Pullman Strike of 1894, the Colorado Coalfield War of 1914, the suppression of the Bonus Army (1932), the inner-city uprisings of 1967 and 1968, and the riots following the acquittal of Rodney King's police assailants in 1992. Trump and his follower, Senator Tom Cotton, invoked its spirit in 2020 when they called activists protesting the police killing of George Floyd "insurrectionists, anarchists, rioters and looters," vowed to show them "no quarter," and advocated defunding "anarchist cities."[17]

The State is also more than willing to supplement policing with a program of "irregular" violence when it's deemed necessary. Beginning with slave patrols in colonial America, continuing into the nineteenth century with paramilitary forces such as the Texas Rangers (whose principal job then was to dispossess and expel Spanish-speaking residents from the new state); the twentieth century with ultranationalist terror groups like tsarist Russia's Black Hundreds, Germany's Brown Shirts, and Northern Ireland's Ulster Volunteer Force; and the twenty-first century with the United States' right-wing militias˙ and India's youth militia, Hindu Yuva Vahini, violent extremist organizations have been tolerated and sometimes maintain informal partnerships with regular police, the military, and other elements of the State, even in countries with democratic governments.˙

As highly nationalistic governments took hold in the early twenty-first century, such arrangements naturally deepened. A 2020 report by Michael German, a former agent of the Federal Bureau of Investigation, found that white supremacist groups had infiltrated police in every region of the United States; indeed, FBI internal documents reveal that militia groups the agency had investigated had "active ties" to law enforcement. Nevertheless, German told the *Guardian*, "nobody is collecting the data and nobody is actively looking for these law enforcement officers," and there was no national strategy for identifying and weeding them out.[18] In Germany, meanwhile, local and regional police forces are honeycombed with members of violent ultraright groups; in 2020, the defense minister had to partially disband an elite commando force that had been taken over by right-wing extremists.[19]

Often, these actors claim they are defending the rights and protecting the security of the Core Identity Group; in reality, this means disrupting and driving out "undesirable" groups by sowing terror among them. A July 2020 report by the Center for Strategic and International Studies that reviewed twenty-five years of data on incidents of what it defined as domestic terrorism in the United States

*   Private militias are illegal in all fifty U.S. states. The Supreme Court, in a 2008 decision authored by conservative justice Antonin Scalia, ruled that the Constitution confirms that the states have the right to prohibit them. Mary B. McCord, "The Plot against Gretchen Whitmer Shows the Danger of Private Militias," *New York Times*, October 8, 2020. Yet these laws are seldom enforced, even though membership in paramilitary groups is overwhelmingly white and far-right.

†   A 2019 survey of readers of the independent publication *Military Times* found that 36 percent of U.S. active-duty soldiers "had personally witnessed examples of white nationalism or ideological-driven racism in recent months." And while the Defense Department has forbidden "active participation" in white supremacist and other extremist groups since 1996, membership is not prohibited. Lois Beckett, "How the US Military Has Failed to Address White Supremacy in Its Ranks," *Guardian UK*, June 24, 2020.

found that the majority had been launched by far-right groups, and that proportion was growing: two-thirds in 2019 and 90 percent in 2020 thus far were committed by such groups. Running far behind were "Salafi Jihadists," the group whose crimes were the pretext for the creation of a vast Department of Homeland Security (DHS) after 9/11.[20] In January 2020, at the height of Trump's popularity, a survey of Republicans and Republican-leaning independents by sociologist Larry M. Bartels found over 40 percent agreeing that "a time will come when patriotic Americans have to take the law into their own hands." There was nothing generalized or unspecific about these people's assertions, Bartels stressed; "rather, they are grounded in real political values—specifically, and overwhelmingly, in Republicans' ethnocentric concerns about the political and social role of immigrants, African-Americans, and Latinos in a context of significant demographic and cultural change."[21]

The pattern is a familiar one: the tsarist regime tolerated pogroms against Jews and other crimes by ultranationalists prior to World War I, and the German government was likewise lenient toward reactionary thugs like the Nazi Brown Shirts in the decade before Hitler's accession to power. This is because these groups were understood to provide support for the existing order, unlike dissident groups on the other end of the political spectrum.

At the end of April 2020, for instance, armed protesters broke into the legislative chamber of the Michigan statehouse to oppose economic shutdown measures advocated by the state's Democratic governor. Armed men stood over the lawmakers. When the right-wing mob returned to the building two weeks later, the legislative session was canceled. No one was arrested either time, and the state took no legal action. Two months later, during Black Lives Matter street protests in Portland, Oregon, Customs and Border Protection agents, federal marshals, and DHS security were deployed, allegedly to protect federal buildings from vandalism by activists. The agents grabbed a number of activists from peaceful demonstrations, stuffed them into unmarked vans, and took them to locations where identifying information was recorded. They were then released without having been told what they had done or why they were targeted.[22]

Unlike the militia who stormed the Michigan legislature, the

Portland activists appear to have been tagged for inclusion in a database of dissidents the Trump Justice Department was assembling. Following the first wave of antiracist protest marches against the police killing of George Floyd, the Department of Justice claimed to have intelligence of coordination between "extremist" groups, including Antifa—even though no incidents of violence or vandalism had been publicly attributed to the antifascist alliance. "We're mining that data now," said an official. "A lot of this has been happening on social media, so we've got to run it down."

In other words, the violence that took place at many of the demonstrations and marches, the vast majority of which was instigated or provoked by police or far-right counterprotesters, would be used as another excuse to spy on leftists and anarchists, violating their privacy and further criminalizing dissent. One of the few major arrests following the marches in late May, ironically, was of "three alleged members of a militarized far-right movement" who were accused of "plotting to bomb government property and to stoke violence at a Black Lives Matter protest using Molotov cocktails," according to the *Wall Street Journal*.[23]

"Populist" violence may bubble up from below, but seldom without encouragement from the State. In any society managed from the top down, either by an authoritarian ruler or a meritocratic elite, culture, including the place of violence in the society, is defined at the top. Judith Butler said the following about Donald Trump's characteristic model of communication:

> The tweet acts as an incitation but also as a virtual attack with consequences. It gives the public license to violence. He models a kind of entitlement that positions him above the law. Those who support him, even love him, want to live in that zone with him. He is a sovereign unchecked by the rule of law he represents, and many think that is the most free and courageous kind of liberation. But it is liberation from all social obligation, a self-aggrandizing sovereignty of the individual.[24]

Trump's communications with his followers are only a more blatant example of a dangerous cultural transmission that takes place all the time as politicians, CEOs, military leaders, and other role models of the State communicate with and are observed by members of the public. One of the most important functions of the State, in fact, is to normalize violence and criminality not for the public but for its leaders. "Indifference to life," notes the African American writer ZZ Packer, referring to the police murder of a Louisville, Kentucky, emergency medical technician, Breonna Taylor, in her bed, "seems to matter when using a weapon, but not so much when using the much vaster powers of the state as a weapon."[25]

While we tend to think of Hitler or Stalin as fitting this pattern, the more frightening reality is that many sociopaths in high places behave quite normally in other contexts. "It is characteristic of political psychopathy today that grossly delinquent public policies may coexist with good private adjustment," wrote Alex Comfort. "The suggestion that those who order public frauds, massacres or deportation must necessarily be criminal or sadistic in their private relationships has no support in theory or in observation."[26] Would Barack Obama, as a private citizen, be capable of ordering assassinations of people he only vaguely knew about? Probably not, but the power of the presidency enveloped him in an atmosphere and a set of advisers that gave him permission to do so—and so he did.

These examples of the true "banality of evil" should make us more concerned rather than less about our future under the State. Obvious criminal lunatics are typically not needed to engineer sociopathic outcomes; fundamentally sane individuals, once in office and having embraced the norms of power, are quite capable of ordering up deprivation and death. "Be assured of one thing: whichever candidate you choose at the polls in November, you aren't just electing a president of the United States; you are also electing an assassin-in-chief," *Tom-Dispatch*'s Tom Engelhardt warned in 2012, referring to an ostensibly liberal administration's increasingly routine use of drones to assassinate the leadership of groups fighting the U.S. occupation of Afghanistan and Iraq.[27]

When viewed from a bird's-eye perspective, the history of the modern State often looks dramatically like the career of a sociopath.

Not surprisingly, then, when viewed from a bird's-eye perspective, the history of the modern State often looks dramatically like the career of a sociopath. Almost as soon as it appeared, wars involving state actors of unprecedented geographic reach broke out in Europe, starting with the War of the League of Cambrai in 1508; these continued semiregularly for centuries. Violence has always been the State's most frequent means of getting its way on other fronts as well, beginning with the enclosure of the commons, the violent enforcement of property rights, and the capture and management of enslaved populations in the New World and elsewhere. The State subdued, subjected, and in some cases wiped out Indigenous populations in Asia, Africa, and the Americas through a deadly combination of what anthropologist Jared Diamond neatly summed up as "guns, germs, and steel."

The process quickened in the nineteenth and twentieth centuries with the invention of reservations for Indigenous groups, concentration camps for dissident populations, forced labor camps for political and "common" criminals, the death camps of Nazi Germany, and death squads, which are sometimes employed by the State, sometimes by capital, and sometimes by the State with corporate subsidies, as in the case of Colombia, where global oil companies paid government security forces to provide private protection for their facilities.[28] Today, as police become more and more like the robocops seen in the movies and drone warfare mechanizes killing, the death machine no longer needs traditional human actors; it can be operated remotely or by cops trained to think and operate as automatons.

The motivation behind these increasingly sophisticated, technocratic applications is complex and individual, but there are always three common purposes: to control and manage populations, to impress State authority, and to fulfill the State's vision of an orderly, harmonious, and productive society. This vision, then, is built on violence. If the State exercises a monopoly on the use of force, however, that doesn't mean it's the only entity allowed to inflict it. The State gives individuals within the Core Identity Group—even extreme groups like right-wing militias—wide latitude to commit acts of violence against less favored groups, in part to maintain a racial caste system and in part to reassure the Core Identity Group of their special role within the State. So long as we have the State, this is not a feature that can be reformed out of existence; the violent reinforcement of racism, gender inequality, homophobia, and transphobia, and the marginalization of specific religious groups is basic to the system.

* * *

There is no such thing as a homogeneous state; humanity always inclines toward diversity and difference. Even Norway and Sweden have the Sami or "Lapps," Myanmar the Rohingya, Japan the Ainu as well as a denigrated Korean minority, and most European nations the Roma, Travellers, or a visible Muslim minority. Arguably, the large majority of states—especially the largest ones—are the product of long-term campaigns of subjugation or elimination of Indigenous groups by the Core Identity Group, campaigns that shaped the personality and outlook of the Core Identity Group itself. Managing subject populations is one of the tasks of the State, which it generally performs by harnessing them to low-skill, low-paying jobs that help keep labor costs down. In addition, in colonial states such as the United States, Australia, and Israel, pressure is exerted either to confine racially nonconforming groups to certain segregated areas, force them to assimilate, or induce them to leave.

Perhaps more important, the State understands that the disposition of the Core Identity Group depends to a great extent on the relative status of racial minorities. If minorities were treated equally—provided with quality education, health care, good housing, sanitary conditions, and access to careers and jobs—then the Core Identity Group's claim to higher standing would no longer apply; sections of it might begin to question their loyalty to the State. Attempts by the State to alleviate conditions for subject racial groups in response to rebellions and refusals by those groups never fully achieve their objective and always face a fierce backlash from elements within the Core Identity Group.

This has a profound impact on people's vision of themselves as a community—or lack thereof. "Freedom," to the Core Identity Group, always means freedom from mutual obligation, the right to

care about only one's own identity group. In the United States before the end of slavery, whiteness was a precious resource, to be
guarded jealously. "Because whites could not be enslaved or held as
slaves," legal scholar Cheryl Harris writes, "the racial line between
white and Black was extremely critical; it became a line of protection
and demarcation from the potential threat of commodification, and
it determined the allocation of benefits and burdens of this form of
property. White identity and whiteness were sources of privilege and
protection; their absence meant being an object of property."[29]

After the American Civil War, of course, the threat to formerly enslaved people was somewhat different: segregation, consignment to
inferior jobs and living conditions, persecution, lynching, arbitrary
imprisonment, and the perpetual monitoring gaze of white people.
A more complicated version of the game is played with immigrants,
and especially those without strong racial or cultural ties to the dominant group. These people are welcomed by capital as another supply
of cheap labor, but they face the same unequal treatment as anyone
not deemed part of the Core Identity Group.

For the State, the system works because it keeps working people divided from each other, even when the privileges much of the
Core Identity Group enjoy are meager. For the people, however, the
cost is the ongoing inculcation of racism—overt or covert, genteel or
crude—and the social dysfunction it creates.

The State also has a vested interest in maintaining, if not promoting, sexism, gender inequity, homophobia, and transphobia. Since
the beginning of the modern era, the State has worked to convert individuals who once worked in extended communities—as agrarians
or as members of urban guilds and other formations, not to mention as serfs on rural manors—into waged workers, as a better way to
organize labor under a capitalist system focused on growth. It took
centuries for this social structure to fully assert itself, but as the process continued, the family or household emerged as the other vital
component of the system.

These units were necessary to reproduce labor, to generate consumption as communities became less self-sufficient, and to give the
(male) worker the time needed to labor away from home. This ce-
mented a regime in place that tied women to the home as unpaid

domestic labor and deprived them of the economic freedom neces-sary to decide their own futures. The system resulted in a new brand of sexual tyranny as well, as men who worked outside the home took the cue from their bosses to impose a hierarchical structure in the home that paralleled the structure at work by asserting the para-mountcy of their own needs.

The marginalization of gay and other sexually nonconformist people relates to the State's promotion of the family or household structure as well. Because these individuals did not fit easily into this system, they were either forced to conform to it anyway, what-ever their preferences, or else funneled into the few social spaces that could more easily accommodate them, such as the church. As the worker-headed family became the norm in the eighteenth and nineteenth centuries, sexual nonconformists faced more outright persecution. While much of the rhetoric and hate speech against gay people took a moral or ideological line (homosexuality was a crime in the Soviet Union from 1933 until the dissolution of the USSR), their material offense in the eyes of the State was more practical: their failure to contribute to either the reproduction of labor or the worker-family-household system of productive economic growth.

The result was a growing body of laws and customs tying women to the home, subordinating their rights to their parents and hus-bands, and suppressing or criminalizing sexual nonconformism. While many of these have been swept away by some governments, the balance of power remains tilted in favor of straight men even in ostensibly enlightened societies.

The State didn't invent racism, sexism, or homophobia; these had existed in various forms, often reinforced by organized religion, for many centuries. But they quickly joined the ranks of its supports and enablers. As with its efforts to act against racism, the State's support for women's rights and gay rights has never gone far enough and has repeatedly been stymied by powerful forces it contains within itself. As long as the State remains our society's fundamental organizing principle, these forms of oppression can never be fully rooted out.

The State's policy of catering to the preferences and prejudices of the Core Identity Group—a constituency it has always defined and molded as well—pushes social development toward a monoculture built to the order of that group. The traditional family as well as a host of other traditions, often of rather recent provenance, are endlessly celebrated. In the case of America's Core Identity Group, these include Christmas, the automobile, fried food, police, and the U.S. military. This dovetails with the desire of capital and the State to encourage consumption, the worker-headed household, the family, and the security state. Diversity in values and traditions—including economic models, entertainment preferences, and habits of household formation and child-raising—is discouraged because a more diverse society may be messier and less efficient, doesn't necessarily promote the capitalist model of ever-faster economic growth, and would risk the displeasure of the dominant group. New developments—from hip-hop to Asian fusion cuisine to world music—regularly add a semblance of diversity to the dominant culture, but rarely are the people who actually create these innovations admitted to membership in the Core Identity Group.

In a more sinister vein, popular culture promotes the State's preoccupation with efficiency and automation by giving us cyberheroes like the Terminator, himself a machine; "action" heroes like Jack Bauer, Jack Reacher, and Ethan Hunt, who, as government employees or ex-government employees with perfect physiques and coolly efficient, split-second responses to any situation, might as well be machines; and the many video game protagonists derived from them. Men are coaxed to model themselves after these quasiautomatons, who also fit in nicely with the postindustrial economy's drive for "frictionless" production and performance.

* * *

The larger role of popular culture is to cement the public's allegiance to the State and deflect blame for its failings. This reveals itself most dramatically in the portrayal of police and the military in TV and movies, mass-market paperback novels, and news media. With government itself in increasingly ill repute, affection for police and the military has become one of the primary cultural props of loyalty to the State.

The virtue and heroism of our armed guardians is celebrated non-stop. From the United States to Scandinavia, police procedurals portray cops as not just crime solvers but defenders of the innocent, the front line in the battle against a chaotic and dangerous society, heroic wrestlers with God and morality; often, they are martyrs in this existential struggle with "the element." Cop culture reaches a fever pitch in the United States, of course, but because of the power of American popular culture worldwide, it's worth focusing on this important topic for a moment longer.

As people—even many of the Core Identity Group—have become more cynical about government and their own ability to influence State decision-making, police have become more alluring figures, not just because they represent the law but because of their ability to operate outside it. Cops are different from us: they carry guns and can use them; they roam the city streets freely rather than being tied to an office or a workstation; they can inflict pain and punishment, even death; and they belong to a brotherhood solemnly pledged to protect each other. Police are hypnotic figures for much of the public, representing a fantasy of empowerment that most people know can never be achieved in most other walks of life.

The bulk of their support comes from the Core Identity Group. Even amid the outrage over the police murder of George Floyd, when a Gallup poll found that only 48 percent of Americans felt confident in police—a historic low—a solid 56 percent of white adults expressed confidence, compared with just 19 percent of Black adults.[30]

In popular culture, cops are humanized—portrayed with plenty of human flaws, from alcoholism to depression to adultery—while the criminals they hunt are cast essentially as social problems or pathological cases. "We demonstrated moral ambiguities," an actor in the series *The Wire* tweeted defensively after a critic for *The Hollywood Reporter*, responding to the death of George Floyd at the hands of Minneapolis cops, wrote that the series gave police violence a "heroic gloss."[31] Viewers and readers—almost always assumed to be the Core Identity Group—are encouraged to identify with the police as representatives of the best of their community, despite the individual officer's flaws, and as emblematic of their own good intentions and good values.

Sometimes they're lovable comic characters. "If you—as I have—worked on a TV show or movie in which police are portrayed as lovable goofballs, you have contributed to the larger acceptance that cops are implicitly the good guys," Tom Scharpling, an executive producer of the TV series *Monk*, tweeted in June 2020, after the wave of police brutality following Floyd's death provoked a backlash against the cop genre.[32] That would include legions of writers and directors dating back to the bumbling Keystone Kops flicks of the early silent-film era, more than one hundred years earlier.

Cop culture has been drilled deep into the American psyche for as long as anyone alive can remember, starting with the FBI-inspired "Junior G-Men" of the 1930s and continuing in the postwar years through the radio and TV series *Dragnet* and *Gang Busters*. "America is run and governed by people who grew up on TV cops," wrote the media critic James Poniewozik. "The police built prime time. . . . Good times, bad times, liberal eras, conservative eras—crime shows were a constant." The underlying message is always the same: "It's a sick, sad world, and if you're going to step out in it, you need protection. . . . When a politician goes on Twitter or stands at a convention declaring for 'LAW & ORDER!' those viewers have an enormous library of images to illustrate the slogan." Poniewozik expressed doubt whether producers and screenwriters could avoid falling back on the tried-and-true police-story formula once the latest wave of anger over killings by cops ran its course.[33]

Along with saintly cops, lovable cops, and cops who die for our sins, we've grown accustomed to popular fiction, movies, and TV that valorize "our" soldiers as heroes protecting us from a dangerous world beyond our borders and embodying the best values of "our" society—that is, of the Core Identity Group. In the United States, the movie industry has partnered with the State to propagate this vision almost from its inception, and it's been one of Hollywood's most successful storylines for many years.

After releasing a number of commercially unsuccessful films that told stories critical of the post-9/11 U.S. wars in the Middle East, such as *Jarhead*, *Lions for Lambs*, and *Redacted*, Hollywood followed with a series of quite different films, including *The Hurt Locker*, *The Messenger*, and, in 2014, the spectacularly successful *American Sniper*. That film showed American soldiers in Iraq in an unreservedly heroic and sympathetic light, never broached the subject of Washington's reasons for being there—to be a good soldier is never to sully oneself by asking—and hardly acknowledged their enemies as human. All of these essentially prowar, promilitary films were acclaimed by critics as real, raw, and human.

Such stories are not concocted out of thin air by producers, screenwriters, and hack novelists; they are products of a close partnership between the police and military and the media and entertainment industries. To achieve authenticity requires storytellers to befriend cops and learn to see the world through their eyes. The New York Police Department in particular has developed a sophisticated capability for working with "creatives" to make sure cop stories are told the way it wants them to be.[34] The Pentagon has done the same, when it comes to war or combat stories.[35] Anyone who presumes to tell these stories the "wrong" way risks losing access to and cooperation from the force or the services.

The public come to see a multitude of problems, from drug peddling to homelessness to foreign opposition to American imperialism, through the eyes of police and the military, which is to say, as dangers that need to be addressed with force rather than as social or political issues. Individuals, broken families, low-income communities, and occupied countries collapsing into civil war—generally, people and societies that don't fit the Core Identity Group's self-image—are to blame for their ills, and the burden of recovery and regeneration is on them.

The military and the police, on the other hand, are the last institutions of the State that exercise a strong emotional appeal to a substantial segment of the population. They project an aura of efficiency and trustworthiness. Since they are recruited primarily from the working class, they appeal to a lingering feeling of cultural or class solidarity. And they meet a need, constantly stoked by the State and the military and police themselves through popular culture, for protection against perceived threats, both internal and external.

"Former Vice President Biden was wrong when he said that the majority of Americans condemn the actions of the police," poet and novelist Ishmael Reed wrote in 2020 following George Floyd's murder. "The police feel that the majority of white Americans have given them the mandate to do whatever they wish to minorities. They're right."[36]

The result is that conservatives' worship of the national state and the Left's focus on building state-sponsored social provisions are replaced by a fetishization of uniformed guardians whose real function is always to protect the State and capitalism.

A large chunk of people hate these institutions, of course, but those in the Core Identity Group tend to identify fiercely with them, even if they don't think they are identifying with the State itself. When a controversy broke out in 2020 over the naming of military bases in the American South after Confederate army officers, the *New York Times* noted that "the base names were agreed upon as part of broader accommodations in which the military embraced segregation so as not to offend Southerners by treating African-Americans as equals."[37] In other words, the base names were selected to secure the Core Identity Group's allegiance in the South. In every state in 2020, the military command structure continues to be thoroughly dominated by the Core Identity Group. In the United States, for example, when 43 percent of men and women on active duty in 2020 were people of color, all but two of forty-one senior commanders were white.[38]

As a practical matter, this viewpoint coaxes the public and the courts to grant police and military—in the United States, increasingly overlapping categories, as veterans fill the police ranks—an extraordinary amount of covert as well as overt authority. A 2020 investigation by Reuters of five hundred cases that went before the Supreme Court since 2005 found that the court was 3.5 times more likely to intervene on behalf of a police officer than a civilian and that the justices almost always ruled in favor of the cop.[39] That's because of the doctrine of qualified immunity, which says that an officer can't even be put on trial for excessive force unless a prior case with exactly the same set of facts already established that the conduct was illegal; Justice Sonia Sotomayor has called this doctrine "an absolute shield for law enforcement officers, gutting the deterrent effect of the Fourth Amendment" to the Constitution.

When policing and armed conflict are not involved, the weight of responsibility falls quite differently. Rather than focusing on the failure of the State and capital to pursue the large-scale, global solutions required to address climate change, for example, narratives in popular journalism and consumer culture encourage us to think of this life-or-death matter as something that's "up to us," something we can overcome by buying the right kind of car, favoring the right types of food, and buying the right kinds of cleaning products. The response can never be to question a State system based on endless economic growth; instead, we must find new, more "ethical" ways to consume and new ways to generate wealth for the State and for capital.

The other part of popular culture's mission is to celebrate what's considered normal and typical, thus supporting the State's preference for an orderly, economically productive society. This determines the portrayal of women, of sexual nonconformists, and of people of color in TV, films, and popular fiction, where they most frequently appear as wives, friends, or sidekicks of white male characters, as exotics, or, even in a presumably more enlightened period, as sources of danger. When they are presented as more fully rounded characters, often their uniqueness is sanded off so that they resemble the white male paradigm as much as possible, once again reinforcing the socioeconomic vision the State wishes to sell to the public.

The news media's approach to reporting is typically informed by similar impulses: to affirm the State's basic goodness, deflect blame for its failings, and celebrate the normal and typical. This is for three reasons. First, even in their public-service role of reporting and interpreting the news, media like newspapers, TV networks, blogs, and websites—not to mention Twitter and Facebook—appeal to their readers as entertainment. Their primary audience is always the Core Identity Group, who like to see news framed in ways that conform to their preferred view of the world.

Second, just like the purveyors of fictional crime and war stories, the major news media depend on components of the State for much of their day-to-day reporting and many of their better yarns. Reporters on the crime beat everywhere rely on police for inside information about their activities and investigations.[40] In the United States, the Washington press corps are tied umbilically to their sources on Pennsylvania Avenue and on K Street. Battlefield reporters bond with the troops they embed and sometimes train with. Business reporters depend on contacts with executives to know what's going on in any industry from financial services to fossil fuels to high tech.

Relying on these sources as they do, the vast majority of journalists adopt their perspectives and attitudes, which are then regurgitated in broadcasts, newspaper accounts and op-eds, blogs, and TV roundtables. In some respects, this is a matter of survival: reporting uncomfortable facts or exposing hostile viewpoints would quickly push many once-favored journalists into exile—or, in the case of WikiLeaks's Julian Assange, something worse.

Third, most major media are business enterprises, often owned by diversified corporations or investors with other business interests; a prime example is the *Washington Post*, owned by Amazon founder and chair Jeff Bezos. These owners aren't anxious for their employees to publish anything that undermines their sources of wealth, or the institutions that protect and aid them as they accumulate it. The bottom line, then, is that news media are just as much a part of the State as any capital-fueled activity, with a deep commitment to defending and legitimizing it. While they can often be critical of government, corporations, and social injustice, they seldom delve deep into the systemic causes of the problems they report, and they always affirm that these can be corrected by a few reforms implemented by wise leaders. The State itself, in other words, is never the problem, always part of the solution, and the news media's primary job is to confirm that belief.

When elements of the media and public opinion refuse to play along, or need to be manipulated to do so, the State has traditionally resorted to subterfuge and disinformation, for which government-orchestrated trolling, bots, and other high-tech tools are merely the latest helpful resources. States have always leveraged lies, slander, and manipulation of the facts to get their way, including by intervening in each other's party politics and elections. The tools the State has developed to manipulate public opinion—propaganda is the polite word—are closely related to those the private sector uses in marketing and advertising; the two have cross-pollinated for many years. State lies are justified as necessary to persuade a public with limited knowledge to go along with policies that their wise leaders have designed in their best interest. In practice, these lies supply excuses for the State to increase its latitude to wage war, attack internal enemies, bail out capitalists, and concentrate power in the elite.

* * *

The eminent German jurist and political theorist (and enthusiastic Nazi) Carl Schmitt argued that all key elements of modern State theory are secular versions of theological concepts, since the modern State is the successor to the medieval church as the embodiment as well as the controlling "mind" of society. From a single transcendent God, embodied in the church, we moved to a "single transcendent power" or "political apparatus."* Sovereignty, denoting supreme rank or power, is something that every state claims, no matter how democratic it professes to be, and it has proved a remarkably supple and useful concept for the State. It was "functional to the development of monarchic absolutism," observed the Marxist political scientists Toni Negri and Michael Hardt, who drew some of their thinking from Schmitt. "But in fact its transcendental schema could be applied equally to various forms of government: monarchy, oligarchy, and democracy. . . . Democratic, plural, or popular political forms might be declared, but modern sovereignty really has only one political figure: a single transcendent power."[41]

What is the "theology" of this "sovereign" power, the State? According to Schmitt, one of its key doctrines is that humans are fundamentally evil and need a strong state, with strong leaders, to keep them from destroying themselves.[42] To make this work, however, the State must establish a friend/enemy framework through which the public—implicitly, the Core Identity Group—can view the world. In other words, the State's mission to hold society together can only be legitimated if there's an Other to hold it together against.[43]

---

* "When the Pilgrims formed their 'body politic' [by signing the Mayflower Compact prior to landing in what is now Massachusetts], they referred to it as a 'covenant.' The notion was congruent with their religious principles." John G. Turner, "The Mayflower Compact at 400," *Wall Street Journal*, November 21–22, 2020.

This assertion poses a dilemma for the State. On the one hand, it aspires to transcendence: to comprehend everything, to leave nothing outside its orbit, to be all things to all people. Yet the State requires hostile externalities, Others, to maintain the tension that keeps the Core Identity Group believing in its necessity. So, the State's highest desire for itself can only be met at the risk of losing its grip on its primary audience. Continually identifying and constructing an Other is an essential task of the State, whether it likes it or not.

Much of the time, the Other is an external power, but, all too often, it's an enemy within—migrants, Indigenous peoples, religious minorities, people of color, the poor, radicals. The State, by way of (in the United States) the police, the National Guard, the Drug Enforcement Agency (DEA), ICE, and other agencies, is our protector against them. "We are not your enemy," the National Fraternal Order of Police said in a November 2020 social media post urging its followers to reelect Trump, "we are the Thin Blue Line. And we are the only thing that stands between order and anarchy."[44] Naturally, we identify closely with our protectors. What this arrangement reveals is that violence and the threat of violence are integral to the State's modus operandi, making it all the more critical for the State to control the narrative that the public receives and absorbs when violence occurs.

Since the modern world has grown more enveloping, bewildering, and violent, a narrative that makes sense of it all has become more elusive—and much more in demand. "Daily life is becoming a kaleidoscope of incidents and accidents, catastrophes and cataclysms," writes Virilio, "in which we are endlessly running up against the unexpected, which occurs out of the blue, so to speak. In a shattered mirror, we must learn to discern what is impending more and more often—but above all more and more quickly, those events coming upon us inopportunely, if not indeed simultaneously."[45]

We've just reviewed some of the ways the State makes sense of this sensory overload: by encouraging us to identify deeply with the police and military, to value security above all else, to place our hopes in leadership—in the elite—and to place the supposed values and lifestyle of the Core Identity Group at the center of our aspirations. But to control the narrative—to keep us focused in the preferred direction and divert attention from the ways in which the State itself destabilizes society and marginalizes our needs and desires—the State engages in a kind of double game that feigns sympathy for those concerns while making sure its interests are not compromised.

Rule by a self-selecting elite is camouflaged by democratic elections, and popular outrage at the elite's excesses is placated by right-wing pseudopopulists—Trump, Orbán, and Brazilian president Jair Bolsonaro among them—whose substantive policies never rock the boat excessively and who can be removed if they prove inconvenient or incompetent.* Reliance on cheap migrant labor and the resentments this engenders is addressed by tolerating if not encouraging periodic bursts of racism and xenophobia, resulting in crackdowns, abuse, and human tragedy—but never any change in employers' or the State's labor policies. Rapid economic globalization destabilizes communities and households; the elite deals with the ensuing rage through dramatic actions like jacking up tariffs, then renegotiates existing trade treaties—but in so doing, it leaves all the fundamental issues unaddressed. Meanwhile, rapid social change—women's emancipation, in particular—linked to economic transformation and new technologies erodes patriarchy and heteronormativity, enraging reactionaries and prompting right-wing politicians to launch a Kulturkampf that predictably fails but nevertheless helps keep right-wing politicians in office.

The State gets away with this sleight of hand in part by toggling between different definitions of itself. To progressives, the State is still the social-democratic or welfare state, and politics is about returning it to that model. To reactionaries, the State is the national state, and right-wing politicians are happy to encourage them to believe it still is. Capitalists embrace the neoliberal state, and the State works hard to make this model a reality, but with occasional nods to the older models as needed.

For the most part, the trick works, making the State our most effective—and slipperiest—storyteller. Control of the narrative allows it to set the terms by which its own success is judged.

One way it does so is through numbers. The modern State has

---

* The appeal to grievances against "elites" is just one of the wag-the-dog techniques these figures borrow from earlier right-wing populists like Hitler and Mussolini.

always encouraged us to judge it based on its success at producing economic growth, but this tendency went into hyperdrive in the last century as tools proliferated for quantifying productivity, trade volumes, market ups and downs, and other gauges of economic performance. Some of these tools tell stories that upset us: about increasingly unequal distribution of wealth, greed-fueled speculative collapses, environmental despoliation. But as populations expand and economies grow over time, GDP tends to grow as well. The State and capital can claim credit while promising to right any wrongs that might develop with a few well-targeted reforms.

The other way the State controls the narrative is through the drama of government itself. The passage of historic laws, the issuing of landmark court decisions, the signing of executive orders, and the deployment of troops in emergencies—real or alleged—are a few of the ways the three branches demonstrate to the public that their needs and desires are noted and responded to. The implicit message each time is that the story has ended happily, the State can continue its work as before, and the enraged masses can all go home.

Passage of the Civil Rights Act and the Voting Rights Act in 1964 and 1965, for example, certainly were watershed events for the U.S. Civil Rights Movement, the moment when activists' demands were finally addressed by the broader society, but this framing also allowed the Core Identity Group to assure itself that the "story" was over and it could now move on. What should have been only the first steps in a broader effort to correct the political and economic injustices that African Americans faced instead marked the end of the drama for most of the public and gave the State permission to shift its gaze elsewhere. It took the urban uprisings of the following years to refocus the State's attention—and then only temporarily.

We've seen the same thing happen countless times in countless places, from the constitutional amendments following the American Civil War to the election of the first national representative body in Russia following the 1905 revolution to the adoption of the liberal Weimar Constitution in Germany following World War I. On each occasion, a revolutionary upheaval led to a significant gesture of reform by the State, which demobilized all or much of the movement behind the upheaval, supplying a seemingly tidy ending to the drama but bringing about little or no deep change. As this book goes to press, we're waiting to see if the wave of revulsion at police misconduct in the wake of another string of killings of African Americans will devolve into the same sad scenario. (Cancellation of the egregious police "reality" show *Cops*, after airing for thirty-two seasons, was admittedly a positive move, although it soon found another home; less so was Amazon.com's announcement that it was forbidding police use of its facial recognition software—but only for one year.)

The State's control of the narrative imposes a series of false choices that force us to debate our future only on the State's terms. Order versus chaos, economic growth versus poverty, democracy versus autocracy, peaceful demonstration versus violent protest are just a few of these. The first compels us to choose the State over any other possible organizing principle, for fear that human society will otherwise collapse in a wretched heap. The second teaches us that the inevitable result of adopting a less wasteful, more sustainable economic system will be deprivation. The third tells us that the only alternative to the corrupt electoral systems that the "free" world lives under is an authoritarian, one-party state like China. The fourth would have us believe that we only possess the right to protest if we play by the rules the police—the State—set: march and rally only where they allow us to, make only as much noise as they allow, and never push back physically against police violence and abuse of power.

In each case, the message is that we have only one choice; the State is our defense against chaos, poverty, autocracy, and mob rule. We have no rights without the State, can never get justice without the State, and no abuse can ever delegitimize the State to the point of justifying forcible defiance or overthrow.

Another false choice revolves around economic growth. Is it thanks to government policies or free-market initiative? The question is meant to force us to conclude that without free-market capitalism, society would give way to socialism or worse, and we'd all descend into poverty (those of us who aren't already there). Capitalism represents freedom in opposition to the controlling and bureaucratic State.

In reality—and as every prominent politician, corporate chieftain, banker, and economist surely understands—the question is an exercise in misdirection. As we noted earlier, the State is an economic unit, and while capital is a vital component, it will always need the protection and subsidies the State provides. Corporate interests complain incessantly about "regulatory overreach" and inconvenient laws, but law and regulation, not to mention tax breaks, allow many sectors, notably financial services, oil and gas, and defense, to maintain their privileged position in the economy. Government bonds are an enormous source of business—and profit—for banks and a store of wealth for investors. And the government-run social safety net keeps consumption—and sales—from cratering during economic downturns.

> The State's control of the narrative imposes a series of false choices that force us to debate our future only on the State's terms. Order versus chaos, economic growth versus poverty, democracy versus autocracy, peaceful protest versus violent protest are just a few of these.

When corporate interests and many so-called libertarians attack big government and the "deep state," their real target is not government or the State; often, they are enthusiastic fans of the harshest (and most expensive) forms of policing, immigration suppression, and military response. What they are really attacking is any form of collective or cooperative system of social provision or commitment: public health, old-age provision, economic safety nets, basic human rights like housing and health care. In mainstream political economy, public pensions and unemployment benefits, publicly owned utilities and postal services, and public education, for example, are dubious forms of "socialism" while the United States Defense Department's cost-plus contracting system, which essentially guarantees profits to defense contractors, is somehow a perfectly acceptable free-market practice.*

---

* "Between 2008 and 2019, the Department of Defense spent over $1.2 trillion on . . . cost-type contracts, none of which were subject to the cost-reducing pressures of private markets. Other contracts include lifetime service agreements and sole-supplier contracts, which effectively create monopolies." Heidi Peltier, "The Growth of the 'Camo Economy' and the Commercialization of the Post-9/11 Wars," Boston University, Pardee Center for the Study of the Longer-Range Future, June 30, 2020, 2.

While the State chose to offer pensions and unemployment benefits to workers in the years when it was concerned about the destabilizing effects of industrial-worker unrest, it doesn't see them fitting into the new model of the neoliberal state; appeals to neoliberal economic doctrine provide ideological justification for the State to either eliminate them or reduce them to irrelevancy. The government-versus-private-sector debate enables the State to marginalize groups demanding that it commit more substantially to programs that support social and economic justice or calling for it to abandon the State-capital model for one based on economic democracy.

This is the most harmful aspect of the State's reliance on false choices: we find ourselves unable or afraid to acknowledge our interdependence and unable to see that the elements of the State that work best for us are founded on a cooperative rather than a competitive model. In the United States, for example, Social Security and Medicare are contributory programs that collect payroll taxes from younger workers to supply benefits to retirees and survivors. They belong to the people who participate in the two systems and fund them. The basic idea behind these social insurance programs was the anarchist principle of mutual aid; the French anarchist Pierre-Joseph Proudhon was one of the first to propose a system of society-wide insurance against "disease, old age and death."[46] Over sixty million Americans—one in five—received benefits from Social Security in January 2020, and forty-four million were enrolled in Medicare; the programs are crucial to keeping many of these millions out of poverty.

Yet the right and center-right had been laboring for more than forty years to reframe Social Security and Medicare as "welfare" programs that rob us of individual control of our wealth and thus of the chance to create value with that money in the free market. Americans on the progressive side who want to defend these programs find themselves championing the State as a provider of social welfare, rather than perceiving the programs as what they are: a form of mutual aid that doesn't need the State to function and therefore could help establish the basis for a stateless, cooperative economy.

This foreclosing of possibilities and narrowing of our collective imagination makes it extremely hard to discuss any number of other

topics—restorative justice, sustainable agriculture, social housing—
without running aground on the questions of how they would work
as components of the State and how any decision to implement them
can be massaged to gain acceptance from capital and the other elements of the elite. We are to assume we can get everything we need
or desire in the way of security, identity, and material well-being
in one of only two ways: by purchasing it in the free market—if it's
available and we can afford it—or by petitioning the State. The same
goes for social justice.

Even in a democratic system, where laws are made by elected
representatives, the dilemma is the same: we have to demonstrate
to the State that our demands are strong enough and urgent enough
that they can't be ignored. Once our representatives are in office,
it's up to them whether they listen, and we face a lot of competition
from capital and from other powerful components of the State like
the police and military. We are supplicants, and in the framework of
the State, only two modes of supplication are acceptable: lobbying
and public demonstrations. Lobbying is expensive. As for demonstrations, "theoretically," the English novelist and critic John Berger
wrote, they "are an appeal to the democratic conscience of the State.
But this presupposes a conscience which is very unlikely to exist. If
the State authority is open to democratic influence, the demonstration will hardly be necessary; if it is not, it is unlikely to be influenced
by an empty show of force containing no real threat."[47]

When the State insists that only "peaceful, nonviolent" protest is
acceptable, then, it's demanding that the people's relationship to it
remain that of a supplicant: easy to ignore, easy to dismiss. It's telling us, implicitly, that reform or redress of wrongs is only possible if
there is no cost to be paid by society or the segments of society that
benefited from past injustices. This position reverberates in the continuing refusal of the U.S. government to consider reparations for the
descendants of formerly enslaved people, but the pattern goes back
much farther. Earlier, it was this refusal is visible in the federal government's decision not to grant freedmen and freedwomen the forty
acres and a mule that might have given them a reasonable chance to
launch themselves, and instead to give the land back to their former
owners; it was visible in the tsar's insistence that individuals who

had lived under serfdom pay a "redemption bond" to compensate landowners for their loss; and it was evident in France's forcible extraction of some $21 billion from Haiti over a period of 122 years for the privilege of being acknowledged as a free country. In each case, the State reiterates that the economic and property interests of the owners are more important than the rights of the human beings they injured—and that no amount of peaceful reform can ever change this basic principle.

Unless one speaks for a key component of the elite, or can persuade a very large chunk of the Core Identity Group to show support, supplication and petition are unlikely to be effective against the State, whether or not the specific governmental system is democratic. Occasionally, a dramatic event like the murder of George Floyd provokes a dramatic, possibly transformative change of attitude within the Core Identity Group, but then the hard work of turning that new perspective into legislation that permanently changes society still involves appealing to the State. A similar change happened in middle America in the 1960s when southern racists lashed back violently against civil rights activists—but keeping American lawmakers focused on implementing the needed changes in succeeding decades proved impossible.

Journalist Natasha Lennard points out that the State is comfortable talking about rights but far less comfortable talking about justice. This is because it can decide what rights to recognize—in legislation, in the courts—and which to override, while justice is a far broader concept that the State can't by itself define. "When we're forced to play the state's game—that is, to bring a case to court—there's no avoiding state logic," Lennard writes. "Under a rights framework, the state can have its punitive way with any protester if that protester has violated some mythical social contract with 'bad' or 'violent' behavior."

According to right-wing theorists of the State, this is not a bug in the system but a feature. Carl Schmitt defined the sovereign—in the case of the United States, the executive branch—as "he [sic] who decides on the exception," that is, who has the power to step outside the rule of law, including both legal and moral rights, in the public interest. Otherwise, Schmitt reasoned, no state can act decisively when necessary. Whatever form the modern State takes, either dictatorship or representative democracy, its authority is sovereign: that is, absolute. *

Obedience to the State always rests on a distinctly one-sided social contract—the operating system's "user agreement"—by which the masses agree to live their lives within an environment devised by government, capital, and a hierarchical social structure in return for (as we've seen) security, a sense of identity, and a path to material comfort. If we object to the State's conduct, we can protest, we can petition, and we can vote, but any rights we may win for ourselves can always be taken back. Neither are we allowed to replace the State—that is, to back out of the user agreement. "The irony," says Lennard, "is that true believers in the social contract ought, according to their political philosophy, to withdraw their submission to a government they believe has vitiated the contract's terms. But faith in the ultimate legitimacy of the state, based in liberal contractualism, is inherently unrevolutionary: such a belief relies on appeals to a government's better nature."[48]

When, if ever, can the State go "too far" and fundamentally violate its "contract" with us—that is, forfeit its legitimacy? In the eyes of the State itself, it never can, and the foreclosing of possibilities it inculcates in us virtually shuts down any discussion of when that might be, despite centuries of genocide, enslavement, economic subjugation, and terror.

---

* In the U.S., for example, for more than sixty years the Justice Department has created and regularly updated Presidential Emergency Action Documents (PEADs), many of which are unconstitutional but that claim to authorize the president to take actions in case of a national emergency: suspend habeas corpus, declare martial law, order censorship of news reports, detain enemy aliens or other dangerous persons. According to the Brennan Center for Justice at New York University Law School, PEADs are not "subject to congressional oversight. Although the law requires the executive branch to report even the most sensitive covert military and intelligence operations to at least some members of Congress, there is no such disclosure requirement for PEADs, and no evidence that the documents have ever been shared with relevant congressional committees." Brennan Center, "Presidential Emergency Action Documents," May 6, 2020. PEADs may have been one basis for President Trump's repeated declarations that his "authority is total," extending to powers "at a level nobody has ever seen before."

But why, one might ask, does that discussion have to take place? Isn't it possible that we can reform the State and make it work for us rather than for its elites? This would only be the case if the State really was transcendent, as it claims to be, if it really did exist on a plane over and above all human existence, such that it perfectly comprehends and can legislate for every aspect of human life and society satisfactorily and equitably at any given time. It isn't, and it doesn't. It's the product of a particular five-hundred-year period of history, and its principal skill at any given moment is its own survival.

This is all the more unfortunate since the problems the State has created are becoming more severe, not less. Wholesale stripping of natural resources, which began with the early modern State's consuming quest for gold and silver, has escalated in vulnerable regions like the Amazon and parts of Indonesia, threatening to make the earth's atmosphere unbreathable. The State's intrusion into our personal lives, growing ever more sophisticated, now threatens to entirely destroy privacy and create the most efficient police state in history; in 2020, the coronavirus pandemic provided yet another handy excuse to take this capability further. The revival of the nuclear arms race and the expansion of the "family" of nuclear-armed countries has made the State an existential threat to life on this planet; right away in 1945, the State established that it was willing to use such weapons.

All of these developments took place within the past one hundred years. We're already getting a glimpse of the next stage.

In May 2020, President Trump held an Oval Office ceremony to unveil the official flag of the newest branch of the U.S. armed forces: the Space Force. Calling it a "very special moment," Trump congratulated his administration for having "worked very hard on this and it's so important from a defensive standpoint, from an offensive standpoint, from every standpoint there is," thereby admitting up front that U.S. militarization of outer space was aggressive in intent. "We have developed some of the most incredible weapons anyone's ever seen," including a new "super-duper missile," he enthused, "and it's moving along very rapidly."[49] The new Space Force amounted to an abrogation of the Outer Space Treaty that the United States and other governments signed in 1967 to prevent "a new form of colonial competition" and to bar the use of outer space for military purposes.

The same month that Trump held his flag ceremony, the White House announced that the United States would begin negotiating accords with other governments including Canada, Japan, the United Arab Emirates, and European countries with "like-minded" interests in mining the moon. The "Artemis Accords," as the projected agreement was named, would include "safety zones" surrounding future moon bases to prevent damage or interference from rival countries—or companies. These would presumably include Russia, which was pointedly left out of the negotiations.[50]

Neither of these developments should have been the least bit surprising, despite more than half a century of protestations that no state was interested in turning outer space into a battlefield, a shooting gallery, or another natural resource to be despoiled. It never was within the logic of the State to stick to any such pledge, and there should be no doubt that these initiatives will continue, in the United States and elsewhere, outlasting parties, individual politicians, and shifts in alliances.*

The larger implications are also clear: the State refuses to be bound to one planet or one environment. It is greater than the earth, and greater than any human population. If it turns this planet into an unlivable husk through environmental depredation, race war, or nuclear holocaust, so be it; the State will find other worlds to shape to its will, other settings in which to reproduce itself.

* * *

The State has one final argument for its existence: as long as there are powerful states in the world, we—as individuals and communities—can't afford not to have its protection. Somalis, without a state, are

---

* Amazon mogul Jeff Bezos has promoted a rather different idea: "rezoning" Earth for "residential and light industry" and moving "heavy industry, polluting industry" onto artificial, orbiting space stations. Overflow population, too, could move onto separate space stations with perfect weather—"Maui on its best day, no rain, no storms, no earthquakes"—perhaps replicating "historical cities" on Earth. "Going to Space to Benefit Earth," May 9, 2019 presentation, posted to YouTube by Blue Origin, https://www.youtube.com/watch?v=GQ98hGUe6FM.

vulnerable to any armed outsider that wants to invade and abuse them. Without Israel, Jews would have no certain refuge from anti-Semitism. Even the citizens of much less beleaguered countries need the State; what would a Mexican migrant do if the Mexican government wasn't there to protest her mistreatment at the hands of ICE in the United States? Statelessness, lack of citizenship, is a dangerously exposed condition in today's world.

Rather than proving the necessity of the State, however, this is another reason to ask why states exist to abuse Somalis, Jews, and Mexicans in the first place. Such a world is one the State itself created; it offers us protection only if we play by its rules, and often not even then. While seeming to settle the issue, this argument simply kicks the can down the road, to be raised again for the millionth time when we're faced with the next military atrocity, corporate crime, or ratcheting-up of surveillance and population control.

Why, then, would one make such an argument? Because it reinforces a view of humanity that is basic to the State itself and that's generally called classical realist. "The human condition was always going to be one of interest conflict, and this condition was capable of palliation but resistant to cure," says political scientist Chandran Kukathas. "But there is no particular balance to be struck, for every point on the scale is a possible equilibrium point, each with its own advantages and disadvantages. To understand the state is to recognize that we are in this predicament and that there is no final resolution."[51]

What is "this predicament," and what does it imply about the political and social orientation of the modern State? Is the State intrinsically right or left, liberal or conservative? Certainly, the State has accepted or initiated numerous progressive changes over the past five centuries, from higher living standards even for the poor to better public health to more widespread education to—relatively speaking—greater acceptance of racial and gender equality. Most often, however, it has had to be scared into doing so. The State is fundamentally conservative for a variety of reasons. Hierarchy and inequality are baked into its economic and governing models. A political and social equilibrium built around a Core Identity Group literally depends for its survival on perpetuating a traditionalist mythology in which that group are the only "true" and "authentic" people, marginalizing all others; an aversion to cooperative or collective economic solutions makes altering this balance very difficult. The State's conservatism extends to another, more basic level as well.

In the centuries since the monarchical State began to give way to the national State, a vast literature on sovereignty and government has grown up. Whereas James I of Great Britain liked to boast of his "kingcraft," the scholars and practitioners who followed him spoke of "statecraft"; two pillars of the system, former British prime minister Margaret Thatcher and U.S. diplomat Dennis Ross, wrote books with that word as the title within five years of each other (in 2003 and 2008, respectively). Since World War II, one of the most widely admired books in this genre has been *Politics among Nations* by Hans Morgenthau, a German-born American academic. In his book, Morgenthau argued that human nature "has not changed since the classical philosophies of China, India and Greece"; that states are the main actors in politics; and that the best we can hope for in the political world is therefore a balance of power between states.

This philosophical position represents a distillation of realpolitik, the doctrine that politics or diplomacy should be based on consideration of given circumstances and factors, not on ideological notions or moral and ethical premises. The underlying assumption is that the State is transcendent and all-encompassing, a culmination rather than an episode in human history, and that this supposed reality alone must guide public policy. As a result, Morgenthau's analysis is often portrayed as tragic because it asks humanity to resign itself to living with evil and to make a conscious choice to focus on national interest rather than universal ideals in international relations.

---

* The 2017 Game Expo Best Card Game Winner was *Statecraft: The Political Card Game*, which invites players to "build a political party in a familiar but fictional world, recruiting politicians to your cause, developing your manifesto of winning ideas, campaigning for the support of the public and firing off salvos of slander and sabotage at your cunning rivals, and surviving catastrophic events that shake up the nation you're playing the game of politics in." Statecraft: The Political Card Game (2017), Board Game Geek, https://boardgamegeek.com/boardgame/193500/statecraft -political-card-game.

There is no hope for fundamental improvement; this is always the way it's going to be.

This is a false choice. Universal ideals (like liberal democracy, the public interest, and civic virtue) and national interest are both concepts hatched by political elites to persuade us of their own essential role: both require a State, a System of States, and strong leaders to pursue them. In reality, humanity has organized itself successfully in a vast number of ways that do not require a State, often with mutual aid rather than self-interest (in the modern sense) as a guiding principle in which "national interest" has no meaning. But this is not a world that Morgenthau or other acolytes of the State (Henry Kissinger was one of his most devoted followers) are interested in or deem credible. The grim contest between states actually represents a kind of earthly perfection for conservative defenders of the State, in part because it provides a stage on which leaders can act out a heroic, never-ending chess game of national rivalry.

"The statesman [sic] must think in terms of the national interest," Morgenthau wrote, "conceived as power among other powers. The popular mind, unaware of the fine distinctions of the statesman's thinking, reasons more often than not in the simple moralistic and legalistic terms of absolute good and absolute evil."[52] This may not be true, but it's a fair summary of the working assumptions that every member of the State's elite absorbs, consciously or not. And while not everyone in policymaking circles accepts Morgenthau's theoretical framework, the wide respect it's accorded suggests just how conservative, undemocratic, and elitist the modern State really is.

VIII

Shaking Off the State

It is therefore certain that government and capital will not allow them-
selves to be quietly abolished if they can help it; nor will they miraculously
"disappear" of themselves, as some people pretend to believe. It will require
a revolution to get rid of them.
—Alexander Berkman, *Now and After:*
The ABC of Communist Anarchism

While very few people outside policy-wonk circles "love" the State anymore, passive acceptance may be at an all-time high; its resources for isolating and managing troublesome populations through surveillance, geographic control, and media manipulation have never been more sophisticated and effective. Neoliberal capitalism, while it tears societies apart and has created spectacular levels of inequality and environmental destruction, works efficiently to force more and more people and communities into the economic framework of the State, turning them into productive assets. Above all, the State convinces us that it is what there is.

But we have misgivings. During the crisis in policing precipitated by the string of killings that culminated in the death of George Floyd, more of the public in more parts of the world were forced to confront the reality—or at least the possibility—that racism isn't something that can be reformed away and that institutions like the police might be fundamentally racist.

From there, it's just a step to considering the possibility that those institutions are part of a wider system of racism and to then ask what function racism plays in the logic of the State, something we addressed in the previous chapter. Within weeks after Floyd's death, the *New York Times* noted the proliferating use of the term "systemic" in "boardrooms, classrooms, streets and stadiums" while Merriam-Webster was "revising its entry on racism to illustrate ways it 'can be systemic.'"[1]

In an essay on Albert Camus's novel *The Plague*, British scholar Jacqueline Rose notes that when the State claims a monopoly of violence, "the responsibility of the citizen for his [*sic*] own violence is not diminished by such fraudulence but intensified, since it confronts him with what the state enacts in his name." The plague—the depredations that humans inflict on each other and on their world—"will continue to crawl out of the woodwork . . . as long as human subjects do not question the cruelty and injustice of their social arrangements."[2]

Despite its power and pervasiveness, then, the State exists because we choose to let it. "A nation's existence is, if you will pardon the metaphor, a daily plebiscite, just as an individual's existence is a perpetual affirmation of life," the French historian Ernest Renan wrote in 1882, and this could be applied also to the State, which gives the idea of the nation substance and force in the modern world. We created the State, and we re-create it every minute of every day. We can, of course, decide not to.

"We can't reform the police. The only way to diminish police violence is to reduce contact between the public and the police," writes Mariame Kaba, director of Project NIA, which works to end youth incarceration in the United States. "When you see a police officer pressing his knee into a Black man's neck until he dies, that's the logical result of policing in America. When a police officer brutalizes a Black person, he is doing what he sees as his job," a job that was given to him or her, along with all its explicit and tacit privileges and powers, by the State.[3]

At the time Kaba wrote, many people were denouncing the United States and the other dominant world powers for their shockingly incompetent and opportunistic response to COVID-19. "The manner and disorder of the hegemonic players' responses to the crisis proves beyond a shadow of doubt that the old order can no longer be restored and its ruling classes can no longer administer society in the old way," declared the Laban ng Masa coalition in its "Socialist Manifesto for a Post-Covid 19 Philippines."[4]

Change in this direction is most likely to come from below. The Movement for Black Lives raised the question of how far rage would drive activists in their demand for change. Would they settle for cosmetic reforms, which politicians eagerly began offering, many of them retreads of approaches that had failed to bring about change in the past? Or would the demand to abolish the police take hold?

And if it did, would it be accompanied by a demand to abolish prisons, to end the domination of the justice system by abusive prosecutors, to decriminalize drugs, and to abolish ICE and the DEA? Law enforcement, especially in urban areas, is complex; the police are only one part of an interlocking network within the State that also includes prosecutors, courts, politicians, police fraternal and public-support organizations, prison-guard unions, private prison operators, and even the media. Would the groundswell provoked by George Floyd's murder lead to a grappling with this larger system?

If not, the system surely would recuperate. "I can see the potential good that can come from dismantling or defunding the police," writes former CIA case officer and whistleblower Jeffrey Sterling, "but whatever system that will step in the blighted steps of the police will be no better if its foundation remains the same laws and system that have plagued racial equality in this country. . . . As an African American, it is an unmistakable, and far too often repeated and professional truth that this country regards us as inmates, in or out of prison."[5]

It's understandable nonetheless that even in the first weeks after Floyd's death, many people—especially in elite circles—were trying hard to change the subject. The State has survived more severe crises, including the Great Depression, the Russian and Chinese revolutions, and numerous other police outrages, and it quickly turned to some of its tried-and-true tools in response to this one. Washington, D.C., mayor Muriel Bowser, who became something of a hero for defying Trump's claim to control the streets of the capital, ordered "Black Lives Matter" painted on a street leading down to the White House—but also requested a $45 million budget hike for the D.C. police.[6] Democratic presidential candidate Joe Biden, too, was calling for an additional $300 million for police forces around the country. Once again, the State saw the further refinement of its own techniques of control and persuasion as the solution to a problem it had created.

In the past, this has worked well. As we've seen, the State is not just an administrative unit or a system of economic production and consumption; it's an imitation of life, a virtual and actual world mixing hard reality and pure illusion to convince people that nothing they could ever want or need exists outside it. Like a computer operating system, it becomes the air we breathe, and it's calculated to make our lives difficult if we try to live them elsewhere or otherwise. It adapts and absorbs new vital elements as long as enough people have soaked up its logic and tend to its cultivation and reproduction. The solution must lie with the State because that's all there is. Revolution is comparatively easy, since it's like replacing iOS with Windows—swapping one version of the State for another—although it does raise people's hopes.

> The State is not just an administrative unit or a system of economic production and consumption; it's an imitation of life, a virtual and actual world mixing hard reality and pure illusion to convince people that nothing they could ever want or need exists outside it.

Maybe this time it's different. The State is still with us in part because it's adept at sweeping so many conflicts, contradictions, and injustices—from racism, sexism, and economic inequality to the status of Indigenous peoples—under the rug of public discourse. But the State itself has created crises it's not equipped to address and that are no longer amenable to being hidden. Climate change can't be finessed; neither can the frictions of the genuinely multicultural society that economic globalization is creating or the rising inequality that's the product of neoliberalism. Pandemics are, in part, the product of both climate change and neoliberal globalization; more technologically sophisticated—and violent—policing is the State's response to inequality and a more economically integrated world. If these problems are to be solved in a way that's not inconceivably brutal, we'll have to address them outside the framework of the State—and we'll almost certainly have to push aside the State and its conflicting set of interests to do so. Have we reached that point?

By the time you read this book, we may know the answer, at least for the short term. In the longer run, shaking off the tyranny of the State—disconnecting the operating system, not simply replacing it with another that does largely the same thing, and then organizing our lives outside the State—requires testing its limits in two ways: first, organizing more of our individual and collective lives outside it, and, second, making reasonable demands it can't meet. We're used to thinking of revolution as an event, a decisive break with the past; in practice, it never is. To succeed, it has to be part of a process, not an end point. That process is social revolution, which doesn't start with a violent overthrow of existing governmental authority (which is only one component of the State) but much earlier, with grassroots efforts to transform all aspects of society.

* * *

For a social revolution to succeed, we first have to free our minds of the State. We must understand that it is something broader and deeper than "government," and we must learn to think outside it. We must lose the false assumption that the material advances made over the past five hundred years—and anything humans might achieve in the future—could only have been made within the ambit of the State. A social revolution "must first take place in the ideas and opinions of the people, in the minds of men [sic]," wrote anarchist Alexander Berkman. "The social revolution must be prepared: prepared in the sense of furthering evolutionary process, of enlightening the people about the evils of present-day society and convincing them of the desirability and possibility, of the justice and practicability, of a social life based on liberty."[7]

What's "reasonable" but, in the logic of the State, "impossible"?

In the United States, a Green New Deal was proposed that would provide a job with a family-sustaining wage to all people; affordable, safe, and adequate housing; and guaranteed higher education. At the same time, it would shift the whole country to clean, renewable, and zero-emissions energy sources and eliminate greenhouse gas emissions from manufacturing and agriculture. Such a proposal is hardly revolutionary. It would produce a better-educated, more productive population of workers, build whole new energy-efficient and nonpolluting industries, and forestall more drastic steps down the road. But it would require owners of capital to surrender an enormous chunk of their profits and redistribute wealth from the 1 percent to the lower tiers of society. That, in a word, would be "impossible." When a Green New Deal resolution was introduced in the U.S. Senate in 2019, it was defeated 0–57, most Democrats voting "present" rather than risk being stuck with the label.

Degrowth is an entirely reasonable approach that uses "well-being" rather than "standard of living" as a measure to evaluate economic activity and development. Rather than basing humanity's entire operating model on the extraction and burning of fossil fuels to the point of no return, it proposes to repair ecosystems, restoring earth's stock of water, food, and oxygen. But this implies moving away from rapid economic growth as the overriding goal of the State and capital; degrowth therefore is "impossible" to accept.

In the wake of the lightning-fast collapse of vital supply chains following the novel coronavirus outbreak, deglobalization also makes great sense. Countries and regions could become more self-sufficient with respect to vital goods, building up stockpiles in case of crises rather than sacrificing such precautions in the name of a precarious low-cost efficiency. Food sovereignty, a related concept developed by members of Via Campesina, the international organization of peasants, small farmers, and Indigenous rural communities, proposes that people who produce, distribute, and consume food should control the means of production. It also asserts that the food culture of the people consuming it should determine what's available to them. Food sovereignty is not a revolutionary concept either; a richly diverse global food culture doesn't discourage economic growth but promotes it. But deglobalization and food sovereignty, too, would prevent capital from squeezing maximum profit from every instance of production. Because a global monoculture will always be more capital-efficient, food sovereignty and self-sufficiency are "impossible" ideas.

The philosophy or developmental perspective known as *buen vivir*, which derives from the worldview of the Quechua people of the Andes and emphasizes a community-centered, ecologically balanced, and culturally sensitive route to well-being, embraces much of the above.[8] It's even expressed in the constitution that Ecuador adopted in 2008, which declares, "We . . . hereby decide to build a new form of public coexistence, in diversity and in harmony with nature, to achieve the good way of living." But this *buen vivir* is "impossible" on the face of it, since it presupposes that Indigenous peoples—and all peoples—have a right to determine their own path to development and does not assume rapid economic growth as the overriding goal.

What about abolishing the police? This is certainly "reasonable" if our goal is for communities outside the Core Identity Group to control their own neighborhoods and especially if abolition is accompanied by community control and adequate social investment in education, health care, and access to jobs. Collectively, these measures would enable communities of color to participate more fully in the mainstream capitalist economy, enjoy more of its benefits through consumption, and contribute greater productive capacity. The problem is that these communities would no longer be as ready a source of cheap labor and of pretexts for the State to expand its security apparatus (which would instead shrink). That makes abolishing the police "impossible."

One thing that capitalists appear to have in common with advocates for migrant workers is a disdain for borders. Borders separate families, often brutally; maintain a geographic division of wealth that leaves many countries—and peoples—impoverished; and foment antagonism between workers who should be organizing industry-wide across the globe rather than against each other. They also make it more difficult for capital to allocate labor resources where they're needed and to hold down wages in sectors such as agriculture and construction. That would seem to make abolishing borders, or at least substituting a less ruthless regime of border control, a "reasonable" goal for everybody.

But not for the State. Borders, as we've seen, aren't just physical lines in the ground, fences, or customs posts. Borders stretch deep into the geography of the political unit and are a critical part of its capability to control and manage populations, which is one of the State's principal mandates. Borders expand the State's ability to lock down or expel undesirable populations, surveil them, and exploit underground activities such as black markets, drug smuggling, and human trafficking. In no other context except prison does the State have as much power over individuals as when they are in proximity to borders or to the authorities connected with them, such as ICE. Abolishing borders, therefore, is "impossible."

What most of the initiatives we've just surveyed have in common is that they reject one-size-fits-all solutions for the problems of a diverse global society whose economic, environmental, and human trajectories are colliding disastrously. None of them is or has to be revolutionary. But together they challenge the State's drive to impose itself—its operating system—on every aspect of society and to harness the earth's resources in service to its model. They stand in the path of the totalization that's always been the State's objective, instead encouraging a multitude of forms of political, social, and economic organization directly managed by the community and unmediated by elites. As that implies, they stand a far better chance of being achieved outside the State, with its profoundly different priorities.

The other way we can begin to shake off the State is to withdraw from it by organizing more of our individual and collective lives outside it. The more relationships we build that the State has no role in shaping, the more the State's grip is loosened. This is a slippery matter. The present-day network of culture and socialization, with its webs of communication and social media, is denser and more consuming than ever, far fewer people live apart from it, and pulling oneself away can feel isolating and alienating. Many of the New Left, who used the mainstream media skillfully to spread their message, eventually found themselves overmastered and controlled by it. Labor unions, many of which began outside and sometimes in opposition to the State, can be neutralized, folded into it, and used to further reproduce it.

Even economic communities constructed on a noncapitalist model can be neutralized, their withdrawal rendered ineffective. The United Society of Believers in Christ's Second Appearing, or Shakers, developed successful cooperative communities, many of which lasted well over a century, but much of their success was based on the design and sale of popular consumer products to non-Shakers. This made them moderately wealthy but linked them closely to the capitalist economy; their transformative mission grew more inward and faded. Something similar has happened to cooperatives in other contexts; after enjoying a degree of success navigating the market system, their imperative tends to shift in the direction of perpetuating that success, which in turn leads them to adopt a more appropriately corporate structure and to hire executive leadership in tune with that approach.

Starting some 150 years ago, as we've seen, the State began creating social insurance and welfare programs that borrowed from and effectively absorbed the practices of mutual aid that had long existed in traditional communities and were being adapted by members of the new urban working class for the industrial age. Like other laws and institutions of the State, these "developed from the nucleus of customs useful to human communities," Kropotkin wrote, "and have been turned to account by rulers to sanctify their own domination."[9]

The institutions of the social-democratic or welfare state grew out of this tendency: old-age pensions and survivors' benefits; unemployment compensation and family and child support; public housing; public transportation; public health, nutrition, and sanitation; free public education; and publicly supported and maintained green spaces, wilderness, and cultural establishments. Each of these adapted some function that local communities had once supplied for themselves: pensions and survivors' benefits and public-health programs[10] from fraternal or mutual aid societies and earlier communal practices; public education from village schools; and public parks from common lands and forests, for example. Not surprisingly, these "inherited" institutions, which help people and communities directly and in humanly essential ways, are the best the State has to offer us.

But they are constantly threatened as the State prefers to support functions that reinforce its power, like schools that mold the elite, a bloated military establishment, increasingly militarized police forces, and subsidized business development. Nor are the benefits even of the functions that the State adapted from mutual aid shared equally. The State is relatively happy to provide social support for households of the Core Identity Group, but reluctant when the recipients are people of color or other populations considered marginal. Inherited institutions that carry the seeds of resistance, meanwhile, must be contained and controlled.

* * *

In medieval England, historian Peter Linebaugh writes, juries were not simply panels assembled to sit submissively while being lectured by judges, harangued by patronizing lawyers, sequestered, overseen by bailiffs, and compelled to render verdicts on the narrowest of grounds according to often outrageous laws they had no role in creating. "In its origins," Linebaugh writes, the jury "adjudicated other kinds of disputes, especially concerning the commons, or the usufructs of the land"—that is, the right to use or derive profit from the land. It was not "a balancing of interests, as in possessive individualism, but a means of asserting communality and constituting subjectivities."[11] Such an institution had to be brought to heel by the modern State, and it was.

Part of the challenge of shaking off the State is devising ways to take back institutions like the jury, old-age pensions, and public or social housing so that they once again reflect the principle of mutual aid, creating autonomous services that provide for households' essential needs rather than sanctifying the dominion of the State.

This may not be as difficult as it sounds, since the neoliberal state is whittling down or privatizing many social services, offering people less reason to remain loyal to a system that leaves them without essential economic supports. Reenergizing mutual aid outside the State gives individuals and communities direct democratic control of these initiatives, further instilling the habit of managing themselves rather than letting an elite do it for them—and it's absolutely necessary if we're not to fall back on rebuilding the State.

Prefigurative politics, which originated with nineteenth-century anarchists and has been an ideal of much of the radical Left since the 1960s, is defined as "the embodiment within the ongoing political practice of a movement, of those forms of social relations, decision-making, culture, and human experience that are the ultimate goal."[12] This approach necessarily has mutual aid at its core. In the early months of the COVID-19 outbreak, when neighbors and activists were organizing mutual aid projects across the United States and many other places in the world, Mariame Kaba said,

> I think one of the most important parts about mutual aid has to do with changing the social relationships that we have amongst each other, in order to be able to fight beyond this current moment, beyond the current crisis, beyond the current form of a disaster that we're trying to overcome. . . . One of the beautiful aspects is that you really don't know where the connections are going to take you. You're going to make and build new relationships that will kind of lead to new projects and will lead to new understandings, that will shape the potential future of, you know, your community and beyond. . . . And it provides a foundation for future political action, if it's done in a good way where people feel good about it and good about each other.[13]

Because the State is fundamentally an economic unit, organizing economic life to meet human needs rather than to increase capital and grow the State's own power is essential to building up expertise and creating a culture capable of operating outside its boundaries. Unions, cooperatives, and other formations outside the State, organized here and now, ensure that "when the Revolution, brought about by the natural force of circumstances, breaks out, there will be a real force at hand which knows what to do and by virtue thereof is capable of taking the Revolution into its own hands and imparting to it a direction salutary for the people," the Russian anarchist Mikhail Bakunin argued.[14]

Recent examples exist of communities that have organized on a basis of mutual aid rather than profit maximization, sometimes in extremely difficult circumstances and sometimes with considerable success. The Local Coordination Committees of Syria began setting up councils that placed power directly in the hands of local communities in the months after the Arab Spring uprising began in 2011. The movement's foundational document was "The Organization of Local Councils," by the Syrian economist and anarchist Omar Aziz, who died in an Assad-regime prison two years later. It set forth three main goals:

- To support human beings in managing their lives autonomously, without state institutions or structures (even if this autonomy is not complete).
- To create space for collective expression that can reinforce cooperation among individuals and that can encompass more necessary tasks as political engagement grows.
- To incite social revolutionary activities on a regional level while unifying supporting structures.[15]

The Autonomous Administration of North and East Syria, or Rojava, was a higher-profile effort, along somewhat similar lines, established by mainly Kurdish political parties and insurgents in 2012. It was organized as a loose federation, with a great deal of power concentrated in local cantons, and the court system included elements of restorative justice: focusing on repairing harm rather than inflicting retribution. Some three-quarters of property in the Rojava confederation was placed under community ownership, and a third of production was directly managed by workers' councils, although the process of transfer was much more gradual.[16]

The political philosophy of the Rojava experiment was eclectic. It reflected the evolution of the Kurdish nationalist leader Abdullah Öcalan from Marxist-Leninism to a form of libertarian socialism or anarchism derived from Murray Bookchin's writings and influenced by some of Aziz's ideas, but it also foregrounded respect for diverse cultural practices and traditions, an important feature given that the Rojava enclave was organizing in a multiethnic region with a wide assortment of religious faiths.

Rojava's organizational development has come in for plenty of criticism, including for the cult of personality around Öcalan, the deference paid to traditional tribal leaders in decision-making, and some crackdowns on dissidents that turned deadly. Much of this, however, should be understood against the backdrop of the continual security crisis in which Rojava operated, especially from a Turkish army that was determined to dismember it. Even a critic like Italian journalist Andrea Glioti allowed that this "Syrian lab" was a "politically innovative experience" that bore watching. One reason was the very different place that women claimed in the society being built in Rojava. "Civil marriages in Syria were introduced here thanks to a new legislation, a woman's testimony was made equal to a man's in spite of widely accepted Islamic norms, and the presence of women is encouraged in both political and military institutions as nowhere else in the country," Glioti wrote.[17]

That represented a dramatic break from most traditional societies in the Middle East and suggests the transformative potential of a social revolution built on a nonhierarchical, cooperative model that, quite significantly, declared its lack of intention to form a state. Once command of their collective future is placed in the hands of people on a local level, free of a rigid operating environment, communities often are more willing to engage with an egalitarianism that empowers women, other ethnicities, and other religions. Nothing guarantees that this will always be the case, but it suggests the degree to which even entrenched social attitudes can change, given the right circumstances and opportunity. It also highlights the need for activists to look, sometimes in unexpected places, for developments that fundamentally challenge the State and then to support those efforts.

Almost 250 years into the era of revolutions that began in France in 1789, this can still be difficult for Europeans and white North Americans to grasp. They continue to assume that revolutions happen in "advanced" states and that upheavals that occur in developing or colonial societies are less relevant or are dead ends. The reality, however, is that many if not most of the history-making revolutions of the past century have broken out in poorer, less developed societies, including Mexico (1911), Russia (1917), Vietnam (1945), China (1949), Iran (1979), and Mexico again (the Zapatista uprising, 1994).

Revolution is actually more difficult, it appears, in places where the modern State is firmly established. That doesn't mean it can't happen in Europe or North America, but it suggests that people living in so-called advanced societies have a harder time losing the habits of mind that the State inculcates and must look for the inspiration and tools to oppose the State effectively in resistance movements that already exist elsewhere.

While the State covers more of the globe than ever before and has absorbed the vast majority of the world's population, it's still not universal; Indigenous peoples in the Amazon, in the Zapatista liberated territory in Mexico, in the Bolivian highlands, and in other places continue to organize based at least in part on traditional approaches to agriculture, production, and community. Learning from traditional communities has always been part of the program of anarchism; the Russians Lev Tolstoi and Alexander Herzen emphasized the lessons to be learned from the *obshchina* or *mir*, peasant communities that held land in common and governed themselves cooperatively until they were legislated out of existence by the procapitalist Stolypin reforms during the decade before World War I. More recently, the Indigenous movement that led to the end of oligarchic rule in Bolivia and to the presidency of Evo Morales Ayma drew its organizing strength from the *ayllus*, a centuries-old Andean form of community that includes rotating leadership, an ethic built on mutual aid, and a distinctive set of agricultural practices fitted to a diverse ecology.[18]

What this tells us is that Indigenous communities can and do reclaim their culture and organize around it successfully, even in the world of the modern State. In the process, they open up new possibilities of social, political, and economic organization for all of us: the path anarchist theory and organizing have been pointing to for almost two centuries.

When Western people open themselves to the practices of nonstate peoples, the first thing they notice is the vast range of social organization available, leading them to realize that the one-size-fits-all model they've been accustomed to is not inevitable. The second thing they notice is that many of these other methods rely very little on leaders and leadership yet have effective strategies for making important decisions. The third thing that reveals itself is that less prescriptive approaches to social organization are more consonant with the nature of human society, which tends toward pluralism. And if they examine their own history deeply enough, they realize that every important advance in working people's material well-being and political status, from free public education to decent pay and dignity for industrial workers to racial equality, has been thanks to social movements that first formed outside the State and in opposition to its power structure, and that these advances were lost when those social movements atrophied or were subsumed by the State.

> Every important advance in working people's material well-being and political status has been thanks to social movements that first formed outside the State and in opposition to its power structure.

"Inquiry into the social life of a complex society discloses an immense number of social groups, social activities, social interests, an immense diversity in these and a process of change which, at varying rates, all are undergoing," wrote the Australian anthropologist Kenneth Maddock.

> This plurality is recalcitrant to reduction to any monolithic principle (except when the terms of the principle are so vague that they can be made to cover any situation whatsoever), it defies organization by policies derived from any such principle. Acceptance of monolithic principles implies deception, including self-deception, and policies derived from such principles serve to advance particular interests by misrepresenting them as general interests.[19]

Practices and institutions like the *mir* were not perfect; neither were the Native American tribes or First Nations, the medieval German free cities, or the communalism practiced in different parts of sub-Saharan Africa before the colonial era.[20] What's important is that there was nothing about these structures—certainly not their relative lack of hierarchy or their noncapitalist economies—that made them naturally inferior to the State as methods of social organization. They were living traditions following their own path of development, and they would have continued to do so if they hadn't been seized and bent to conform to the pattern of the State. If we want to shake off the State and build a society with deeper connections to the earth and deeper respect for nature and each other, we can start by learning from them.

Direct action is the tool that enables us to put all of this to-gether—directly challenging the State, organizing outside it, and learning from other social structures and resistance movements, past and present. This can take any number of forms: the general strike, the boycott, hacktivism, occupying land or facilities belonging to the government or private business. Direct action can sidestep the State completely—setting up a cooperative farm or factory, creating an autonomous community off the grid, squatting in an abandoned building, farming a vacant city lot—so long as people are prepared to defend the community's right to practice it. Either way, direct action prepares us to both think and act outside of and in contradiction to the State and to capitalism every single day.

"Direct action is a way of life and lens through which to view the world," writes longtime activist Lisa Fithian. "It is not about asking permission but rather doing what needs to be done to accomplish your goal as efficiently and effectively as possible. It means work-ing together, democratically, to take care of the problems we face, instead of waiting for others to make the change. Direct action is empowering, in the purest sense of the word. It allows people and communities to assert their power, to exercise their freedom. And to draw on their own wisdom to transform their lives."[21]

Above all, direct action takes us out of the habit of asking—which is the attitude the State always wants us to assume when we want something—and instead accustoms us to working directly, and col-lectively, to get what we want and need. Direct action also puts us back in intimate, purposeful contact with each other as a commu-nity, reversing the atomization that the modern State encourages. Socialism, Daniel Guérin argued after seeing fascist populism in ac-tion, cannot win by insisting on the material side of life and ignoring the emotional, idealistic, spiritual side. People could be turned away from "fascist mysticism," he thought, but only if those same impulses could be directed toward a new "idealism," specifically the "highly 'spiritual' purpose of ending man's [sic] alienation."[22]

* * *

However we do it, constructing relationships outside the State enables us—compels us—to build a body of knowledge and experience that adds up, in Bakunin's words, to "a real force at hand which knows what to do" when the opportunity presents itself to shake off the State.

But where does that opportunity come from and how do we seize it? States have disappeared or been overthrown multiple times in living memory; the collapse of the USSR and the disintegration of the Libyan and Somali states are examples. The Islamic State of ISIS arose, created a semiviable system of administration and finance, and then disintegrated in just a few short years. Drug cartels in Colombia and Mexico have carved out quasi-states that sometimes interact as equal players with governments and powerful agencies like the CIA. But in modern times, no revolution has ever overthrown the State: *not yet*. Each time, the next regime, whatever it calls itself, has replicated the form and its components: military, police, governmental structure, financial system, cultural institutions, and more.

What does it take for a large enough mass of people to conclude that they are better off abandoning the State and organizing outside it?

No revolution has ever been successful unless it was against a system that had discredited itself in the eyes of a large portion of the population. When that happens, small acts of resistance—everything from civil disobedience, mass protests, and tree-sits to various forms of industrial, military, and digital sabotage—can mushroom into mass uprising. The Russian Revolution succeeded because the tsarist regime had been completely discredited by its disastrous performance in World War I. The Soviet regime was discredited when it led the people into an unwinnable war in Afghanistan and failed for over twenty years to solve the problems pulling down its economic structure. The Irish revolution against British rule succeeded because the Crown discredited itself when it decided to execute the leaders of the Easter Rising, losing the loyalty of the majority of people. The Republic of Vietnam (South Vietnam) failed almost from the start to secure its people's allegiance due to its spectacular corruption and incompetence.

For the State itself to be discredited, it must fail in all three of the ways it needs to legitimize itself. It must

- fail to provide a degree of personal security;
- fail to establish a shared identity and a sense that one's voice is being heard; and
- fail to provide a path to material well-being.

When a state disgraces itself in any one of these dimensions, it becomes vulnerable to overthrow and replacement by another version of the State. If the crisis is severe enough, and particularly if it fails in all three, the entire edifice of the State could be at risk. Of course, states have recovered from such disasters plenty of times: after the tsarist empire fell and was dismantled, the new Soviet regime essentially put it back together again in just a few years. But it's up to the people to initiate the social revolution that will prepare them to abolish the State once it discredits itself—and not to let another new, improved version take its place in their psyche.

The current moment is promising because, for perhaps the first time and in part thanks to the increasing interconnectedness of every national economy, it's no longer individual states that are failing to perform in these three areas; it's the State itself, and the System of States that supports it. In the face of global warming and the COVID-19 pandemic, the State has failed to provide security. As nearly every country becomes more multiethnic and multicultural, the State has failed to expand its definition of identity and has actually narrowed the space for people outside the Core Identity Group to have a voice. By clinging to neoliberal policies, it has exposed vast portions of humanity to poverty or economic precarity, further destabilizing them socially and geographically.

How long can this continue? In the developed world, the Core Identity Group itself is shrinking, creating a growing problem for the State. According to 2020 U.S. Census Bureau numbers, the white portion of the U.S. population was 60.1 percent, down from 69.1 percent in 2000 and from almost 80 percent in 1980. In 2019, for the first time, more than half of the population under age sixteen was a racial or ethnic minority, signaling that racial diversity in the United States is accelerating. The previous decade was the first in which the white population did not grow, which means that population expansion was entirely because of growth in the nonwhite segment. "Racial and ethnic diversity will be an essential ingredient of America's future," wrote William H. Frey, a senior fellow at the Brookings Institution, yet anti-immigrant, nativist movements are growing within white America.[23]

Europe, the birthplace of the modern State, is also becoming more racially and culturally diverse—and more xenophobic as members of the Core Identity Group feel increasingly under siege. France and Germany, which were close to all-white decades ago, are now 8.8 percent and 6.1 percent Muslim, respectively, and becoming more so. As these societies become more multicultural, xenophobia has spread. In eastern European countries, which have vanishingly small nonwhite and non-Judeo-Christian populations, paranoia about migration and ethnic variety is, if anything, even stronger. This has exacerbated anti-Jewish and anti-Roma sentiment as well. At the same time, the population of almost every large continental European country is declining, suggesting that immigrants and ethnic minorities will assume a higher profile in coming decades.[24]

Ethnic diversity is not a problem in and of itself, providing the society accepts it and is open to accepting new populations on an equal footing. But it is a severe problem for the State, whose legitimacy, not to mention its power base, is lodged in the Core Identity Group. This is evident in countries like Hungary, Croatia, Italy, and Japan, all of which have shrinking populations and are among the most reluctant to accept immigrants. New populations might not be as likely to accept the State's legitimacy or lend it their support; if the State reaches out to these new groups, on the other hand, it risks alienating the Core Identity Group. In some places, ethnic and cultural minorities have been increasingly accepted over time— Irish, Jewish, and southern and eastern European immigrants in the United States were eventually accepted as "white," for example—but new groups have never been accepted from such a wide variety of backgrounds and in such numbers as at present. Thanks to the disruptions wrought by neoliberalism and a more mobile global population, the world's future is multicultural; but the State, in country after country, is less prepared to accommodate the shift.

A century or even a half century ago, when the world was less interconnected, these problems could conceivably be handled by individual governments through their own administrative and economic processes. Now they can only be solved through governmental cooperation across borders and a massive rethinking of the State's priorities by the global elite. Following World War II, the State created institutions aimed at helping the System of States to solve global problems or at least providing the appearance that it could. In recent decades, those institutions have either been dismantled or allowed to atrophy. The result has been the sad farce around the Paris Agreement on climate change, the tragic failure to establish a global strategy on migration or pandemics, the continuing refusal of institutions like the World Bank, the World Trade Organization, and the U.S. Treasury Department to accept any new thinking about global economic policy, and the European Union's stubborn adherence to austerity in the midst of economic hardship. Creating a functioning world government that's able to address these problems within the context of the State—the ideal of thinkers from Dante and Kant to Bahá'u'lláh and H. G. Wells—is one step the State shows no sign of taking.

Shaking off the State, then, will require both organizing locally to achieve the "impossible" and connecting local with global struggles to find solutions to the problems for which the State has abdicated responsibility. It also means being prepared for the worst. The State has spent centuries creating a vast web of control, assimilation, and identity. Like any living organism, it will fight to preserve itself at all costs. This will include both a physical and a psychological dimension: violent repression as well as strong appeals to the identities the State creates for us, fostering fear of the unknown and of each other. There will almost certainly be an armed struggle at some point as activists confront a violent reaction and the majority of the population either stays loyal to the present system or else stops cooperating with it. But the State will not go away until we force it to.

CONCLUSION

We Create Our Own Reality

We are told we need leaders.
—Jeffrey St. Clair, *Counterpunch*

According to an old cliché, every American child wants to be president. Why? Not because they want the responsibility, the 24/7 schedule, or the requirement to travel to obscure towns and cities and make the same banal speeches over and over, but because of the freedom it offers. The president can do *anything*: not literally, in any and every circumstance, but in the popular imagination. (If not, why would Donald J. Trump ever have considered running?)

Once the child grows up, their ambitions expand. History looms. And the State, we are given to believe, is the Engine of History. If being president is not possible, then some other high-level post in an administration, or CEO of a major corporation (which confer power and wealth greater than many states wield). The point is to be a molder and maker of events and epochs, not a subject, and, in so doing, to free oneself of the constraints of community that tie ordinary human beings together. To be able to do *anything*. Paradoxically, the highest ambitions one can achieve through the operating system that is the State free a person, to some extent, from the control of the State—or, at least, feed their desire to be free of it. Here's what a White House aide told *New York Times* reporter Ron Suskind during the months following the Iraq invasion:

> The aide said that guys like me were "in what we call the reality-based community," which he defined as people who "believe that solutions emerge from your judicious study of discernible reality." . . . "That's not the way the world really works anymore," he continued. "We're an empire now, and when we act, we create our own reality. And while you're studying that reality—judiciously, as you will—we'll act again, creating other new realities, which you can study too, and that's how things will sort out. We're history's actors . . . and you, all of you, will be left to just study what we do."[1]

Note that the speaker was a figure of some authority in a liberal democracy—the world's most powerful, and the institutional model for many if not most other contemporary states. Every statesperson, every influence peddler, every corporate executive or financier in every state partakes to some extent of the same breathless megalomania. The State instills this quality in its subjects—at least those who inhabit the Core Identity Group—because it needs individuals as its leaders who understand that to leave one's mark on history is to reproduce and extend the State.

In the world as it is today, they are not wrong. The last century offers example after example of stuff the State has given us that nobody outside the political and economic elite really wanted but that humanity accepted anyway. Not just misguided adventures like the Iraq invasion, but *stuff*: nuclear weapons, genetically modified foods, island-nation tax havens, private equity funds, thousands upon thousands of steel-and-glass skyscrapers, millions of tons of toxic waste with nowhere to go, surveillance cameras, migrant detention centers, and much more. Each by itself is appalling, but together they make up much of the infrastructure and furniture of the world—the utopia?—that the State and capital are busy foisting upon us. They make it. We take it. And we watch as they proceed to the next iteration or upgrade.

The ancient Greek term *hubris* came to be understood as "overweening presumption that leads a person to disregard the divinely fixed limits on human action in an ordered cosmos."[2] The modern State may be the ultimate expression of hubris, since it presumes to replace any such divine order with an order—an operating system—generated by human beings themselves. But the original meaning of the word, as it was understood by the Athenians, was more specific: Hubris is inherently violent and "consists in doing and saying things that cause shame to the victim," Aristotle said in the *Rhetoric*, "simply for the pleasure of it." For example, "young men and the rich are hubristic because they think they are better than other people."

The modern State is the most ambitious reflection of a presumed human impulse to conquer and exploit nature, not coexist with it, and to treat our own communities, our own cultures, as useful only insofar as they contribute to this project.

The modern State, too, reproduces and extends itself through violence: physical, cultural, economic, and social. It is the most ambitious reflection of a presumed human impulse to conquer and exploit nature, not coexist with it, and to treat our own communities, our own cultures, as useful only insofar as they contribute to this project. This is the path the modern world decisively took once the State came to define it.

The flip side is a deep fear of what lies outside its boundaries. While Mussolini declared that nothing outside the (fascist) State has value, our leaders are just as likely to see anyone outside of it as wasters or destroyers of value: at worst, as vortices that will suck the State in and destroy it if they aren't subdued, ordered, and subjected to the discipline to which the rest of the world conforms. Failed states, lawless frontiers, and areas given over to Indigenous communities have been a problem for the State going back to the times when, for example, escaped slaves took refuge with Native American nations across the vaguely defined colonial frontier and sailors and pirates went native in Polynesia, Madagascar, and other remote places. Today, slums and ghettos are at once spaces to segregate unwanted or exploitable populations and enticing zones of possibility, difference, and sometimes revolt.

We see examples of State policy toward these zones of resistance in the treatment meted out to any community that overtly or implicitly sets itself up against the State: when China reportedly carries out sterilizations of Uighur women[3] or when the United States imposes sanctions on Venezuela and North Korea that precipitate or aggravate humanitarian disasters. We see it domestically in the United States when Trump and Republican leaders swear, under cover of suppressing "violence," to show "no quarter" against "insurrectionists, anarchists, rioters and looters."[4]

Similar treatment is administered even to states with all the characteristics that define the model but that stand outside behavioral boundaries set by the System of States or the most powerful actors. States like Cuba, Venezuela, North Korea, and Iran, for example, become pariahs, and any criminal act perpetrated against them becomes acceptable. Both domestically and internationally, we are trained to think of "terrorism" as lawless acts of violence committed by forces operating outside the proper boundaries of the State—by ISIS, by the FARC, by Hamas or Islamic Jihad—but never by states in good standing, and certainly not the United States, even when their actions fit the definition.

Such policies are—have always been—born of anxiety and fear as much as megalomania. They emerge from anxiety about the State's strength and durability, especially when economic inequality no longer seems natural and acceptable, and from fear that it can't coexist or even survive in the presence of any system other than its own. We know this in part from its mania for tracking, surveilling, and prying into more and more aspects of our lives, and also because the work of so many public thinkers and artists from Machiavelli and Shakespeare to the present is drenched in fear that the "system" can't hold, that it's right on the brink of chaos.

We detect this anxiety in the events that take place when a state collapses or falls into serious crisis, as in the case of Haiti, Somalia, or Russia and the Warsaw Pact states after the Soviet Union fell. Other governments immediately dispatch economists, technocrats, and other advisers to assist in setting that state back on its feet, always with their economic policies "reformed" along neoliberal lines.

It's essential, then, for the State to encourage the same fears in the Core Identity Group, to convince them to equate the repression of resistance with the preservation of society itself. Over the past fifty years, "terrorism" has been the prime bogeyman supporting this strategy. One such campaign, launched after 9/11, persuaded Americans to tolerate "fusion centers" bringing together local police and federal law enforcement in the name of stamping out terrorism, along with increased surveillance, including of email and other electronic communications.

A similar ratcheting-up took place in Europe. According to a 2017 report by Amnesty International, after a spate of violent attacks in the EU, "Individual EU states and regional bodies have responded to the attacks by proposing, adopting and implementing wave after wave of counter-terrorism measures that have eroded the rule of law, enhanced executive powers, peeled away judicial controls, restricted freedom of expression and exposed everyone to government surveillance. Brick by brick, the edifice of rights protection that was so carefully constructed after World War II, is being dismantled."[5]

While "self-determination" is a right to which nearly every state gives lip service, it does not extend to the choice not to live in the State at all. Every citizen has the right to vote and to petition, but never the right to demand, however just the cause. And not everyone has the right to be a citizen; the State frequently holds non-natives and certain classes of native-born in some variety of legal limbo, for its own security and economic profit. The State professes to guarantee security by enforcing a reasonable and consistent set of laws; in reality, it stands above the law (even in supposedly democratic countries, the state habitually makes decisions without public input to which the public would never agree) and holds many categories of miscreants harmless when they disobey, including owners of capital and strategic assets, organized nationalist and racialist thugs, and other criminals who can render a service to the State.

These are not errors or glitches that can be reformed; they are basic and time-honored features of the operating system without which it couldn't pursue its project.

The institution to which civil rights leaders, civil libertarians, union organizers, feminist and LGBTQ activists, and immigrants seeking asylum have appealed for so many years to do the right thing and give them justice is, ultimately, the biggest obstacle in their struggle. In each case, the injustice is inherent in the State.

But the injuries accumulate, and behind every major crisis lies an injustice that demands to be corrected. When a Black man is pinned to the ground by his neck until he dies, all over a $20 bill, the injustice is racism, accepted and systematized by the State. When climate change threatens to bring about mass extinction and render much or all of the earth uninhabitable by humans, the injustice is headlong industrial growth, consumption, and fossil-fuel extraction, promoted and facilitated by the State. When streams of migrants are allowed to die at sea or are confined indefinitely to squalid camps, the injustice begins with military intervention and economic exploitation of their countries of origin by states more powerful than their own and the financial and commercial interests that benefit from those interventions.

In each case, the injustice began with the State. The institution to which civil rights leaders, civil libertarians, union organizers, feminist and LGBTQ activists, and immigrants seeking asylum have appealed for so many years to do the right thing and give them justice is, ultimately, the biggest obstacle in their struggle. This is a hard truth for people who have lived their entire lives within the operating system called the State and can't conceive of a pathway to justice that doesn't pass through it.

But the unspoken presumption is that it can all go on forever: that unlike previous forms of social organization, the modern State is supremely adept at exploiting nature and the human population while keeping the latter in line and that capital can forever tie the people to its side by creating new consumer desires and aspirations to preoccupy them while the corporate economy continues to expand. If new frontiers are needed, they can be found, perhaps underground, perhaps elsewhere in the galaxy; time will tell.

Nature, at least, may have other ideas. In June 2020, a report published in *Proceedings of the National Academy of Sciences* found that biodiversity is collapsing so fast that in ten to fifteen years, the opportunity for preventing the mass loss of species will close; some five hundred more terrestrial vertebrates will go extinct and total losses will equal those that have occurred naturally over the past ten thousand years. This will have a devastating impact on ecosystems, including fresh water, pollination, and pest control.[6] Expect usable water supplies to dwindle, food sources to narrow, epidemics and pandemics to become more frequent and devastating, and the poor and communities outside the Core Identity Group to bear the brunt.

This can only be reversed by shaking off the State. In the last chapter, we argued that it's necessary to begin a social revolution before launching a political revolution; otherwise, the end result is another iteration of the State and a neutralization of radical politics. By the same token, no social revolution can be fulfilled without a political revolution to consolidate it. As a result, the only proper meaning of revolution in our time is, as Kropotkin wrote, "to abolish the State and not to reform it."

History tells us that just like a computer operating system such as Windows, which by now has gone through countless upgrades and iterations while retaining command of its programmers and users, systems of human organization are highly adaptable. Seemingly moribund systems can hang on, make do, and muddle through by making small adjustments for a very long time before they meet a crisis they can't address and then collapse or are toppled. This time, it's different: not because the State can't hang on—it can—but because the problems it has created are more urgent and destabilizing and, for the first time in human history, they are global.

There's never been a more urgent time for revolution: one that frees us to shake off the operating system of the State and build a directly democratic community that can then address our problems honestly and equitably. The trick is to do it in such a way that the State can't absorb the insurrectionists and continue to rebuild and reinvent itself. Plenty of tools are at hand: the general strike, mutiny within the armed forces, seizure of government facilities and key businesses, and mass refusal to cooperate with the State. Then add the fact that working people's ability to communicate, cooperate, and organize across vast distances and across cultural barriers is greater than ever today, thanks in part to technology the State itself has nurtured. With these tools, humanity has the power to save itself, save its world, and bring down the "coldest of all cold monsters." This is doable; nothing about the State makes it immortal, and the future is another country—or, perhaps, no country.

Notes

Introduction: Toward an Anarchist Theory of the State

1. Nicholas Bogel-Burroughs, "U.S. Deaths Top 150,000, Far Eclipsing Projections," *New York Times*, July 29, 2020.

2. "More Than 70,000 Killed in Yemen's Civil War: ACLED," *Al Jazeera News*, April 19, 2019, https://www.aljazeera.com/news/2019/4/19/more-than-70000-killed-in-yemens-civil-war-acled.

3. "Documented Civilian Deaths from Violence," Iraq Body Count, https://www.iraqbodycount.org/database.

4. Niall McCarthy, "U.S. Police Shootings: Blacks Disproportionately Affected," Statista, July 15, 2020, https://www.statista.com/chart/21857/people-killed-in-police-shootings-in-the-us.

5. "Catherine Malabou to Hold This Year's Spinoza Chair," University of Amsterdam, February 4, 2019, https://www.uva.nl/en/shared-content/faculteiten/en/faculteit-der-geesteswetenschappen/news/2019/02/spinoza-chair-catherine-malabou.html.

6. Randall Amster et al., eds., *Contemporary Anarchist Studies: An Introductory Anthology of Anarchy in the Academy* (London: Routledge, 2019).

7. Nick Estes, *Our History Is the Future: Standing Rock versus the Dakota Access Pipeline, and the Long Tradition of Indigenous Resistance* (New York: Verso, 2019).

8. Daniel Bergner, "Whiteness Lessons," *New York Times Sunday Magazine*, July 19, 2020.

9. Matt Simon, "Capitalism Made This Mess, and This Mess Will Ruin Capitalism," *Wired*, September 20, 2019, https://www.wired.com/story/capitalocene.

10. Éric Pineault, "The Capitalist Pressure to Extract: The Ecological and

Political Economy of Extreme Oil in Canada," *Studies in Political Economy* 99, no. 2 (2018): 130–50.

11. Mariana Mazzucato, "Coronavirus and Capitalism: How Will the Virus Change the Way the World Works?," World Economic Forum, April 2, 2020, https://www.weforum.org/agenda/2020/04/coronavirus -covid19-business-economics-society-economics-change.

12. Rafael Soriano and Débora Nunes, "Transforming Society as Capitalism Crumbles: Lessons from Brazil's Peasant Movement," *In These Times*, September 14, 2017, http://inthesetimes.com/working/entry/ 20521/Brazil-MST-Landless-Workers-Peasants-coup-capitalism.

I: The State and COVID-19

1. Ralph Miliband, *The State and Capitalist Society* (New York: Basic Books, 1969), 270.

2. See Daniel Kahneman, Jack Knetsch, and Richard Thaler, "Anomalies: The Endowment Effect, Loss Aversion, and Status Quo Bias," *Journal of Economic Perspectives* 5, no. 1 (1991); and William Samuelson and Richard Zeckhauser, "Status Quo Bias in Decision Making," *Journal of Risk and Uncertainty* 1 (1988): 7–59.

3. Jack Rasmus, "Market 'Solutions' to the COVID-19 Crisis," *Z Magazine*, May 2020.

4. H. Patricia Hynes, "Trump Budget Winners and Losers," *Z Magazine*, May 2020.

5. Data cited in Jeneen Interlandi, "Why We're Losing the Battle with COVID-19," *New York Times Sunday Magazine*, July 19, 2020.

6. Interlandi, "Why We're Losing the Battle with COVID-19."

7. Deb Riechmann, "Trump Disbanded NSC Pandemic Unit That Experts Had Praised," Associated Press, March 14, 2020.

8. Hynes, "Trump Budget Winners and Losers"; Keya Vakil, "Obama Prepared for a Potential Pandemic. Trump Gutted His Work," *Courier Newsroom*, April 15, 2020.

9. Carwil Bjork-James with Chuck Munson, "An Anarchist Response to Ebola, Part One: What Went Wrong?," Anarchistagency.org, November 29, 2014.

10. Paper referenced in Stephen Chen, "Coronavirus: US Death Toll Would Have Been Halved if the Government Acted 4 Days Sooner, According to Study," *South China Morning Post*, May 8, 2020.

11. Betsy McKay and Phred Dvorak, "A Pandemic Was Inevitable. Why Was No One Ready?" *Wall Street Journal*, August 15–16, 2020.

12. Jack Rasmus, "Second COVID-19 Wave and the U.S. Economy," *Z Magazine*, July 2020.

13. Siobhan Hughes and Jacob Gershman, "Liability Shield Is Next Coronavirus Aid Battle in Congress," *Wall Street Journal*, May 4, 2020.

14. See Milton Friedman, *Capitalism and Freedom*, 40th anniversary ed. (Chicago: University of Chicago Press, 2002).

15. Stuart Blume, "The Global Fight over Vaccines," *New York Times*, May 3, 2020.

16. Casey Newton, "Apple and Google Have a Clever Way of Encouraging People to Install Contact-Tracing Apps for COVID-19," *Verge*, April 14, 2020.

17. Kira Lerner, "Government Enforcement of Quarantine Raises Concerns about Increased Surveillance," *Appeal*, April 10, 2020.

18. Ben Burgis, "Your Boss Is Spying on You," *Jacobin*, April 14, 2020.

19. Trone Dowd, "Edward Snowden: Governments Are Using Coronavirus to Build 'the Architecture of Oppression,'" *VICE*, April 11, 2020.

20. Natalie Kitroeff, "Young Leader Vowed Change in El Salvador but Wields Same Heavy Hand," *New York Times*, May 5, 2020.

21. Leon Sverdlov, "Benjamin Netanyahu Suggests Microchipping Kids, Slammed by Experts," *Jerusalem Post*, May 8, 2020.

22. "Everything's under Control: The State in the Time of COVID-19," *Economist*, March 26, 2020.

23. Abrahm Lustgarten, "Refugees from the Earth," *New York Times Sunday Magazine*, July 26, 2020.

24. Lustgarten, "Refugees from the Earth."

25. Loukas Karabarbounis and Brent Neiman, "The Global Decline of the Labor Share," National Bureau of Economic Research, June 2013.

26. "Income Inequality," Inequality.org (Institute for Policy Studies), https://inequality.org/facts/income-inequality/#income-inequality.

27. Lustgarten, "Refugees from the Earth."

28. "Global Trends: Forced Displacement in 2019," UNHCR: The UN Refugee Agency, https://www.unhcr.org/globaltrends2019.

29. "New Costs of War Study: 37 Million Displaced by U.S. Post-9/11 Wars," Watson Institute of International & Public Affairs, Brown University, September 8, 2020.

II: Understanding the State

1. Bernard Avishai, "The Pandemic Isn't a Black Swan but a Portent of a More Fragile Global System," *New Yorker*, April 21, 2020.

2. Courtney Johnson, "Trust in the Military Exceeds Trust in Other Institutions in Western Europe and U.S.," Pew Research Center, September 4, 2018, https://www.pewresearch.org/fact-tank/2018/09/04/trust-in-the-military-exceeds-trust-in-other-institutions-in-western-europe-and-u-s.

3. "Public Trust in Government: 1958–2019," Pew Research Center, April 11, 2019, https://www.pewresearch.org/politics/2019/04/11/public-trust-in-government-1958-2019.

4. "Corruption in the USA: The Difference a Year Makes," Transparency International, December 12, 2017, https://www.transparency.org/news /feature/corruption_in_the_usa_the_difference_a_year_makes.

5. Lydia Saad, "Military, Small Business, Police Still Stir Most Confidence," Gallup, June 28, 2018, https://news.gallup.com/poll/236243/ military-small-business-police-stir-confidence.aspx.

6. International Monetary Fund Fiscal Affairs Department data, cited in Esteban Ortiz-Ospina and Max Roser, "Government Spending," Our World in Data, 2016, https://ourworldindata.org/government -spending#all-charts-preview.

7. Nan Tian, Aude Fleurant, Alexandra Kuimova, Pieter D. Wezeman, and Siemon T. Wezeman, "Trends in World Military Expenditure, 2018," Stockholm International Peace Research Institute, April 2019.

8. Natasha Sarin and Lawrence H. Summers, "A Broader Tax Base That Closes Loopholes Would Raise More Money Than Plans by Ocasio-Cortez and Warren," Larrysummers.com, March 28, 2019, http://larrysummers.com/2019/03/28/a-broader-tax-base-that-closes -loopholes-would-raise-more-money-than-plans-by-ocasio-cortez -and-warren.

9. Nicholas Shaxson, "Tackling Tax Havens," *Finance & Development* (International Monetary Fund) 56, no. 3 (September 2019): 6–10.

10. Matthew Sherman, *The Alphabet Soup Explained: An Analysis of the Special Lending Facilities at the Federal Reserve* (Washington, D.C.: Center for Economic and Policy Research, July 2009).

11. Dion Rabouin, "Fed Chair: 'There's No Limit' to Coronavirus Stimulus Response," Axios, May 18, 2020, https://www.axios.com/jerome -powell-coronavirus-stimulus-response-d94cd03a-af34–4f30-a620 -e5ccc03c28cf.html.

12. Max Weber, "Politics as a Vocation," lecture, 1918.

13. The phrase was first used by Engels; Lenin discussed it fully in *The State and Revolution* (1917).

14. Peter Kropotkin, *Evolution and Environment* (Montreal: Black Rose Books, 1995), 94.

15. Michel Foucault, *Sécurité, territoire, population: Cours au Collège de France, 1977–78* (Paris: Gallimard Seuil, 2004), 294, 282.

16. Joe Painter and Alex Jeffrey, *Political Geography*, 2nd ed. (London: SAGE, 2009), 22–24.

17. See Bernard E. Harcourt, *Exposed: Desire and Disobedience in the Digital Age* (Cambridge, MA: Harvard University Press, 2015), 62–64, 164–65.

18. Philipp Staab, "Enclosing the Market," Social Europe, September 17, 2020, https://www.socialeurope.eu/enclosing-the-market.

19. Erica L. Green, "DeVos Will Push for Public Schools to Share Aid with Private Institutions," *New York Times*, May 28, 2020.

20. See Eric Laursen, *The People's Pension: The Struggle to Defend Social*

Security Since Reagan (Oakland: AK Press, 2012).

21. National Research Council, *Funding a Revolution: Government Support for Computing Research* (Washington, D.C.: National Academy Press, 1999), 138.

22. Errico Malatesta, *Anarchy*, trans. Vernon Richards (London: Freedom Press, 1994), 25.

23. Karl Marx, *The German Ideology* (London: Lawrence & Wishart, 1965), 42.

24. David Graeber, *Fragments of an Anarchist Anthropology* (Chicago: Prickly Paradigm, 2004), 65.

25. Emily Glazer and Liz Hoffman, "As Harris Joins Biden Ticket, Wall Street Exhales in Relief," *Wall Street Journal*, August 13, 2020.

26. Ralph Dum, Jeffrey Johnson, "Global Systems Science and Policy," in *Non-Equilibrium Social Science and Policy: Introduction and Essays on New and Changing Paradigms in Socio-Economic Thinking*, Jeffrey Johnson et al., eds. (Cham, Switzerland: Springer Nature, 2017), 209.

27. For more on recent theories of societal or state collapse, see Ben Ehrenreich, "Why Societies Fall Apart," *New York Times Magazine*, November 8, 2020.

III: Versions of the Operating System

1. See Corey Robin, "Why Did Liberals Support the Iraq War?," *Crooked Timber*, March 25, 2013.

2. Quoted in Ferdinand Mount, "You Are a Milksop," *London Review of Books*, May 7, 2020.

3. Quoted in Uri Avnery, "Manifest Destiny and Israel," *Counterpunch*, April 15, 2008.

4. Peter Kropotkin, *Anarchism*, 215, quoted in "An Anarchist FAQ (03/17)," section "B.2.1 What Is [the] Main Function of the State?," Anarchist Library, https://theanarchistlibrary.org/library/the-anarchist-faq-editorial-collective-an-anarchist-faq-03-17#toc10.

5. Excerpted in Larry DeWitt, Daniel Béland, and Edward D. Berkowitz, eds., *Social Security: A Documentary History* (Washington, D.C.: CQ Press, 2008), 34.

6. Anton Hemerijck and Robin Huguenot-Noël, "Just Transition: The Pensions Analogy," Social Europe, February 5, 2020, https://www.socialeurope.eu/just-transition-the-pensions-analogy.

7. Philip Bobbitt, quoted in Art Kleiner, "Philip Bobbitt: The Thought Leader Interview," *Strategy+Business*, no. 34 (2004).

8. See Valeria Pulignano, "Including the Precariat," Social Europe, September 9, 2020, https://www.socialeurope.eu/including-the-precariat.

9. Pankaj Mishra, "The Rise of China and the Fall of the 'Free Trade' Myth," *New York Times*, February 7, 2018; Mishra, "Flailing States,"

London Review of Books, July 16, 2020.

10. Data (through 2018) from the Organisation for Economic Co-operation and Development (OECD).

11. Philipp Heimberger and Nikolaus Krowall, "Seven 'Surprising' Facts about the Italian Economy," Social Europe, June 25, 2020, https://www.socialeurope.eu/seven-surprising-facts-about-the-italian-economy.

12. Lisa Pelling, "Sweden, the Pandemic and Precarious Working Conditions," Social Europe, June 10, 2010, https://www.socialeurope.eu/sweden-the-pandemic-and-precarious-working-conditions.

13. Avantika Chilkoti and Gabriele Steinhauser, "Covid's Next Economic Crisis: Developing Nation Debt," *Wall Street Journal*, July 26, 2020.

14. Peter S. Goodman, "In Pandemic, Rich Nations Have Failed the Poorest," *New York Times*, November 2, 2020.

15. Tim Blanning, "Princes, Poets and Prussians," review of *Germany: A Nation in Its Time* by Helmut Walser Smith, *Wall Street Journal*, April 18–19, 2020.

16. Mark O'Connell, *Notes from an Apocalypse* (New York: Doubleday, 2020), quoted in Toby Lichtig, "The Truly Final Frontier," *Wall Street Journal*, April 11–12, 2020.

IV: Characteristics of the System, 1: Ways and Means

1. Stefan Zweig, *The World of Yesterday* (London: Pushkin Press, 2011), quoted in Yaroslav Trofimov, "A World of Hardening Borders," *Wall Street Journal*, April 17, 2020.

2. Judith Butler, interviewed by Masha Gessen, "Judith Butler Wants Us to Reshape Our Rage," *New Yorker*, February 13, 2020.

3. Quoted in Charles M. Blow, "The Politics of a Pandemic," *New York Times*, March 30, 2020.

4. See Branko Marcetic, "The CIA's Secret Global War against the Left," *Jacobin*, December 1, 2020.

5. Tilly, *Coercion, Capital, and European States*, 66.

6. "Global Military Expenditure Sees Largest Annual Increase in a Decade" (press release), Stockholm International Peace Research Institute, April 27, 2020, https://www.sipri.org/media/press-release/2020/global-military-expenditure-sees-largest-annual-increase-decade-says-sipri-reaching-1917-billion.

7. Greg Shupak, "The Weapons Industry Doesn't Care Who's President," *Nation*, October 30, 2020.

8. Gilles Deleuze, "Instincts and Institutions," in *Two Regimes of Madness: Essays and Interviews, 1975–1995*, ed. David Lapoujade and trans. Ames Hodges and Mike Taormina (Los Angeles: Semiotext(e), 2007), 19.

9. Kenan Malik, "When Refugees in Libya Are Being Starved, Europe's Plans Are Working," *Guardian*, November 30, 2019.

10. Raja Shehadeh, "Occupying Palestine Is Rotting Israel from Inside. No Trump Deal Can Hide That," *Guardian UK*, September 17, 2020.

11. "Summary of the Opinion Concerning Unauthorized Outposts-Talya Sason, Adv.," Israel Ministry of Foreign Affairs, March 5, 2005.

12. "Israel 'Funded Illegal Outposts,'" BBC News, March 9, 2005.

13. Roxane Gay, "Ugly Truths about America," *New York Times*, January 10, 2021.

14. Constanza Dalla Porta and Pablo Pryluka, "Argentina's Dictatorship Was Not a 'Dirty War.' It Was State Terrorism," *Jacobin*, June 10, 2020.

V: Characteristics of the System, 2: Motivations and Drivers

1. Third All-Russian Congress of Trade Unions: Stenographic Report, Moscow, 1920, 87–97.

2. Peter Wade, "Trump Economic Adviser Reduces Workers to 'Human Capital Stock,'" *Rolling Stone*, May 27, 2020.

3. Blue Origin, "Going to Space to Benefit Earth," YouTube, May 9, 2019, https://www.youtube.com/watch?v=GQ98hGUe6FM&feature=emb_logo.

4. Robert Lee Hotz and Kevin Hand, "Building a Better Athlete," *Wall Street Journal*, March 12, 2020.

5. Leon Trotsky, *Terrorism and Communism* (Ann Arbor: University of Michigan Press, 1961), 131.

6. Charles Tilly, "War Making and State Making as Organized Crime," in *Bringing the State Back In*, ed. Peter B. Evans, Dietrich Rueschemeyer, and Theda Skocpol (New York: Cambridge University Press, 1985), 169–91.

7. Tilly, "War Making and State Making," 172.

8. Deborah Barrett and Charles Kurzman, "Globalizing Social Movement Theory: The Case of Eugenics," *Theory and Society* 33, no. 5 (October 2004): 487–527.

9. Ying-kit Chan, "Eugenics in Postcolonial Singapore," Blynkt.com, no. 1, October 4, 2016; John Rawls, *A Theory of Justice*, rev. ed. (Cambridge, MA: Harvard University Press, 1999), 92.

10. Corey G. Johnson, "Female Inmates Sterilized in California Prisons without Approval," *Reveal*, Center for Investigative Reporting, July 7, 2013, https://revealnews.org/article/female-inmates-sterilized-in-california-prisons-without-approval.

11. Caitlin Dickerson, Seth Freed Wessler, and Miriam Jordan, "ICE Detainees Recall Pressure to Get Surgery," *New York Times*, September 30, 2020; Victoria Bekiempis, "More Immigrant Women Say They Were Abused by ICE Gynecologist," *Guardian UK*, December 23, 2020.

12. Carter Sherman, "Staggering Number of Hysterectomies Happening at ICE Facility, Whistleblower Says," *VICE*, September 15, 2020, https://

www.vice.com/en/article/93578d/staggering-number-of-hysterect omies-happening-at-ice-facility-whistleblower-say.

13. Russell Kirk, *The Conservative Mind: From Burke to Santayana* (Chicago: Henry Regnery Company, 1953), 280, 395.

14. Katharina Pistor, "Limited Liability Is Causing Unlimited Harm," *Social Europe*, February 11, 2020, https://www.socialeurope.eu/limited-liability-is-causing-unlimited-harm.

15. Abrahm Lustgarten, "How Climate Change Will Remap Where Americans Live," *New York Times Sunday Magazine*, September 20, 2020.

16. "C.I.A. Covert Activities Abroad Shielded by Major U.S. Companies," *New York Times*, May 11, 1975.

17. Caitlin Dickerson, "A Private Security Company Is Detaining Migrant Children at Hotels," *New York Times*, August 16, 2020.

18. Gavin Grindon, "Art Brought to You by Guns and Big Oil," *New York Times*, May 31, 2020.

19. Kate Conger and Cade Metz, "'I Could Solve Most of Your Problems,'" *New York Times*, May 3, 2020.

20. Andrew Phillips and J. C. Sharman, "The Danger of Companies That Act Like States," *Wall Street Journal*, July 11–12, 2020.

21. Raymond Zhong, "In Halting Ant's I.P.O., China Sends a Warning to Business," *New York Times*, November 6, 2020.

22. Leslie Wayne, "The Shrinking Military Complex," *New York Times*, February 27, 1998.

23. Jing Yang, Quentin Webb, and Frances Yoon, "Hong Kong Endures as Finance Hub," *Wall Street Journal*, July 14, 2020.

24. David Harvey, "Capitalism Is Not the Solution to Urban America's Problems—Capitalism Itself Is the Problem," *Jacobin*, June 3, 2020.

25. Karl Marx and Friedrich Engels, *The German Ideology (1846)*, https://www.marxists.org/archive/marx/works/1845/german-ideology/cho1b.htm.

26. Michael Herzfeld, "Boundaries, Embarrassments, and Social Injustice: Fredrik Barth and the Nation-State," in *Ethnic Groups and Boundaries Today: A Legacy of Fifty Years*, Thomas Hylland Eriksen and Marek Jakoubek, eds. (London: Routledge, 2018), 74.

27. Isabel Wilkerson, "America's Enduring Caste System," *New York Times Sunday Magazine*, July 5, 2020.

28. Michael Herzfeld, "Boundaries, Embarrassments, and Social Injustice," 68–9.

29. Peter Fritzsche, *Hitler's First Hundred Days* (New York: Basic Books, 2020), cited in Andrew Stuttaford, "High-Speed History," *Wall Street Journal*, June 13–14, 2020.

30. George Orwell, "Review of *Mein Kampf* by Adolf Hitler (unabridged translation)," *New English Weekly*, March 21, 1940, in *My Country Right or Left: The Collected Essays, Journalism and Letters of George Orwell, 1940–1943* (London: Penguin Books, 1970), 29.

31. Daniel Guérin, *Fascism and Big Business* (New York: Pathinder, 2010), 88.

32. "German Car Parts Giant Confronts Nazi Past," *Deutsche Welle*, August 27, 2020, https://www.dw.com/en/germany-nazi-past-continental-tires/a-54719878; Jack Ewing, "Automotive Company Admits Link to Nazis," *New York Times*, August 27, 2020.

33. Stevphen Shukaitis, "Whose Precarity Is It Anyway?," *Fifth Estate*, Winter 2006/2007.

34. Nikole Hannah-Jones, "What Is Owed," *New York Times Sunday Magazine*, June 30, 2020.

35. Laura Davidson, "IRS Fails to Pursue Thousands of Rich Tax Cheats, Watchdog Says," *Bloomberg*, June 5, 2020.

36. Volin, *The Unknown Revolution, 1917–21* (New York: Free Life Editions, 1974).

37. Quoted in Geoff Mann, "The Inequality Engine," *London Review of Books*, June 4, 2020.

38. John Micklethwait and Adrian Wooldridge, *The Fourth Revolution: The Global Race to Reinvent the State* (New York: Penguin Books, 2015), 1–4.

39. R. F. Foster, *Modern Ireland 1600–1972* (London: Penguin Books, 1988), 522.

VI: Characteristics of the System, 3: Distinguishing Features and Preferences

1. Graeber, *Fragments of an Anarchist Anthropology*, 65.

2. "Trump Administration Revokes Tribe's Reservation Status in 'Power Grab,'" *Guardian*, April 1, 2020.

3. "Against the Coronavirus and the Opportunism of the State," CrimethInc., March 12, 2020, https://crimethinc.com/2020/03/12/against-the-coronavirus-and-the-opportunism-of-the-state-anarchists-in-italy-report-on-the-spread-of-the-virus-and-the-quarantine.

4. Quoted in Phil Karp, "Human Experience Can't Be Quantified," *New York Times*, November 8, 2020.

5. Lewis Fried, *Makers of the City* (Amherst: University of Massachusetts Press, 1990), 115.

6. Lewis Mumford, *The Myth of the Machine: The Pentagon of Power* (New York: Harcourt Brace Jovanovich, 1970), 324.

7. Shawn M. Powers and Michael Jablonski, *The Real Cyber War* (Champaign: University of Illinois Press, 2015), 63–69.

8. Jeff Nesbit, "Google's True Origin Partly Lies in CIA and NSA Research Grants for Mass Surveillance," Quartz, December 8, 2017, https://qz.com/1145669/googles-true-origin-partly-lies-in-cia-and-nsa-research-grants-for-mass-surveillance.

9. Leslie Collins, "Former Google Exec Sheds Light on KC Startups, Kansas Tech Scene," *Kansas City Business Journal*, January 15, 2020.

10. Patrick Tucker, "Russia, US Are in a Military Exoskeleton Race," *Defense One*, August 30, 2018, https://www.defenseone.com/technology/2018/08/russia-us-are-military-exoskeleton-race/150939.

11. "Joint All-Domain Command and Control (JADC2)," Congressional Research Service report, September 28, 2020.

12. Michael T. Klare, "Robot Generals: Will They Make Better Decisions Than Humans—Or Worse?" TomDispatch.com, August 26, 2020, https://tomdispatch.com/michael-klare-artificial-un-intelligence-and-the-u-s-military.

13. Sudha Setty, "Litigating Secrets: Comparative Perspectives on the State Secrets Privilege," Digital Commons @ Western New England University School of Law, 75, no. 1 (2009): 229.

14. See Garry Wills, *Bomb Power: The Modern Presidency and the National Security State* (New York: Penguin Press, 2010).

15. Alice Speri, "Homeland Security Wants to Erase Its History of Misconduct," *Intercept*, October 7, 2020.

16. Matthew Connelly, "Closing the Court of History," *New York Times*, February 5, 2020.

17. Nicholson Baker, *Baseless* (New York: Penguin, 2020), quoted in Tunku Varadarajan, "Information, Please," *Wall Street Journal*, July 25–26, 2020.

18. Joshua Cho, "WaPo Backing Limited Impeachment Was Constitutional Disaster," FAIR.org, February 27, 2020.

19. "The Iran–Contra Hearings: Excerpts: Plausible Deniability . . . Is Not Any Printed Doctrine or Dogma, Simply a Concept," *Los Angeles Times*, July 22, 1987.

20. Martin Jay, author of *The Virtues of Mendacity: On Lying in Politics*, quoted in "Why Politicians Should Lie," *U.S. News and World Report*, May 6, 2010.

21. Barry Glassner, "Take It from a Magician: Trump Isn't Trying to Distract Us, He's Misdirecting Us," *Los Angeles Times*, April 19, 2019.

22. See Joshua Frank, "Russia's Forgotten Nuclear Disaster," *Counterpunch*, December 13, 2020.

23. Shoshana Zuboff, "The Known Unknown," *New York Times*, January 26, 2020.

24. Chip Cutter and Rachel Feintzeig, "Smile! Your Boss Is Tracking Your Happiness," *Wall Street Journal*, March 7–8, 2020.

25. Patentscope, "WO2020060606 - Cryptocurrency System Using Body Activity Data," https://patentscope.wipo.int/search/en/detail.jsf?docId=WO2020060606.

26. Nate Berg, "Predicting Crime, LAPD-Style," *Guardian*, June 25, 2014.

27. Kevin Gosztola, "NYPD Chief Bill Bratton: 'Minority Report' Is Modern Fact, Not Fiction," Shadowproof, August 3, 2015, https://shadowproof.com/2015/08/03/nypd-chief-bill-bratton-minority

-report-is-modern-fact-not-fiction.

28. Jill Lepore, *If Then: How the Simulmatics Corporation Invented the Future* (New York: Liveright, 2020), 5.

29. Zach Campbell and Chris Jones, "Leaked Reports Show EU Police Are Planning a Pan-European Network of Facial Recognition Databases," *Intercept*, February 22, 2020.

30. Maurice Brinton, "Revolutionary Organization," *Agitator*, March and April 1961.

31. Thomas L. Friedman, "America, We Break It, It's Gone," *New York Times*, June 3, 2020.

32. Steven M. Lieberman, "COVID-19's Painful Lesson in Leadership," *Baltimore Sun*, March 22, 2020.

33. Walter Russell Mead, "The Imperial Presidency Will Outlast Trump," *Wall Street Journal*, June 23, 2020.

34. Alex Comfort, *Authority and Delinquency: A Study in the Psychology of Power*, rev. ed. (London: Sphere Books, 1970), 110.

35. "The Pursuit of Gender Equality: An Uphill Battle" (Paris: OECD Publishing, 2017), 22, 28.

36. Rosa Cho and Gail Cooper, *Gender Lens on Poverty*, 2nd ed. (re:gender, March 2014), 4.

37. Silvia Federici, *Caliban and the Witch: Women, the Body, and Primitive Accumulation* (New York: Autonomedia, 2004), 11.

38. Federici, *Caliban and the Witch*, 173; Natasha Heenan, "Silvia Federici, *Caliban and the Witch*," Progress in Political Economy, November 6, 2017, https://www.ppesydney.net/silvia-federici-caliban-witch.

39. See, for example, *Full Circles: Geographies of Women over the Life Course*, Cindi Katz and Janice Monk, eds. (London: Routledge, 1993).

40. "Snowden-Interview: Transcript," Norddeutscher Rundfunk, January 26, 2014.

41. "Tony Blair," Wikipedia, https://en.wikipedia.org/wiki/Tony_Blair #Post-premiership_(since_2007).

42. See, for example, Michael Kimmage, *The Abandonment of the West* (New York: Basic Books, 2020).

43. Alex Williams, "Friend or Flying Foe?," *New York Times*, May 28, 2020.

44. Susan Eisenhower, *How Ike Led* (New York: Thomas Dunne, 2020), quoted in David L. Roll, "Unity of Purpose," *Wall Street Journal*, August 1–2, 2020.

45. James C. Scott, *Seeing Like a State: How Certain Schemes to Improve the Human Condition Have Failed* (New Haven: Yale University Press, 1998), 4–5.

46. U.S. Department of Defense News Transcript, "Secretary Rumsfeld Media Availability en Route to Chile," November 18, 2002, available from the Federation of American Scientists, https://fas.org/sgp/news/2002/11/dod111802.html.

VII: Why Are We against the State?

1. Francis Fukuyama, "The Thing That Determines a Country's Resistance to the Coronavirus," *Atlantic*, March 30, 2020.

2. For a revealing account of how the two-party system subverts genuine political choice in electoral democracy, see Ralph Nader, *Crashing the Party: Taking on the Corporate Government in an Age of Surrender* (New York: St. Martin's, 2002).

3. See Eric Laursen, "Why I'm Not Voting," *Counterpunch*, November 5, 2018.

4. Hannah Arendt, *The Origins of Totalitarianism* (Orlando, FL: Harcourt, 1968), vii.

5. Paul Virilio, *Unknown Quantity* (New York: Thames & Hudson, 2003), 41.

6. David Quammen, "We Made the Coronavirus," *New York Times*, January 20, 2020.

7. Naomi Klein, "Puerto Ricans and Ultrarich 'Puertopians' Are Locked in a Pitched Struggle over How to Remake the Island," *Intercept*, March 20, 2018.

8. David Segal, "Logistics: We're Flunking a Test That We Wrote," *New York Times*, May 24, 2020.

9. Meadhbh Bolger, "Overconsumption, Globalised Supply Chains and the COVID-19 Crisis," Social Europe, May 6, 2020, https://www.socialeurope.eu/overconsumption-globalised-supply-chains-and-the-covid-19-crisis.

10. Virilio, *Unknown Quantity*, 133.

11. See Atossa Araxia Abrahamian, *The Cosmopolites: The Coming of the Global Citizen* (New York: Columbia Global Reports, 2015).

12. Quoted in Alleen Brown, "Tilting at Windmills: The FBI Chased Imagined Eco-Activist Enemies, Documents Reveal," *Intercept*, August 24, 2020.

13. Thomas Frank, "It's the Healthcare System, Stupid," *Le Monde Diplomatique*, August 2, 2020.

14. Timothy McLaughlin, "Lessons for American Police from Hong Kong," *Atlantic*, June 5, 2020.

15. David Cohen, "Portland Mayor to Trump Administration: We Want You to Leave," *Politico*, July 19, 2020.

16. University of Chicago Law School, International Human Rights Clinic, *Deadly Discretion: The Failure of Police Use of Force Policies to Meet Fundamental International Human Rights Laws and Standards* (Chicago: Global Human Rights Clinic, 2020).

17. C. J. Chivers, "Home Front," *New York Times Sunday Magazine*, June 28, 2020; Matthew Choi, "Trump Floats Pulling Federal Money from 'Anarchist Cities,'" *Politico*, September 2, 2020.

18. Sam Levin, "White Supremacists and Militias Have Infiltrated Police

across U.S., Report Says," *Guardian UK*, August 28, 2020.

19. "Germany Far Right: Police Suspended for Sharing Neo-Nazi Images," BBC News Daily, September 16, 2020.

20. Jason Wilson, "Violence by Far-Right Is among US's Most Dangerous Terrorist Threats, Study Finds," *Guardian UK*, June 27, 2020.

21. Larry M. Bartels, "Ethnic Antagonism Erodes Republicans' Commitment to Democracy," *Proceedings of the National Academy of Sciences of the United States of America*, August 31, 2020.

22. Juan Cole, "Trump's Secret Police Whisk Portland Protesters into Unmarked Cars, but Allowed Right Wing Armed Militiamen to Invade Michigan State House," *Informed Comment*, July 20, 2020.

23. Rebecca Davis O'Brien, Andrew Tangel, and Ben Chapman, "Picture Hazy on Violence Perpetrators," *Wall Street Journal*, June 9, 2020.

24. Judith Butler, interviewed by Masha Gessen, "Judith Butler Wants Us to Reshape Our Rage."

25. ZZ Packer, "The Empty Facts of the Breonna Taylor Decision," *New Yorker*, September 27, 2020.

26. Alex Comfort, *Authority and Delinquency: A Study in the Psychology of Power*, 29.

27. Tom Engelhardt, "Praying at the Church of St. Drone," TomDispatch .com, June 5, 2012, https://www.tomdispatch.com/post/175551/tom gram%3A_engelhardt,_assassin-in-chief.

28. Michael Gillard, Ignacio Gomez, and Melissa Jones, "BP Hands 'Tarred in Pipeline Dirty War,'" *Guardian*, October 17, 1998.

29. Cheryl Harris, "Whiteness as Property," *Harvard Law Review*, 1993, quoted in Jamelle Bouie, "A Twisted Conception of Liberty," *New York Times*, May 10, 2020.

30. N'dea Yancey-Bragg, "Poll: Americans' Confidence in Police Falls to Historic Low," *USA TODAY*, August 13, 2020.

31. Amanda Hess, "Backlash on the Portrayal of 'Good Cops,'" *New York Times*, June 11, 2020.

32. Hess, "Backlash on the Portrayal of 'Good Cops.'"

33. James Poniewozik, "'Cops': Off TV, but Still in the Air," *New York Times*, June 13, 2020.

34. Tatiana Siegel, "Hollywood and the Police: A Deep, Complicated and Now Strained Relationship," *Hollywood Reporter*, July 1, 2020.

35. See Sebastian Kaempf, "'A Relationship of Mutual Exploitation': The Evolving Ties between the Pentagon, Hollywood, and the Commercial Gaming Sector," *Social Identities* 25, no. 4 (2019): 542–58.

36. Ishmael Reed, "Why Killer Cops Go Free," *Counterpunch*, June 19, 2020.

37. Editorial, "Why Does the U.S. Military Celebrate White Supremacy?," *New York Times*, May 24, 2020.

38. Medea Benjamin and Zoltan Grossman, "10 Reasons Why Defunding Police Should Lead to Defunding War," *Z Magazine*, August 2020.

39. Andrew Chung, Lawrence Hurley, Jackie Botts, Andrea Januta, and Guillermo Gomez, "For Cops Who Kill, Special Supreme Court Protection," Reuters, May 8, 2020.

40. See Rodney Stark, *Police Riots: Collective Violence and Law Enforcement* (Belmont, CA: Wadsworth, 1972).

41. Michael Hardt and Antonio Negri, *Empire* (Cambridge, MA: Harvard University Press, 2000), 85.

42. Carl Schmitt, *Political Theology: Four Chapters on the Concept of Sovereignty* (1922), trans. George Schwab (Chicago: University of Chicago Press, 2005), 36–52, cited in *The Stanford Encyclopedia of Philosophy*, https://plato.stanford.edu/entries/schmitt.

43. Carl Schmitt, *The Concept of the Political*, expanded edition (1932), trans. George Schwab (Chicago: University of Chicago Press, 2007), 58–68, cited in *The Stanford Encyclopedia of Philosophy*, Fall 2019 edition, ed. Edward N. Zalta, https://plato.stanford.edu/archives/fall2019/entries/schmitt.

44. Cited in Trone Dowd, "Cops Said a Child Was Lost in Philly's 'Riots.' Video Shows They Took Him from His Mom's Car," *VICE*, November 1, 2020.

45. Virilio, *Unknown Quantity*, 5.

46. Pierre-Joseph Proudhon, "The Political Capacity of the Working Classes," in *Property Is Theft! A Pierre-Joseph Proudhon Anthology*, ed. Iain McKay (Oakland: AK Press, 2011), 757.

47. John Berger, "The Nature of Mass Demonstrations," *New Society*, no. 34 (Autumn 1968).

48. Natasha Lennard, "An Appeal to the 'Democratic Conscience of the State' Won't Get You Far," Literary Hub, April 26, 2019, https://lithub.com/an-appeal-to-the-democratic-conscience-of-the-state-wont-get-you-far.

49. Barbara Sprunt, "Trump, Unveiling Space Force Flag, Touts What He Calls New 'Super-Duper Missile,'" NPR, May 15, 2020.

50. Joey Roulette, "Trump Administration Drafting 'Artemis Accords' Pact for Moon Mining," Reuters, May 5, 2020.

51. Chandran Kukathas, "A Definition of the State," paper presented at the "Dominations and Powers: The Nature of the State" conference, University of Wisconsin, Madison, March 29, 2008.

52. Hans J. Morgenthau and Kenneth Thompson, *Politics among Nations*, 6th ed. (New York: McGraw-Hill, 1985), 165.

VIII: Shaking Off the State

1. Amy Harmon, Apoorva Mandavilli, Sapna Maheshwari, and Jodi Kantor, "An American Awakening Is Prying at Racism's Grip," *New York Times*, June 14, 2020.

2. Jacqueline Rose, "Pointing the Finger," *London Review of Books*, May 7,

2020.

3. Mariame Kaba, "Yes, We Mean Literally Abolish the Police," *New York Times*, June 14, 2020.

4. Cited in Walden Bello, "The Race to Replace a Dying Neoliberalism," *Counterpunch*, May 19, 2020.

5. Jeffrey Sterling, "Whistleblowing, the Pandemic and a 'Law and Order' System of Injustice," *Z Magazine*, July 2020.

6. Keeanga-Yamahtta Taylor, "The End of Black Politics," *New York Times*, June 14, 2020.

7. Alexander Berkman, *The ABC of Anarchism* (Mineola, NY: Dover, 2005), 38.

8. Oliver Balch, "Buen Vivir: The Social Philosophy Inspiring Movements in South America," *Guardian*, February 4, 2013.

9. Peter Kropotkin, "Law and Authority," in *Kropotkin's Revolutionary Pamphlets*, ed. Roger N. Baldwin (New York: Dover, 1970), 215.

10. Carwil Bjork-James with Chuck Munson, "An Anarchist Response to Ebola, Part Two: Envisioning an Anarchist Alternative," Anarchistagency.com, November 29, 2014.

11. Peter Linebaugh, "Pallas and 'the People's Business,'" in *Uses of a Whirlwind: Movement, Movements, and Contemporary Radical Currents in the United States*, eds. Craig Hughes, Stevie Peace, and Kevin Van Meter (Oakland: AK Press, 2010), 298.

12. Carl Boggs, "Marxism, Prefigurative Communism, and the Problem of Workers' Control," *Radical America 11* (November 1977), 100.

13. Interviewed on *Democracy Now!*, April 21, 2020.

14. *The Political Philosophy of Mikhail Bakunin*, ed. G. P. Maximoff (New York: Free Press, 1953), 323.

15. Omar Aziz, "The Formation of Local Councils: To Live in Revolutionary Time," Anarchist Library, https://theanarchistlibrary.org/library/omar-aziz-the-formation-of-local-councils.

16. Strangers in a Tangled Wilderness, eds., *A Small Key Can Open a Large Door: The Rojava Revolution* (Oakland: Strangers in a Tangled Wilderness, 2015).

17. Andrea Glioti, "Rojava: A Libertarian Myth under Scrutiny," Al Jazeera, August 5, 2016, https://www.aljazeera.com/opinions/2016/8/5/rojava-a-libertarian-myth-under-scrutiny.

18. Benjamin Dangl, "Centuries of Fire: Rebel Memory and Andean Utopias in Bolivia," North American Congress on Latin America (NACLA), April 6, 2020.

19. Kenneth Maddock, "Pluralism and Anarchism," *Red and Black #2*, Winter 1966.

20. See Emmanuel E. Etta, Dimgba Esowe, and Offiong O. Asukwo, "African Communalism and Globalization," *African Research Review* 10, no. 3 (June 2016): 302–16.

21. Lisa Fithian, *Shut It Down: Stories from a Fierce, Loving Resistance* (White River Junction, VT: Chelsea Green, 2019), 10.
22. Daniel Guérin, *Fascism and Big Business*, 88.
23. William H. Frey, "The Nation Is Diversifying Even Faster Than Predicted, According to New Census Data," Brookings Institution, July 1, 2020.
24. World Population Review, "Europe Population 2020," https://world populationreview.com/continents/europe-population.

Conclusion: We Create Our Own Reality

1. Ron Suskind, "Faith, Certainty and the Presidency of George W. Bush," *New York Times Magazine*, October 17, 2004.
2. "Hubris," *Encylopaedia Britannica*, May 18, 2017, https://www.britannica .com/topic/hubris.
3. "China Sterilising Ethnic Minority Women in Xinjiang, Report Says," *Guardian*, June 29, 2020.
4. Quoted in C. J. Chivers, "Home Front," *New York Times*, June 28, 2020.
5. "Dangerously Disproportionate: The Ever-Expanding National Security State in Europe," Amnesty International, 2017, 6.
6. Rachel Nuwer, "Extinctions Are Accelerating, Threatening Human Life," *New York Times*, June 3, 2020.

Index

AK PRESS is small, in terms of staff and resources, but we also manage to be one of the world's most productive anarchist publishing houses. We publish close to twenty books every year, and distribute thousands of other titles published by like-minded independent presses and projects from around the globe. We're entirely worker run and democratically managed. We operate without a corporate structure—no boss, no managers, no bullshit.

The **FRIENDS OF AK PRESS** program is a way you can directly contribute to the continued existence of AK Press, and ensure that we're able to keep publishing books like this one! Friends pay $25 a month directly into our publishing account ($30 for Canada, $35 for international), and receive a copy of every book AK Press publishes for the duration of their membership! Friends also receive a discount on anything they order from our website or buy at a table: 50% on AK titles, and 30% on everything else. We have a Friends of AK ebook program as well: $15 a month gets you an electronic copy of every book we publish for the duration of your membership. *You can even sponsor a very discounted membership for someone in prison.*

Email **friendsofak@akpress.org** for more info, or visit the website: **https://www.akpress.org/friends.html**.

There are always great book projects in the works—so sign up now to become a Friend of AK Press, and let the presses roll!